# THRILLING DAYS OF YESTERYEAR: THE GOLDEN AGE OF RADIO

## BY JOHN RAYBURN

Thrilling Days of Yesteryear: The Golden Age of Radio
By John Rayburn
© 2018 John Rayburn. ALL RIGHTS RESERVED.

All rights reserved. This book may not be reproduced in any form, in whole or in part (beyond that copying permitted by U.S. Copyright Law, Section 107, "fair use" in teaching or research, Section 108, certain library copying, or in published media by reviewers in limited excerpts) without written permission from the publisher.

Published in the USA by:
BearManor Media
P O Box 71426
Albany, Georgia 31708
www.bearmanormedia.com

ISBN: 978-1-62933-310-6
BearManor Media, Albany, Georgia
Printed in the United States of America
Book design by Robbie Adkins, www.adkinsconsult.com
All radio and microphone images provided by stock.adobe.com.

## TABLE OF CONTENTS

Chapter 1 - The Way It Was ............................... 1
Chapter 2 - Durward Kirby................................ 3
Chapter 3 - An Objection Came From Yale University .......... 9
Chapter 4 - Not One Cent for Tribute ..................... 13
Chapter 5 – Roots ....................................... 16
Chapter 6 - He Was Shanghaied........................... 18
Chapter 7 - Why-y-y-y, Daddy? .......................... 19
Chapter 8 - It Was Audience Participation in Name Only ....... 20
Chapter 9 - May 6, 1937, Lakehurst, NJ .................... 24
Chapter 10 - They Were Once Hired to Bolster Broadcasts by
  the Glenn Miller Orchestra............................. 28
Chapter 11 - Nila Mack Didn't Like Children…At First! ....... 30
Chapter 12 – "Cal-l-l for-r-r Philip Mahh-a-a-rees!" ............ 34
Chapter 13 - An Irreverent Introduction for "Spiderlegs" Kalty .... 37
Chapter 14 – Red Was Legal Part of Richard Red Skelton's
  Christened Name .................................... 41
Chapter 15 - She Had No Idea Who They Meant When They
  Said "Arthur Godfrey"................................. 45
Chapter 16 - A Whole Bunch of Charlies, Even Bald-headed Ones .. 49
Chapter 17 - Parley Baer Even Had a Wild Animal Act at One Time ...51
Chapter 18 - Cedric Adams Was a Down-to-Earth Communicator. ..56
Chapter 19 - Parker Fennelly Used His Personal Background
  for a Radio Character ................................. 59
Chapter 20 - Kate Smith: A Song on Her Lips, But "Hurt"
  in Her Heart ........................................ 62
Chapter 21 - Ever Wonder How Some of Radio's Best-Known
  Sponsors Got Their Name?............................. 66
Chapter 22 - A Poem Possibly Inspired By a Lack of Quality
  Programming on Modern Radio......................... 70
Chapter 23 - Three Notes from the Famed NBC Chimes ........ 72
Chapter 24 - Coming, Mother............................. 74
Chapter 25 - "Kissin' a feller with a beard is like a picnic."......... 78
Chapter 26 - Egos on Parade.............................. 80
Chapter 27 - Try This Tongue-Tangler Three Times ............ 83

Chapter 28 - The Voyage of the "Seth Parker"................. 86
Chapter 29 - Tots in Clover................................ 90
Chapter 30 - A Slip of the Lip ............................ 91
Chapter 31 - It…is…later…than…you…think!.............. 92
Chapter 32 - Orson & the Mercury Theater Players Didn't
    Cause Nearly As Much Fuss......................... 94
Chapter 33 - The Ad Read, "Put a Mirror Near Every Radio"...... 96
Chapter 34 - Nowhere in the Pages of History..... ............ 97
Chapter 35 - Death-Dealing, Space-Cleaving, Time-Dissolving
    Devices of the 25th Century.......................... 104
Chapter 36 - Bits 'n' Pieces About Comedy................... 107
Chapter 37 - A Gift of Improvisation ..................... 109
Chapter 38 - Another Star Interview ...................... 111
Chapter 39 - It Was a Case of Turning Imagination Into Money! . 115
Chapter 40 - Gloom Chasers................................ 117
Chapter 41 - Why British Broadcasting Became Non-commercial  119
Chapter 42 - Good Evening, Mr. and Mrs. North America, and
    All the Ships at Sea................................. 120
Chapter 43- The Mystic Voice of the Ether................... 121
Photo Gallery............................................. 123
Chapter 44 - It Was a "First" and It Lasted For an Hour and a Half.. 132
Chapter 45 - Pompous! Arrogant! Pretentious! Windbag!
    Supercilious! Blowhard! .............................. 133
Chapter 46 - The Sound Effects Specialists Were the Unsung
    Heroes of Old Time Radio ........................... 139
Chapter 47 - The Story Behind a Song ..................... 142
Chapter 48 - In the Early 1920s, a Lot of Copper Wire Was
    Wrapped Around Oat Boxes.......................... 144
Chapter 49 - Harry Bartell Appeared on at Least 181 Different
    Radio Series........................................ 147
Chapter 50 - "It might be…it could be…it IS…a home run!"..... 153
Chapter 51 - A Gallon Jug of Milk Played a Part in Getting
    a Career Started! ................................... 156
Chapter 52 - A Pre-Med Course Gave Way to Radio!........... 158
Chapter 53 - Perhaps You Should Call Me, "Mrs. Quiz"......... 159
Chapter 54 - Creative Energy ............................. 161
Chapter 55 - Time Marches On ........................... 163
Chapter 56 - Apocryphal o' Wry ........................... 165

Chapter 57 - Who Was Mrs. Calabash? .................... 166
Chapter 58 - The Witch's Tale............................. 168
Chapter 59 - Another Young Performer .................... 169
Chapter 60 - "Bowes No. 1 Money Man" .................. 171
Chapter 61 - "Who's that little chatter box?................. 172
Chapter 62 - In Show Biz – at age 4? ....................... 174
Chapter 63 - Big Band "Remotes"......................... 175
Chapter 64 - She Was Radio's First Singing Superstar.......... 181
Chapter 65 - The Show Must Go On!...................... 184
Chapter 66 – Critic At Play............................... 185
Chapter 67 - You Ain't Heard Nothin' Yet! .................. 187
Chapter 68 - Good Old Golden Rule Days & What's In a Name?.. 188
Chapter 69 - A *Real* Rolling Stone ........................ 190
Chapter 70 - Give Him Good "Marx" For Humor............. 191
Chapter 71 - "Hello, Anybody, Here's Morgan."............... 192
Chapter 72 - Some Miscellaneous Notes..................... 194
Chapter 73 - Take Two Kirkwoods and Call Me in the Morning.. 196
Chapter 74 - Ever Hear of *The Flotsam Family*? & Speaking
   of Quiz Shows......................................... 197
Chapter 75 - A Long-Ago Bit of Subterfuge ................. 199
Chapter 76 - Aboard the Camel Caravan .................... 201
Chapter 77 - Okay, So They Gave the Election Returns, Then What?. 204
Chapter 78 - What Next? ................................. 205
Chapter 79 - "Duffy Ain't Here" ........................... 207
Chapter 80 - She Got Into Radio as the Result of a Bad Cold.... 209
Chapter 81 - Parody of Commercials and Real Life for That Matter . 210
Chapter 82 - A Well-Deserved Honor ...................... 213
Chapter 83 - Scherzo in a Straitjacket....................... 215
Chapter 84 - "Bill Stern, the Colgate Shave-Cream Man Is
   On the Air............................................ 218
Chapter 85 - Daddy Went on a Trip and Things Changed! ...... 220
Chapter 86 - "The gaudiest, the most violent, the lonesomest
   mile in the world" ..................................... 222
Chapter 87 - In the Right Place at the Right Time............. 224
Chapter 88 - Name Changes Were Common................. 225
Chapter 89 - He Was There When it Happened! .............. 226
Chapter 90 - A Veteran Actress Who May Have Been the Best of All. .231
Chapter 91 - Wonder what they'd think now?................. 233

Chapter 92 - The several gentlemen known as Deems Taylor . . . . . 236
Chapter 93 - Chester and Norris Became Two of Radio's
    Best-Loved Characters . . . . . . . . . . . . . . . . . . . . . . . . . . . . . 239
Chapter 94 - "How 'bout that?" . . . . . . . . . . . . . . . . . . . . . . . . . . . . 244
Chapter 95 - A couple of close friends with compassion. . . . . . . . . 246
Chapter 96 - The Unbelievable "Reach" of Radio . . . . . . . . . . . . . . 247
Chapter 97 - A Different View on Old Time Radio
    and Its Many Uses. . . . . . . . . . . . . . . . . . . . . . . . . . . . . . . . . . 245
Chapter 98 - It Was Probably the Most Popular Radio Show
    of All Time . . . . . . . . . . . . . . . . . . . . . . . . . . . . . . . . . . . . . . . 250
Chapter 99 - "A Day Which Will Live in Infamy." . . . . . . . . . . . . . 254
Index . . . . . . . . . . . . . . . . . . . . . . . . . . . . . . . . . . . . . . . . . . . . . . . . 257
About the Author. . . . . . . . . . . . . . . . . . . . . . . . . . . . . . . . . . . . . . 260

## The Way It Was

Once upon a time, there was a wonderful form of family entertainment called radio. Changing times, changing attitudes, changing technology all blended together to signal the end of the so-called Golden Age of Radio. While it lasted, from approximately 1926 to 1952-54, it was a magical medium providing families with a means of escape from the myriad problems confronting the nation. One of the period's most memorable series, *Inner Sanctum Mysteries*, was produced by a gentleman named Himan Brown. Many years later, at an Old Time Radio convention in Los Angeles, he paraphrased for me a reflective statement that encapsulated what made radio perfect for the times.

"*Of all the forms of theater, radio drama commanded the most effective stage. No medium—not theater, not film, not television—had more sheer space in which to achieve the basic goal of drama, telling a story. Theater is bounded by the bare boards and the footlights and the flats, film by the white screen and television by the comparatively tiny tube. But radio…radio played itself out in boundless space…the listener's mind… your mind. We in radio always called it the theater of imagination. We proudly traced our lineage back to the primitive campfire and the tribal story tellers as the passers-on of legend, heroic adventure, mysteries of nature. They told their stories orally and so did we. We did not show, we told you. We made you believe everything because it was happening before your mind's eye. The basic appeal of radio drama was that you had to listen if you wanted to follow it. It wasn't enough to merely hear it. You had to listen. The word listen implies a conscious effort to pay attention, to participate.*

"*Senses were activated, the curiosity was sparked, the imagination was fired and the listener found himself participating. He was a collaborator. In his brain he matched a face and a body to the voice. In his mind he saw the action. And that was the basic difference between radio and every other visual medium. A good movie, a fine stage play, a television drama, excellent ballet…all those required an appreciative audience, but only radio called for a creative audience, a listener who really worked with the writer, the director, the actors and technicians to give completeness to the creative process."*

My intention is to tell at least part of the way it was, knowing full well it can't be revived, but providing background and anecdotes that hopefully bring to life a fascinating period that covered an all-too-brief segment of little more than a quarter of a century.

In addition to many behind the scenes stories I had the good fortune to meet, interview and sometimes perform in script reenactments of some of the great shows with a lot of the talented individuals from those by-gone days.

## Durward Kirby
### His First Radio Effort (a small one) Came In 1931

The late Durward Kirby died in mid-March of 2000. Some time before that he provided your writer with an exclusive interview and it was a distinct pleasure to chat with one of the all-time nice guys in broadcasting, one of those individuals who decided while in college that radio was the thing he wanted to do in life. And, boy, did he do it! Later, television was his focus and he was equally proficient there. After our delightful conversation he sent us a picture of the first microphone he ever used on the air. It was a "carbon mike" and Durward spoke his first radio words into it on February 19, 1932 at WBAA, West Lafayette, Indiana. Back then, engineers would hit the back of such a mike with a pocket knife before a broadcast to loosen the carbon particles. His first name was often misspelled as Durwood and he was always careful to let the offenders know they were wrong. As a result, I decided to start our talk with information about this name, telling him I thought he was the only Durward I knew.

D.K. D-u-r-w-a-r-d. I've only heard from 11 other men with that name.

J.R. How did you come to get it?

D.K. It was in a play...*Lena Rivers*...which was on Broadway. My folks were then engaged and they were so taken with the leading man's performance that they vowed right there and then that if they had a son his first name was going to be Durward. I struggled for years with that name and a lot of people got it wrong.

J.R. Tell me about WFBM in Indianapolis in 1934.

D.K. I'll start a little ahead of that. I joined the staff of WBAA in 1931. The station was on the air only 2 hours a week, Monday and Friday from 7-8 pm as I recall. I was one of 4 announcers and we were assigned a 15-minute air slot and had to go out and hunt our own performers. The station manager was a history teacher who let me audition. I read out of his history texts. The studio was about 15-feet square...glassed in...heavily draped for acoustical purposes and it was on the third floor of the Electrical Engineering building in West Lafayette, Indiana where I was a student at Purdue University. That's about as far back as I can go.

J.R. So Indianapolis activity came when you decided to make it a career.

D.K. Yes, after I got out of school. A man named Frank Sharp was program manager and he hired me at WFBM in '34 after I had a haunting experience in an audition at WKBF there. I was told I had no comprehension of words, I was a poor reader and my voice wasn't suitable to the medium. As I left, I stood on the curb and looked at the second floor windows that had the call letters painted on them. I vowed right then that *you*, WKBF, within five years will be hearing my voice via a network and I made the dream come true in just four and a half years. I was very much in love with radio and after about two and a half years I thought I had learned everything I could at that station and it was time to move on. So, I went down to Cincinnati and WLW and was auditioned and was hired at $45 a week. It was the most powerful station in the world…500,000 watts…an experimental license. No sooner did they get on the air with it than WOR, New York and WGN, Chicago applied to get that power but were denied. And WLW was eventually cut back to 50,000 watts.

J.R. Then, in 1937 you left to go to NBC in Chicago.

D.K. That's correct. I had covered the terrible Ohio River valley flood that year and after the waters receded I got a nice telegram from Abe Shector in New York (the NBC head of News and Special Events). He congratulated me on the job I'd done covering the flood from an airplane, a Coast Guard boat, from atop buildings, etc. He said if I was ever in Chicago to look up the NBC chief announcer, Everett Mitchell, and perhaps he'd give me an audition that might possibly further my career. I got that wire on a Tuesday and I was in Chicago on Thursday. They hired me and I had moved from just $25 a week in Indianapolis to the $45 in Cincinnati and now to $125 on the network.

J.R. I note in '39 you were on the show *Li'l Abner* that starred John Hodiak. The role of Pappy Yokum was done by Clarence Hartzell who did so well as Uncle Fletcher on *Vic and Sade*, and Ben Withers on *Lum and Abner*. You were working with a great group.

D.K. Oh, yeah. And at that particular time in my career, *Amos 'n' Andy* originated there in the studios and I used to sneak into the control room to watch the performance of those two, Freeman Gosden and Charles Correll. They were remarkable, doing all the voices.

J.R. In that very same year Ransom Sherman's *Club Matinee* had a young guy come in from St. Louis and serve as guest emcee and I guess that's where you first met none other than Garrison Morfit (not yet Garry Moore), the start of a long relationship.

D.K. 29 years together in radio and TV and he was my dearest friend.

J.R. An unusual feature on that show was the Rex Maupin orchestra occasionally playing a number out of tune on purpose.

D.K. Yeah, they'd play along very sweetly and correctly until all of a sudden Rex would give a cue and then guys would go either up or down a tone and play the wrong notes. It was fantastic and really amused the audience.

J.R. So, we find ourselves at 1941 and you were an NBC staff announcer at WENR.

D.K. Yes, and they also had WMAQ. One was the Red Network, the other was the Blue.

J.R. About that time you got the first of your big honors…the first H.P. Davis Memorial Announcers Award given on a nationwide basis by the widow of that Westinghouse pioneer. That must have been a warm feeling.

D.K. I'll say, and it was presented to me on the network by the guy who was then the dean of announcers, Graham McNamee.

J.R. Around then you were on some shows that didn't amount to much nationally. One involved Ransom Sherman again when you were his announcer while he was the proprietor of Crestfallen Manor, "a troubled, rustic hotel."

D.K. Boy, it went nowhere…was called *Hap Hazard*…a terrible title. But, Ransom was a very talented guy way ahead of his time.

J.R. You emceed *Club Matinee* yourself in '43.

D.K. That was because Ransom would turn it over to me when he went on vacation. I also did that with "The Breakfast Club." At one time, Don McNeill told me he started that show making $50 a week but lasted 35 years and he got up to hundreds of thousands of dollars a year.

J.R. One of your later duties was as the announcer on *Alka-Seltzer Time* with Herb Shriner.

D.K. That was a 15-minute show in New York, 3 nights a week. There was a girl singer who became famous…Dorothy…oh, what was her name?

(Note: I assumed it was Dorothy Collins who became well-known on the TV version of *Your Hit Parade*, because music on the Shriner show was by the Raymond Scott Quintet and she eventually married Scott.)

J.R. You were one of a flock of great announcers on the *Henry Morgan Show*…like Ben Grauer, Art Ballinger, Dan Seymour, Ed Herlihy and David Ross…almost a who's who list. Were the changes because Henry couldn't get along with announcers any better than he did with some of the sponsors?

D.K. (Chuckle) That could be. He had his troubles all right but Henry became a good friend of mine.

J.R. Here's one for your memory book…an engaged couples interview show in about 1946 called *Honeymoon in New York*.

D.K. Oh, brother, that was probably the most innocuous show you ever heard of. We used a Silver Anniversary couple and a couple who were engaged and all I did was interview each couple and laid a lot of prizes on them…y'know, toasters, bedwarmers and such…it was the dumbest thing. I was up to my hips in love, love, love five days a week.

J.R. Sounds like a romantic version of Jack Bailey's *Queen for a Day*.

D.K. It wasn't *nearly* as good as Jack Bailey but it got me to New York. I went there and auditioned for that show against a guy who was part of a team…Colonel Stoopnagel…of the show, "Stoopnagel and Budd," and I got the call. The reason I wanted to, get to New York City was because it was prior to the big advent of television, which I knew was coming, and I wanted to be there and get into it.

J.R. Forgive me for skipping around, but let's touch on something that must have been a lot of fun back in the heyday of what we call the Golden Age of Radio and that would be the big band "remotes."

D.K. Oh, I worked a lot of those in Chicago. There was Tommy Dorsey, Jimmy Dorsey, Benny Goodman, Henry Busse, Jan Garber, Harry James, Abe Lyman, Claude Thornhill, Ted Weems, Count Basie, Duke Ellington and a lot of others.

J.R. Were any of those from the famous Aragon and Trianon ballrooms?

D.K. No, that was CBS. I worked at the Marine Room of the Edgewater Beach Hotel, the Panther Room at the Hotel Sherman, the dining room of the Bismarck, the Chez Paree, the plush Ambassador East Hotel, the Congress Casino and just about any other spot that featured a big band. I worked with Henry Busse at the Chez. He had an accent. I'd say "Hi, Dutch," and he hated that, "how's the band tonight?" And he'd say, "Id iss ver' goot..it iss alvays goot, you know." We'd have a list of the music lineup and there could be no deviation because of licensing rules. But, he'd say, "Now den, ven ve get down to number six, I'm putting anudder ting in dere." I'd say, "Look, Dutch, you do that and I'll cut you off the air." He'd come back with, "No, you vouldn't." I told him to try me some time and he did and I gave the cue to the engineer and… blip!...they were off and a stand-by pianist played in the studio.

J.R. Anyone else in your family ever in show business?

D.K. No one. My father was a very good railroad man and my mother was a homemaker. I never was in school plays, never had an acting lesson, just…bang!...there I was. I decided the microphone was my very dearest friend in all the world and my friend had one disadvantage, my friend was completely blind, so that anything I did in the way of adlibbing I had to explain to my friend so that he could see, too, and that went all the way through my radio career. Let me tell you about a radio show with Garry. Andy Rooney was one of our writers for the program that we did for 10 minutes every day, 5 days a week. He would come in with a script that was one sheet of paper with about 5 lines on it and say, "Here's your script." We'd both look at it and it was just a topic. Between the two of us we'd hound-dog that thing for 10 minutes and that was it. Andy would come over and say, "You guys are remarkable. I gave you nothing and you made something out of it. And you do it day after day. How do you do that?" Well, we looked at each other and simultaneously said, "We don't know." That was the real fun of it, working at a trade we loved and getting paid for it, too!

(Note: Durward told me another story about a famous "blooper" that I'd heard attributed to various sources. He said *he* was the one who made the classic goof. He related it this way. "I was the emcee on a show that was featuring a noted banjo player, a former Navy Commander, Eddie Peabody. When it came time for the introduction I blithely said, "Eddie Playbody will now pee for you." Well, I'm 6-4 and Eddie was small, not much over 5-feet, but he looked at me with death in his eyes. He never said goodnight to me after the show, just took his banjo, slapped it into the case, and walked out."

## An Objection Came From Yale University

It all had to do with part of the theme song on *Jack Armstrong, the All-American Boy*, and the sponsor paid heed and changed it!

The Hudson High School song on the program was originally written this way:

"Wave the flag for Hudson High, boys,
Show them how we stand.
Ever shall our team be champions
Known throughout the land. Rah! Rah!
Boola, boola, boola boola,
Boola, boola, boola boo!
Rah! Rah! Rah! Hudson High!"

The song was based on a rouser from the University of Chicago, "Wave the flag for old Chicago," but it was Yale University that didn't like the use of the term "boola" because of the Yale school song. So, that word was dropped.

The sponsor of the program, of course, was "Wheaties, Breakfast of Champions," made by General Mills. That firm came together as the result of business actions that began on the 20$^{th}$ of June, 1928 when 26 different companies combined. The fictional *Jack* was named for a real person of the same name who was familiar to an executive of General Mills. In 1939, that executive once again encountered the real-life Armstrong. The man protested, "I've been swamped with telephone calls from kids asking me when they're going to get the Hike-O-Meters that were advertised on the radio."

Incidentally, the Hike-O-Meter (a pedometer) was first offered nationally on a Thursday broadcast and the following Monday more than 176,000 requests came in. Both the post office at Minneapolis and the General Mills Service Division were filled with consternation. But, their "troubles" were just beginning. More than 70,000 additional requests came in every day that week with a weekend buildup that found 122,000 orders on the second Monday. That was nothing, though, compared to the third Monday (February 27, 1939) when

180,000 more rolled in. It was working out to a ratio of one Hike-O-Meter for every seven kids in America. More than 1,200,000 of the pedometers were eventually mailed to eager Jack Armstrong fans. Naturally, there was a Wheaties box top with every one of those requests, so it was certainly a pleasant problem for the company.

Predecessor of the Armstrong show was the *Skippy* program, which had its final broadcast on a Saturday (July 29, 1933). In order to hold listener attention, *Jack Armstrong* began airing immediately the next Monday. The first announcer was David Owen who had been handling that chore on *Skippy*. A couple of other recognizable names were listed as announcers on the show at one time or another—Truman Bradley and Paul Douglas—but it was Franklyn MacCormack who turned out to be the most remembered.

Since the show had such a prolonged run, there were naturally a great number of actors and actresses who were featured. Jim Ameche was the original Jack and did the part until 1938. The role was handled by Stanley Harris for the better part of a year and three months after that, with Frank Behrens on the job for about half of 1939.

Charles Flynn took over on October 1$^{st}$ of that year and stayed until he was drafted in '43. While he was gone, Rye Billsbury did it, giving way to Flynn upon his return from the service.

It was pretty much the same with other key roles. At least five actors portrayed Jack's good buddy, Billy Fairfield, and five actresses are listed in the role of Billy's sister, Betty. The only role that was never to change throughout the series was that of "Uncle Jim Fairfield"—that was always played by James Goss.

Jim Ameche's brother, Don, briefly played Captain Hughes, but other ambitions took him away. That was just as well because their voices were so similar it was confusing.

Some real life adventures resulted from the radio series. For example, Hudson High went in for some skiing in 1935. One day, during a ski-sailing expedition, one of the younger boys got carried out into the river on a sheet of ice. Jack managed to get him out of the icy water by crawling out to him on a plank. A few weeks after that, three St. Paul boys cut across a pond on the way to school and one of them fell through the ice. Some older lads showed up to help and one of them remembered the episode on *Jack Armstrong*. They found a long board in a nearby garage and used it to pull the young boy to safety. The story came out in the paper and it was told about on the Armstrong show itself the next day. Each of the boys wound up getting a case of Wheaties. Wow! Lots of boxtops!

In case you ever wondered what happened to that vast multitude of envelopes and boxtops that came into General Mills, during the 1930s they were sold as scrap paper. That was working out okay until one day a worker found $9.00 worth of dimes in the bottom of a paper bin. The story has it that efficiency then dropped off as workers spent more of their time looking for money than they did handling the scrap paper. Small wonder, when a lot of men in those days were making maybe $2.00 a day.

The program first became a transcribed set-up in October, 1934, with the transcription being cut three weeks in advance. At the same time there were still live shows on the network and it took about six weeks to set the story with new stations with a separate plot so they could get the background of Jack and his friends, They gradually began working together and were finally synchronized in November. After that, the story was the same on all stations around the nation.

There were some isolated instances when the sponsoring product was something other than Wheaties. In that November of '34 Jack switched to toast for breakfast because of a Bread Letter Contest. Then, a year later, the sponsor for a week was Bisquick when a premium was offered featuring Shirley Temple on a blue glass drinking mug. As usual, the kids were urged to talk their parents into buying Bisquick in order to get the mug at their grocery. The count showed that about 3,600,000 mugs and boxes of Bisquick went out over the nation's counters.

Robert Hardy Andrews, who had been writing the *Skippy* show, is credited with the creation of *Jack Armstrong*. He was also the first writer on *Just Plain Bill* and was once the narrator on *The Shadow* before the role evolved into the central character. Andrews created show called *The Stolen Husband*, produced by Frank and Anne Hummert. It was a soap opera prototype in 1931. He is also credited by some sources as the creator of *Ma Perkins* but that, too, was a

Hummert property and they had a way of getting most of the credit for their many productions. In any event, Andrews did, indeed, put together the original *Jack Armstrong* and it turned into one of the more popular long-running kid serials.

In spite of its popularity, the show did catch considerable heat from schools and mothers, all because Jack never really seemed to attend school much since he was always away on some big adventure. A conservative estimate would have had Jack at least 35-years old before he graduated from high school, even though some pains were taken to, occasionally explain that Jack and Billy and Betty always had their school books along on their big expeditions. And what trips they had! Jack was once carried out into stormy Lake Michigan after a motorboat race at the Chicago World's fair. They faced obstacles of wide variety in Arizona, South America, the Arctic Ocean, Manila, Shanghai, Africa, Zanzibar and the like. For homebound youngsters it was certainly an exciting concept. The final regular program was June 1, 1950. The show went off until the fall when it came back on September 5th as *Armstrong of the Scientific Bureau of Investigation*. It didn't catch on and the program was no longer broadcast after the final *SBI* show on June 28, 1951.

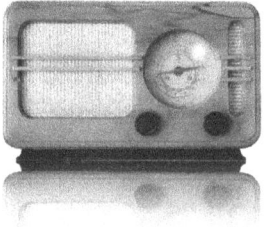

## Not One Cent for Tribute
(Right or wrong, he had the courage of his convictions)

Some of you may have heard the story of why famed movie director Cecil B. DeMille quit serving as "host" on broadcasts of *Lux Radio Theater*. Radio historians Frank Buxton and Bill Owen wrote it was because DeMille wouldn't pay the one dollar assessment by AFRA (American Federation of Radio Artists) to support a campaign in favor of closed shops. Fellow aficionado John Dunning wrote pretty much the same thing, indicating that DeMille's opposition caused him to pursue the matter all the way to the U.S. Supreme Court, where he lost. However, he still refused to pay the dollar and never appeared on the show again.

It all began on August 16, 1944 when DeMille received a letter from AFRA. It informed him that the board of the L.A. local had voted for the one dollar amount to be used in opposing an upcoming November vote on a proposition that would abolish the closed shop in the state and give every Californian the right to get and hold a job whether or not he belonged to a union. He didn't know much about the proposition but, as he said, "I thought I knew something about an American citizen's right to political freedom. I studied Proposition 12 and decided to vote for it. My union was demanding I pay into a fund to help persuade others to vote against it. It was a demand that I cancel my vote with my dollar. I asked myself if any organization had the right to impose such a compulsory assessment."

Many advised him, "Pay the dollar. Don't give up the Lux Show."

DeMille wrote, "To me the issue was clear from the first time I read the letter. What was at stake, as far as I personally was concerned? My job with the *Lux Radio Theater*, which paid me approximately $100,000 a year and which, because of its contact with the American people, meant much more to me than could be measured in money. On the other side of the scale was $1, with my political freedom pinned to it. There are very few men who lightly toss away

$100,000 a year; I am not one. I took advice. Most of it was the advice of appeasement. 'Pay the dollar. Don't give up the Lux show. Fight the thing some other way if you want to, but pay the dollar.'

I saw, moreover, that if I did not pay the dollar, my refusal would become a national issue. That was no exaggerated self-esteem; if a voice that had been listened to by twenty to thirty-million people every Monday evening for nine years was suddenly banned from the air, some of those people would undoubtedly ask why. I was certain that the answer to that question would hurt the union in the public mind, and I had no wish to hurt my union."

So, DeMille held a conference with union officers and offered to contribute to the union, as a voluntary gift, a number of dollars equal to the number of members in the Los Angeles local, if they would rescind the assessment and return their dollars to the members who had paid them under compulsion. The union refused.

When AFRA wouldn't give in, DeMille had to make a final determination on what to do. Again, in his words, "When the issue was finally drawn, when the deadline for paying the assessment passed and the union remained adamant, I sat down for one last discussion of it with Mrs. DeMille, Not since 1913 had we had so serious a decision to make together. I told her again what refusal to pay the assessment would mean to us: the loss of $100,000 a year, the loss of my radio program, the likelihood that I would be pilloried as anti-labor and drawn into a controversy that might last for years, with what effect upon our work and our lives no one could say; and on the other side, the simple solution of paying $1 to a cause in which I did not believe.

"Which,' I asked her, 'should I choose?"

Generations of Adamses, reaching back to the Revolution, spoke in her answer:

"You have no choice."

"I conducted the *Lux Radio Theater of the Air* for the last time on January 22, 1945.

"Since the passage of the Taft-Hartley Act in 1947, no one can be denied the right to work for refusal to pay a political assessment. Not being retroactive, the law is of no benefit to me; but Senator Taft told me that law would not have been enacted if my refusal to pay the dollar had not drawn attention to the abuse of union power."

In March of 1945, DeMille accepted an invitation from Union Pacific president, William Jeffers, to travel to Omaha and take part in a nationwide broadcast from a St. Patrick's Day luncheon to, as Jeffers phrased it, "put before the American people the case of political freedom and the right to work." DeMille made it clear that his host was a good union man and that he himself "did not in any way oppose union thinking." But he insisted on the right of everyone to act freely, citing his own case as an abrogation of that freedom. His closing words were deeply felt:

"May I say that I miss, more than I can tell, my visit in ten million homes every Monday night. The friendship of those unseen millions warmed my heart as nothing in life has ever done, but I would rather never visit them again than visit them as a betrayer of the fundamental right of an individual to make his own choice."

DeMille was listed as producer of the Lux show, as his movie reputation was used as a mark of excellence. In actuality, DeMille was really just a "reader," doing the program introduction and transitions. In spite of the fact he wasn't responsible for the show itself, his courageous stand against something he obviously and strongly felt was wrong, has to be greatly admired.

## Roots

Although generally regarded as basically an American art form, radio had a great many performers in the Golden Age who were born in literally the far corners of the globe. Here are a few of the better known examples with no effort made to list all their credits – just a show or so with which they were more closely identified. In some instances, the births were merely a case of parents being away from their home shores.

First, England: Ronald Colman ("Halls of Ivy"); Peter Donald ("Can You Top This?"); Edgar A. Guest ("The Poet of the People"); Skitch Henderson (conductor); Bob Hope ('nuf said); Hanley Stafford ("Baby Snooks"); Herbert Marshall ("The Man Called X"); orchestra leaders Ray Noble, David Rose and Henry "Hot Lips" Levine; Patricia Ryan ("Let's Pretend"); Les Tremayne ("First Nighter"); and Henry McNaughton ("It Pays to be Ignorant").

How about Russia?:

Commentator Boake Carter; Tim Conway ("The Saint"); conductor Al Goodman; band leader Harry Horlick ("A & P Gypsies"); Al Jolson ("Kraft Music Hall"); conductor Andre Kostelanetz; Minerva Pious ("Allen's Alley"); Arthur Tracy ("The Street Singer") and conductor Mark Warnow ("Your Hit Parade").

Others from Britain included from Scotland announcer Bill Hay ("Amos 'n' Andy"); and William Johnstone ("The Shadow") and pianist Alec Templeton from South Wales.

And, let's not forget Canada:

Announcer Norman Brokenshire; singer Dorothy Collins ("Your Hit Parade"); Charles Coughlin ("The Radio Priest"); conductor Percy Faith; announcer Frank Knight ("The Longines Symphonette"); comedienne Beatrice Lillie; emcee Art Linkletter; orchestra leader Guy Lombardo; Raymond "Abe Lincoln" Massey; Grace Matthews ("The Shadow"); Will Osborne, band leader and Mary Pickford ("America's Sweetheart").

There were a couple born in Rumania – Edward G. Robinson ("Big Town") and conductor Harry Salter ("Mr. District Attorney").

Two from Hungary:
Announcer Alois Havrilla ("Jack Benny") and comedian Joe Penner ("Wanna buy a duck?").

Two from France:
Announcer Andre Baruch ("Your Hit Parade") and opera singer Lily Pons.

Two from Denmark:
Victor Borge ("Kraft Music Hall") and Jean Hersholt ("Dr. Christian").

Two from South Africa:
Newsman and host John Charles Daly ("What's My Line?") and Basil Rathbone ("Sherlock Holmes").

Three from Spain:
Band leader Xavier Cugat; pianist Jose Iturbi and Jinx Falkenburg McCrary ("Tex and Jinx").

Plus, one each from:
Mexico: Nigel Bruce ("Sherlock Holmes").
China: George Fenneman ("You Bet Your Life").
India: Jessica Dragonette ("Palmolive Beauty Box Theater").
Argentina: Singer Dick Haymes.
The Netherlands: Band leader Peter Van Steeden ("Town Hall Tonight").

Perhaps, the most unusual birthplace listing of all would be that for torch singer Gertrude Niesen. She was born in the mid-Atlantic Ocean in 1914. Her parents had been heading out on a belated honeymoon to Europe when they got wind of an impending war and decided to head back home. Gertrude arrived before they made it back. That would make it extremely difficult to give the census taker your home town, wouldn't it?

## HE WAS SHANGHAIED

At the ripe old age of fifteen, William "Bud" Abbott was given a "Mickey Finn" (knockout drops) in a beer joint in Brooklyn. He was shanghaied onto a ship headed for Norway. When they got there, he managed to jump ship and eventually worked his way home. His father got him a job as assistant cashier at a burlesque theater. Abbott saved some money, started some burlesque house in partnership with his brother, couldn't make it work and wound up back in a box office of another Brooklyn theater – the Empire. That's where he met Louis Francis Cristello, who changed his name to Costello after he had some success with a show troupe in St. Joseph, Missouri. Take your choice on how they got together – either a sick Costello straight man with Abbott filling in successfully, or that it was by design and not accident. It has been told both ways. In either case, they made their way around burlesque and lower echelon vaudeville for about nine years before they got noticed and eventually had everyone wondering, "Who's on first?"

## Why-y-y-y, Daddy?

The first actor to play the part of John Perry on *John's Other Wife*, one of the innumerable Frank and Anne Hummert soap opera productions was Hanley Stafford. But, he didn't hang on to the part because he supposedly didn't project enough of a "fatherly image." That was in 1936 and Stafford was followed on that program in the role of the store-owning Perry by the likes of Matt Crowley, Luis Van Rooten, Richard Kollmar, William Post Jr. and Joseph Curtin. I don't know what "fatherly" edge they might have had on Stafford, but he, of course, eventually wound up as the long-suffering "Daddy Higgins on *Baby Snooks* with Fanny Brice.

As some of you may know, Stafford's real name was Alfred John Austin and he was born in Hanley, Staffordshire, England. It's easy to see how he came up with his professional name, but why-y-y-y, Daddy?

## It Was Audience Participation in Name Only
*Can You Top This?*

The audience did take part – sort of, that is. Listeners were invited to send in stories or jokes that were edited in such a way that Peter Donald could then present them to the three-man panel. Donald happened to be a character actor and dialectician who could tell the submitted material in what was generally outrageous fashion. If a listener had a story selected to be used in that manner they would receive ten dollars, not bad with the Great Depression still in existence. Then, if the panel of "Senator" Ed Ford, Harry Hershfield and Joe Laurie, Jr. couldn't top it on a laugh meter activated by studio audience laughter and applause, another five dollars was added to the take. That amount of worthwhile money made the idea even more attractive. The program had begun on WOR in New York in early December, 1940 and there were around 6,000 entries a week. There was absolutely no rehearsal with everything on a spontaneous basis. Not only did the panelists work with no script or notes they had no idea what the jokes were going to be until Donald presented them on the air. At that point, it was up to the trio of jokesmiths to do their best to "top" the submitted material. They seemed to know every joke that had ever been told or written and were absolute masters at doing a "switch," with uncanny ability to take a joke and twist it around into a new gag. All their efforts were funny enough that the program made its way onto NBC in 1942, changed to Mutual in 1948 and got one year reprieves in 1950 (on ABC) and 1953 (back on NBC). The formula was the same in each case, with story- telling, belly laughs and wit. The way they described it was that Hershfield took care of half the story-telling, Laurie handled half the belly laughs and Ford half the wit.

The whole idea came about from joke telling sessions at the famed Lambs Club and Ford created, produced and owned the show. A so-called "thumbnose" sketch by Laurie told that Ford got an after dinner speaking job at the Republican Club in New York. Then-Senator Warren G. Harding spoke ahead of him and the roastmaster followed with an introduction of Ed, "This man is a substitute. I don't know how good he is, but time was short and we had to take what we could get." He facetiously added, "I introduce you to "Senator" Ed Ford." The title was born and stuck forever after. With tongue in cheek later information alleged that Ford supposedly attended grammar school and high school for a few years, then set out to get an education. That background gave him the mental equipment that worked wonderfully well on *Can You Top This?*

On radio, he was the first guest star on *The La Palina Hour* and it was said he was paid with a cigar he was still smoking much later. Pseudo biographical information indicated he may have had an artistic talent and spent a few months on a job at the Academy of Fine Arts, but left when they started using automatic elevators. Another fictional aspect of his activity indicated he was once involved with a harmony quartet and they were hired to sing at a funeral. When they arrived it was discovered the man wasn't dead yet, but they were told to sing until he died. They managed to do the job in less than a chorus.

Harry Hershfield also had an educational struggle, with records indicating he flunked blocks and sandpile in kindergarten, finally achieving the distinction of being the only student in sixth grade that the teacher called "Mister." After finally graduating from grammar school he attended a school of illustration and shortly felt that he was illiterate enough to give the newspaper business a try. It's said all men are created equal, but Harry became a cartoonist. His first effort along this line was a comic strip called *Homeless Hector* in the *Chicago Daily News*, and he eventually did a strip, *Abe Kabibble* that ran for many years.

He did his best to become a failure but was unsuccessful, so he got a start in radio with a nightly program called *One Man's Opinion*, doing theater reviews. He also had an appearance on a Milton Berle radio program called, *If You Heard This One, Stop Me!* They did! By that point, it was said his name meant one thing in radio – shut it off! However, he lucked out and teamed up with Ford and Laurie on *Can You Top This?* Hershfield did much of his speaking with his hands, which meant that if he had a sore throat he didn't have to gargle, he just rinsed his hands. His accent was described as a strange mixture of NBC Oxford and early Bronx. He would often quote himself in order, he said, to add spice to his conversation.

About Joe Laurie, Jr., he *did* attend some school, according to witnesses (nine truant officers). However, when he was faced with printed matter, he would cry out, "I never graduated!," maintaining that if sign language had been good enough for the Indians it was good enough for him. He steadfastly claimed to have held around eighty different jobs at one time or another, starting as a newsboy. He stated he was so honest he bought one of his own papers rather than sneak a peek at the want ads trying to get a real job. Prior to that, his life was apparently as intelligent as a P.S. on a telegram. Once, while leaving an office, it was told that some postage stamps stuck to his sleeve, so he took advantage by writing something on his coat and mailing it.

Laurie actually appeared in several Broadway productions and wrote ten scenes for *Over the Top*, which featured comedian Ed Wynn. His skits gave Fred Astaire his first speaking part, which Joe said was the reason Fred became a dancer! Joe Laurie also wanted it known that he was not related to Annie!

(Note: Tongue-in-cheek material concerning these three humorists was drawn from their own scribblings that served as a lead-in to a book published in 1945 that contained a sampling of jokes used on their program. Times were different and humor was simpler, but their trigger-minded repartee helped provide a nation with laughter when it was sorely needed. Here are a few samples:

"I know an absent-minded nudist who went out one time, with his clothes on!"

-Ford

"A panhandler stopped a fellow on the street, "Please give me three cents for a cup of coffee," he begged. "Three cents for a cup of coffee?," exclaimed the man, "a cup of coffee is five cents. Asked the panhandler, "Who buys retail?"

-Hershfield

"A lawyer got his client a suspended sentence – they hanged him!"

-Laurie, Jr.

"Quite an experience was had by a man on a recent trip to Miami.

"Oh, did I have trouble with my wife," he groaned. "She's one of those fancy ladies who's never satisfied. She had to go to a hotel that charges forty dollars a day for a room, so we got a room for forty dollars a day! The next afternoon she had to go horseback riding. Right away she fell off the horse and got knocked unconscious! I called a doctor and he said she'd be unconscious for twelve weeks!"

"Unconscious for twelve weeks?, gasped a friend who had listened patiently. "What did you do?"

"I moved to a cheaper hotel!"

-Hershfield

"I remember years ago when a horse would see an automobile and get frightened. Now, the only time a horse gets frightened is when he sees another horse!"

-Laurie, Jr.

As the three funnymen maintained, there's no such thing as an old joke. If you've never heard it, it's a new one. They asserted, "You never hear anyone say, 'break a joke to me,"; they say, 'crack a joke,' because jokes are indestructible."

# May 6, 1937, Lakehurst, NJ
# It Was Arguably the Single Most Memorable "Eyewitness" Report in the History of Radio

Herb Morrison of WLS, Chicago, gave the report of the Hindenburg disaster. A friend we met as a result of the online Old Time Radio Digest provided some intimate information about the personal side of this broadcasting icon.

**Herb Morrison:**
**A Memoir and Appreciation**
-By Bill Jaker

In the early 1970s, public television stations around the country were instituting ambitious regular local news programming. At the time, I was producer for WWVU-TV in Morgantown, West Virginia and in charge of putting on *The Mountain Scene Tonight*. To counsel and console us we turned to a local resident with long experience in radio and television news. One day our consultant paused to chat for a moment with some young staffers. After he walked away, one of the videographers asked, "Who was that?"

"Oh, that's Herb Morrison."

"Herb Morrison!," the fellow gasped, gazing wide-eyed toward the short grey-haired man heading briskly down the hall, "Wow, this is like, well, like…meeting Moses!"

Once during a picnic at my house the conversation turned, for some reason, to the 1937 explosion of the dirigible Hindenburg. "I once heard the recording of the radio report where the announcer describes the explosion," a friend of mine remarked. 'Who was it who did that?"

One of the other guests at the picnic table responded matter-of-factly, "It was me."

I think my friend dropped his hotdog.

Herb Morrison will always be remembered for his breathtaking, tearful description of the Hindenburg disaster. The story of that broadcast has been told many times and the experience of announcer

Morrison and his engineer, Charlie Nehlsen, is one of the great adventures of the twentieth century. It gave Herb Morrison the often uncomfortable status of "living legend." To me, he was just a dear friend and neighbor.

Herbert O. Morrison was a staff announcer at WLS in Chicago when he attempted an experiment in transcribed field reporting and went to Lakehurst, New Jersey to record some interviews with Chicago-area passengers arriving on the first anniversary of the dirigible Hindenburg's Atlantic crossings. His whole career would later be viewed in terms of thirty-eight seconds of the most dramatic eyewitness account in the history of broadcasting.

He later worked for WOR/Mutual in New York, served in the U.S. Army Air Corps during World War II and was news director of WTAE-TV in Pittsburgh. At the time I got to know him, Herb was a radio-TV producer for West Virginia University's public information office, probably the least challenging job he'd ever held and one from which he would soon be retired.

Herb and his wife, Jeanne, had moved back to West Virginia and settled in the Morrison family's winterized vacation cottage on a steep hillside above Cheat Lake (you had to climb about sixty steps to reach the porch.) It was a warm and cluttered home and on the couch was a small cushion with a needlepoint depiction of the Hindenburg going up in flames, the handicraft of a friend, and the only visible bit of memorabilia of that event.

My fondest memory of Herb Morrison has nothing to do with broadcasting or news or dirigibles. One night while folding my laundry I somehow tore some back muscles and was almost completely immobilized. After a painful, sleepless night I asked my next-door neighbor to drive me in to an emergency room. He offered to wait for me, but not knowing how long I'd be there I thanked him and said I'd call when I needed a ride home. As it turned out, I was seen quickly, had medication prescribed and was told to go home and rest. But the person who had taken me there must have been running around town because I couldn't reach him. Who could rescue me in my sorry state?

I phoned Herb Morrison. He lived near me and drove a large car that would be easy for me to enter and exit (Herb always liked

Cadillacs and believed that even a "pre-owned" Caddy was better than most new cars). I wasn't sure how Herb, a Christian Scientist, would feel about entering a hospital but he said he'd be right over.

A few minutes later, as I stood in the waiting room (simply sitting down was still painful), Herb came bounding in.

"I know what it's like, Bill. Just take it easy and lean on me. I'll help you out."

With that, the small man in his mid-70s turned around and told me, a guy then in his 30s who stood 6-5, to settle onto his back and in front of dozens of eyes he carried me out to the waiting car. He carefully helped me in and when we arrived at my home pried me out and piggy-backed me into the house.

Once we made it inside, Herb had a suggestion. "Here's how you get those back muscles straightened out." With those words Herb Morrison leaped up and grabbed the top of a door frame. He stretched his full frame and began to swing his feet in the air, a remarkable gymnastic performance. Given my height I'd probably be able to do little more than lean and dangle, but I appreciated the advice.

One day I ran into Herb at the bank and he had a disturbing question, "Did you hear a report that I'd died?"

I had not, and surmised that someone must have confused him with Bret Morrison, the radio actor who played *The Shadow*, and who had recently passed away.

Herb shook his head and then made the most unquestionable statement I ever heard, "People won't hire me if they think I'm dead."

For the first time in his life, he was making money from the Hindenburg broadcast. The original report was produced by WLS on the stipulation that Morrison go to Lakehurst on his day off, and although he was given a gold watch for his accomplishment, he was never paid. But now, he was in demand as a guest speaker – made appearances on David Frost's TV show and on *Good Morning, America*. He was an adviser on the film *Hindenburg*, a genre disaster movie starring George C. Scott. When Herb recounted his and Charlie Nehlsen's experiences and their tangle with German agents who wanted to keep the recording of the explosion off the air, one of the producers commented, "That's the movie we ought to be making."

Herb possessed newsreel film of the tragedy and with his radio report synched to the footage, would show it during lectures. One day he brought it to WWVU-TV to have it transferred to videotape. The engineer on duty told him it would take a few minutes before the film and tape could be set up but that he'd have it for him after Herb's scheduled meeting with the station manager. But, Herb waited in Master Control and never let that reel of film out of sight. Even after it was electronically duplicated it was his most valued physical possession.

On the morning of January 28, 1986, Herb happened to be walking through his living room and again became a witness to a tragic historic event. Jeannie had left the TV set on and even though he hadn't planned to watch, Herb paused for a moment to see CNN's live coverage of the space shuttle Challenger. Within minutes his phone began to ring. News organizations around the world wanted to know his feelings about reports on the Challenger disaster, especially the calm, detached voice of Mission Control as all communication was lost with the exploding rocket. Herb explained that there was really little comparison between a craft several miles in the sky and a dirigible a few hundred feet away. It was obvious, though, that the Hindenburg broadcast was still considered a standard by which to measure other tragic events.

A year later, Morrison returned to Lakehurst for a fiftieth anniversary observance of the final flight of the Hindenburg, and for an interview on ABC Television. His health was failing and travel wasn't easy for him. By then I had moved to New York and on a trip back to West Virginia I went to visit with Herb and Jeannie. The last time I saw him Herb had aged considerably, and not too gracefully. Almost our entire conversation was about the discomfort of the trip to New Jersey, but he brightened a bit when he mentioned the limo driver who came to take him to the airport. "He said he couldn't believe who he was meeting."

Herb Morrison died on January 10, 1989 at age 83. His death was widely reported and Tom Brokaw paid tribute to him on NBC Nightly News. Herb was a gentle and decent man, well remembered as a great broadcasting pioneer. I also like to recall him swinging from the top of my kitchen door."

## They Were Once Hired to Bolster Broadcasts by the Glenn Miller Orchestra

The Andrews Sisters were, without question, one of the most successful and influential female music groups in history. The way they sounded, the way they looked and their overall attitude of optimism were major ingredients that personified the renowned Swing Era. Although the Glenn Miller orchestra was ranked number one in the nation, sponsors decided he might need additional help on the Chesterfield broadcasts from December, 1939 to March, 1940, so the Andrews Sisters were signed on. It was eventually discovered the Miller band didn't need extra help to attract an audience and the two groups went their separate ways.

At the time of this writing, April, 2011, Patty Andrews is the only surviving sister at the age of 93. LaVerne and Maxene were older and passed away previously. When Maxene died at the age of 79 she left behind a book, *Over Here, Over There* that was published by Zebra Books in 1993. This is where she gave some insights into herself and the famed trio. In it she, without hesitation, gave credit to the Boswell sisters, who influenced them and many other singers.

In part, she put it this way, saying it was "in 1932 when the Andrews Sisters debuted as a professional singing act in Minneapolis, Minnesota." (If you're keeping track of the numbers, that means Patty was only fourteen at the time). Maxene went on, "We weren't the first popular girls' singing trio of our day. The Boswell Sisters were a hit act in the early days of radio in the 1920s and became favorites of ours when we were kids."

"We loved them and their music and began imitating their singing style around the house. LaVerne had a wonderful memory for music. She'd listen to a song by the Boswell Sisters and work it out for our own three-part harmony. Patty sang the lead, I sang a higher soprano, and LaVerne took the alto part."

"When we began appearing at various small social events in Minneapolis, word about the three local singing sisters got around quickly. Our first professional contract was with a big 'unit show,' a program with one orchestra and a variety of acts. Unit shows were vaudeville's last gasp and that particular unit proved it. We must have closed every RKO theater in the Midwest."

"We went hungry at times, like anyone else starting out in show business. Mama and Papa traveled with us, helping to save money by cooking meals in our hotel room and doing our laundry. The *Richmond News Leader* ran a feature article describing those early days and our eventual success with *Bei Mir Bist Du Schoen*. The paper said we had been 'an obscure trio on Starvation Street in vaudeville and radio. They believed in each other and soon they were in the four-figure income bracket.'

Maxene also wrote about the big band era being in full force and gave more information about the relatively brief on-air alliance with Glenn Miller. The sisters were doing well on *Your Hit Parade*, and with the Chesterfield sponsors uncertain as to how the Miller sound would go over with the listening audience, they did a couple of things for insurance. They hired the Andrews Sisters and signed a contract for only thirteen weeks, just in case. Well, the program quickly went to three times a week with great response. So much so, that Miller signed for another year, while the Andrews Sisters went back to a personal appearance tour that was already booked.

In her book, Maxene told a great story about her dog, Tyrone, that she took on every trip they made during his 15-year lifetime. He would usually wait offstage, but one night at the Hippodrome Theater in Baltimore, he walked out before the act was over and just sat there looking at them.

As Maxene related, "Finally, Patty put her hands on her hips and said to Tyrone for the first time in his life, 'Now what would you do if *Der Fuehrer* walked in here right now?'

"That little thing got right up from where he was sitting in the middle of the stage, walked to the front, straight to the floor microphone, lifted his leg, and wet the base of the mike. The applause was deafening."

And that was just the way applause was all those years for the close harmony of the Andrews Sisters. It's somewhat sad that we'll never see their like again.

## NILA MACK DIDN'T LIKE CHILDREN...AT FIRST!

That's what we learned about the long-time director of *Let's Pretend*, one of radio's top-notch and long running children's programs, when we spoke with Arthur Anderson. He acted on radio for many years, eighteen of them on *Let's Pretend*, so he had all the first-hand stories concerning the highly successful show. We discovered many facets of the program in an exclusive interview with Arthur.

TDOY (Thrilling Days of Yesteryear:) We listened to a *Let's Pretend* recently with the cast doing a musical version of *Robin Hood* and you were Allan-a-Dale.

A.A. That was one of the shows recorded after the death of the program's creator, Nila Mack.

TDOY: When Johanna Johnston had taken over?

A.A. That's right. Nila took over the show in 1930 when it was originally *The Adventures of Helen and Mary*. In 1934, the title was changed to *Let's Pretend* and Nila Mack continued as its director, it being sustaining all those days, finally becoming sponsored in 1943 and for nine years then by Cream of Wheat. She kept on directing through the loss of our sponsorship at the end of 1952. She died in January, 1953 and I've always thought she died of shock because her child was dying, her child was no longer sponsored and it was obvious that *Let's Pretend* couldn't last much longer because they didn't want to pay all those actors. TV was becoming the glamour boy.

TDOY: It is said that Nila could be pretty demanding during the show because she wanted everything to be right...also that she had a kind of maternalistic approach to all of you when it wasn't actually show time.

A.A. She was both. You never knew which flavor you were going to get. The cast of *Let's Pretend* was originally child actors. When *The Adventures of Helen and Mary* was changed because they decided it was a rather dull children's program, it was also felt someone else needed to take over. When Nila stepped in she agreed it was pretty dull. She was a former actress who wasn't working much but had done some broadcasting for CBS. They eventually remembered her, but it was after she got a Broadway show and then had to leave for her hometown of Arkansas City, Kansas to care for her sick mother. She wound up working for a small Kansas City station, WEEB, and took over as chief writer, chief announcer, sold time on the phone and was practically the whole operation. Six months later, CBS said they had a job for her. Her mother was better so she could leave. She had applied for a permanent writing job because acting jobs were not too easy to come by. The catch was they wanted her to be in charge of children's programs. This was a shock to her. Nila didn't know anything about children. She didn't even *like* children, told friends she didn't. Strange maybe, but it was a job so she took it, went to New York and that became her life.

TDOY: Did she have children of her own?

A.A. No, she married an actor/writer and they never had children. Incidentally, they both wrote scenarios for silent movies, those single lines of dialogue you read on the screen. He later went to Hollywood and died there, so she never had children of her own. By the way, I've written a book about the show titled, *Let's Pretend: Child Actors in the Golden Age of Radio*. (Note: This was published by McFarland & Company in the mid 1990s.) I started out to write my autobiography but when I got to the part of my life when I joined *Let's Pretend*, which was May 5$^{th}$, 1936, that part got longer and longer. So, I said, wait a minute, this book should be about the show; people will want to know, and that's what it became after three years of research and writing. There are detailed biographies of 18 of the child actors who were on *Let's Pretend*. Most of them were very busy on other shows, too. *Variety* would have called them *Moppet Fests*. So, when you tell the story of *Let's Pretend*, you're automatically telling the story of child actors in radio. I did go a little far afield telling their stories, not just on *Let's Pretend*, but what it was like to be a child actor in radio. You were young but you had to take care of business, work out your schedule, be charming and wonderful and not make any mistakes because it was all done live – no tape in those days.

TDOY: Did Nila Mack's approach change from when you were a child to when you became more of an adult on the show?

A.A. Yes, it did because you obviously cannot talk to a six-year old the way you can talk to a grown-up. When we were starting we were so small we had to stand on platforms to reach the microphone. She wouldn't say you're not doing that very well, wouldn't talk negatively because she knew a child might burst into tears or give a rotten performance. She learned to love the children from working with them, the previous dislike being mostly lack of knowledge about youngsters. The children became her family. She trod very delicately. She might say, "Now, wait a minute, that line you just said, you're supposed to be enchanted and this is a real princess you're talking to. Did you ever talk to a movie star or did your mother ever introduce you to a celebrity? Try to think what that was like." When that same six-six year old child had grown up twenty years later, she could say, "Listen, toots, give it a little more pizazz, ok?"

TDOY: As a young performer, did you have awareness of the great attention being given the show, the many awards that were won? Did the effect you were having on the entire country mean anything to you?

A.A. Not very much. I think it's just as well that it didn't because we might have become spoiled brats. It was only in doing research for the book that I became aware of what a great influence the radio program had on the lives of thousands of American families. Everything would stop on Saturday morning and everyone would gather around the radio. You know, Nila had a great sense of humor and she could appreciate a very sophisticated joke, Not on *Let's Pretend*, of course. One time her sense of humor got the best of her; she couldn't restrain herself. A tiny little girl was playing the lady-in-waiting for the princess and she gave her line as, "Your bath is ready, madam." Nina pressed the talk-back button and said, "No, dear, it's not madam, it's madame, *dam* as in God." The kid didn't get it but everyone else broke up. Everybody at CBS liked Nila Mack and her sense of humor was one of the reasons. By the way, she smoked incessantly and laughed a lot.

TDOY: For a while she handled a show called *The March of Games*.

A.A. That was a quiz program for children, in which they had to do tongue-twisters or finish a rhyme or answer some historical question. It was a lot of fun but it never got a sponsor. Let's Pretenders would do little sketches to lead into questions.

TDOY: Some of the stories on *Let's Pretend* had quite a bit of violence. Were there ever any network censorship problems?

A.A. Not from the network and I don't think the public ever objected. The prince would slay the dragon, sometimes people killed each other with their swords but it was the good guys who killed the bad guys. The bad guys might get the upper hand temporarily but they never won. There was plenty of excitement in the violence but it was tastefully done, nothing like you see on TV nowadays.

TDOY: You also worked for Orson Welles on *Mercury* Theater productions. Which gave more enjoyment?

A.A. It's hard to say. Doing the *Mercury* was always thrilling because of the nature of Orson Welles' creativity. There's just no way to really compare the two. It was a great pleasure to work for both of them. Of course, the money was better on *Mercury* because we were paid as adults. On *Pretend* we originally got three and a half dollars a show, which must have been based on the theory that it was so much fun to be on the radio that you surely didn't expect to get paid, too!

## "Cal-l-l for-r-r Philip Mahh-a-a-reees!"

The diminutive bellhop had an insurance policy against growing taller. Prior to March of 1933, the failure of Johnny Roventini to attain full stature was a sort of family skeleton. The clan consisted of father, mother, John and four brothers and sisters, Every dime obtainable was essential to the upkeep of their little home in Brooklyn, Of course, back then there were few jobs available for young men who didn't measure up to what was considered the physical norm. And Johnny never got over 4-feet tall, even as a grown man. There always might have been the circus or a carnival side-show, but the Roventinis were a close-knit family and the struggling parents, unlike some parents who exploit an unusual child, would not fall back on such as that.

As a result, the under-statured boy wound up following the trade of bellhop where his top earnings never exceeded $25 a week. The only thing certain was that Johnny was going to be able to hang on to the job for the simple reason he was considered to be among the most notable of the many pages in the bigger Manhattan hotels. He was employed at the New Yorker and the executives there liked the smiling reaction by customers because of Johnny's highly original style and concise diction. The old better mouse-trap theory was certainly involved although it took a while to be confirmed. His radio sponsors-to-be eventually paved the way for him to leave the hotel job and move up the ladder to affluence and luxurious comfort. The makers of Philip Morris cigarettes wound up making a beaten path to his door, but there were some detours along the way.

The search had begun when the cigarette company came up with an advertising concept that called for a pageboy to be featured on the label. Several brainstorming sessions carried the idea a step further and it was decided that additional attention to the product could be produced by combining the inanimate trademark with a living counterpart.

An official of the advertising agency that was handling the account, Milton Biow, began a mission. He wanted to find someone who could best match up with the artist's creation. The first crop of candidates was supplied by an employment agency. Scores of boys were looked over but none of them measured up to the preconceived qualifications. As a result, Biow began to practically haunt New York hotels, doing his best to find an individual to match the overall person he had in mind. Later on, he told that it was a complete mystery to him how he missed Johnny Roventini in the drawn-out searching process. But somehow he did until finally, almost in despair, he unloaded his problem on the bell captain at the Hotel Commodore. The uniformed employee told him pointblank, "We don't have the boy you want, but I can tell you where to find him. Just go to the New Yorker and look for a boy named Johnny. He's the best pageboy in America and I sure wish he worked for me." That did it, and for all practical purposes the unusual search ended pretty much right then and there, although Biow wanted to convince himself so he made several return trips to the hotel. On one of the visits, it is said Biow asked Johnny to page a man named Philip Morris. Not knowing it was a cigarette name, the bellhop used his unique style to make the call as he moved around the hotel lobby. He came back and said he had gotten no answer. The follow-up visits were pretty much gestures of thoroughness, because as soon as Biow laid eyes on the diminutive bellhop and heard his paging effort he was certain the cigarette company was going to be enamored of Johnny. As it turned out, he was right on all counts.

This mite of a man was just a radio voice to many listeners, but his inimitable "Cal-l-l for-r-r Philip Mahh-a-a-rees," made him into a definite personality around the eastern part of the nation. He received formal invitations from various mayors and he was made a guest of honor at many functions of fraternal and business organizations. No matter where he appeared, his lifetime contract called for him to sing out his widely known page call at least once. During the course of his advertising career unusual things could happen. One amusing incident took place during a broadcast of the *Youth Opportunity Program*. Johnny was due to step up to the microphone and give his famed call. Unfortunately, as he started to move into place he tripped over some wires and fell. There wasn't time to scramble back up so he did his line while flat on his back. His powerful voice made it work okay.

In spite of all the attention that bordered on adulation, Johnny Roventini never forgot his roots and he took part of his higher earnings to purchase and furnish a new home for his family. His watch charm size was no longer a liability. It actually became such an asset that he was eventually insured by Lloyd's of London for one-million dollars *against further growth*! The fame and fortune made life so much easier that Johnny's longevity factor took him until 1988 when he died at the age of 88.

## An Irreverent Introduction for "Spiderlegs" Kalty And Somewhat Surprisingly H.V. Kaltenborn Didn't Seem to Mind

A remarkable commentator/journalist named Mary Margaret McBride established standards during a turbulent two decades from 1935 to 1955 for the hundreds upon hundreds of radio talk shows that would one day exist. Her program was an alternative to afternoon soap operas and showed clearly that female interests went far beyond such things as recipes and cleaning tips. She had an easy-going informality in her unscripted interviews that allowed her to persuade guests to come out with fresh, spontaneous responses. That's undoubtedly why H.V. Kaltenborn didn't seem to mind when she referred to him as "Spiderlegs." She had discovered that some old friends of his had called him that way back in his native Wisconsin. His acceptance of her usage was a trifle unexpected because he was often referred to as the dignified dean of radio correspondents. He had a massive ego to go along with his great adlibbing ability. Kaltenborn had graduated from Harvard cum laude and as a colleague once observed, "never let anyone forget it." He was also a Phi Beta Kappa member and didn't let anyone forget that either.

The McBride chat brought out the story of his really early exposure to radio. In 1921, he was working at the *Brooklyn Daily Eagle* when he took part in an experiment that had a huge impact on his life. He spoke on the radio from Newark, New Jersey and was heard by a small Chamber of Commerce group in Brooklyn that had gathered around for a demonstration of this new invention. He recalled, "The next year I began a series of radio talks on current events, the first spoken editorials ever heard by a radio audience. Hardly a week went by in which there was not some threat to have me put off the air because of my frank expression of opinion."

His recognition factor continued to grow and during twenty days and nights of a 1938 crisis in Czechoslovakia he made 102 broadcasts ranging in length from two minutes to two hours. By that time, portable radio sets had been developed and people listened everywhere with Kaltenborn becoming a household word. As he described it, "News bulletins were handed to me as I talked. Speeches of foreign leaders had to be analyzed and sometimes translated while they were being delivered. I had to keep a constant eye on the control room for signs telling me when I was on or off the air. Sometimes when I had just launched into an analysis of a foreign leader's speech I was given a signal to wind up my talk in exactly one minute. On other occasions I was told to comment on a new development for exactly three minutes before the network switched to a foreign capital. Then, suddenly they would discover that connections with Europe could not be made and the engineer would signal me to continue my comments and expand them until further notice."

Kaltenborn had a stiff-necked appearance and an exaggerated way of speaking that led to an overall feeling of imperiousness about him. That's why it was so amusing when newly-elected President Harry Truman mimicked him after Kaltenborn had declared that Thomas E. Dewey was the winner in the 1948 presidential election.

He had an all-out passion for keen analysis and it was once carried to an extreme when he followed up a prayer for peace by the Pope, with an analysis of the prayer.

He even crossed swords with Edward R. Murrow a few times. One such occurrence came when Murrow was on the air from London with Kaltenborn, Robert Trout and Paul White in the studio in New York. Murrow did his report, Kaltenborn followed with his own and then proceeded to analyze what Murrow had previously said. That didn't sit well with Murrow and when the broadcast was over he called New York on the cue channel and in ice-cold tones, said, "Someone has just been on the air explaining what I said…I don't need anyone explaining what I say!" Trout later told that when that happened, "Redness started at H.V.'s forehead and moved visibly across his glistening dome. Paul White and I didn't dare say a word." And that was in spite of the fact that White was the first CBS news director and had a direct hand in forming the network's news reputation.

Regardless of the incident, Murrow had admiration for Kaltenborn's hard work and dedication to radio and also his stubborn determination to think critically, to have a point of view, no matter how often he was muzzled. It was the Kaltenborn manner that rubbed Murrow the wrong way.

However, any animosity was eased when Kaltenborn, upon leaving CBS to become a "star commentator" on NBC, sent Murrow a letter. The supreme egoist wrote, "…each time I listen my admiration grows. During this past crucial week you have been a tower of strength to millions of Americans who share your belief and mine in the survival of democracy. I find it almost impossible to be as objective as you are, and yet I am three thousand miles away from the bombs that fall at your feet. Well, anyhow, you are doing the greatest job of radio reporting that has so far been performed by anyone, anywhere."

Harking back again to the early days of radio, even as this great new medium of mass communication swept the entire country by storm, it was still very necessary to "measure up," and that meant no immunity for even someone like Kaltenborn. Once he was chided by a teacher for sliding past the first "n" in the word government. It was such remarks that prompted him to comment, "Radio audiences are not only sensitive to what is said, but they are peculiarly sensitive to a speaker's manner and method. Sloven speech is much more offensive on the air than on the platform. Speakers who have been guilty of certain mispronunciations all their lives are likely to hear about them for the first time when they address an invisible audience. Radio speaking is an almost indecent exposure of the personality. Your audience hears you breathe, knows when you turn your head or turn a page, catches the whispered comment intended for *one* ear and not millions."

Kaltenborn was so meticulous about details that early in his career he had his head placed in one of those frame gadgets (similar to those used by early photographers) so his mouth would stay close to the primitive carbon microphones.

Born as Hans von Kaltenborn, he went to the initials only because of the national antipathy concerning German names during the rise of the third Reich.

When Orson Welles and the *Mercury Theater* group performed the renowned *War of the Worlds* broadcast in 1938, Kaltenborn's wife declared she knew it wasn't real because, "If it had been, Hans would have been there!"

## An Unofficial Biography Says Red, Without Quotation Marks, Was Part of Richard Red Skelton's Christened Name

Another note indicates that his mother recalled he was born on time. By that she meant she urged the doctor to hurry because she wanted the baby to be born before his brothers got home from school. So, he entered the world on time at a little past one o'clock in the afternoon on July 18, 1913, according to records in Knox County, Indiana. That date is also shown in most other places, such as his discharge papers from the Army, his passport and marriage licenses. However, Don Ferris, who was music arranger and piano accompanist on the Skelton TV show for years, told a different story. He stated he heard Red say many times that he was actually born in 1906, that he never wavered, saying, "I have one age for the newspapers and one age for reality."

No matter which is correct, he tried very hard for success in his early days. When he was only seven, he sold newspapers for a penny apiece on a Vincennes, Indiana street corner before and after school because, he said, "My family was hungry." Other menial jobs included washing dishes in a diner, ushering in a theater, and racking balls in a pool hall. Sometimes he would hitchhike to other towns to sing and dance on the street for pennies. Seymour Berns, a one-time producer of Skelton's TV show, indicated Red once told him that he was briefly a towel boy in an Indiana whorehouse. Berns did say, though, you couldn't always tell if the comedian was fibbing or trying to be funny by shocking you.

Skelton was only twelve when he ran away from home the first time to join the Doc Lewis Patent Medicine Show. He wanted to sing and dance but Doc wasn't impressed by his talent and instead hired him to help sell bottles of his supposedly health-giving elixir. He quickly sold out his initial batch, went back to the platform to get more, tripped on the steps and took a nose-dive into the medicine bottles. The crowd roared with laughter and Red was hired to keep falling off the stage. That was the beginning of his comic "pratfalls" that he used from then on in his career.

School started up again and Red went home to little or no scholastic success for a couple of years before trying out with a traveling repertory group of actors when he was fourteen. But, when he tried serious roles the audience laughed and he got fired after just a week. He was stranded in a flea-bag hotel along the Missouri River when some luck came his way. A showboat chugged onto the scene and one of its actors had just been shot in an argument with a riverboat gambler. He auditioned and the youngster used several spectacular pratfalls that got him the job. Because of a lack of education he began using more and more pantomime. When a routine wasn't working he would win the audience over by falling into the orchestra pit and reappearing with a drum draped around his neck.

His sight comedy drew far more laughs than any verbal wit and he continued in that manner for several seasons floating up and down the rivers. Without question this experience led to many later critics who considered him better on TV than he ever was on radio. At that time, though, both venues were yet to come and he had one stint as a clown in the same circus where his father had performed years before.

When the stock market crashed, circuses were in trouble and Red took whatever jobs he could get. These were such things as performing in some sleazy carnivals, going on more showboat cruises, and playing one-nighters in crummy tank towns. He was a sideshow barker for a few months and spent a season as a "Mammy" in a minstrel show. It meant often traveling with the dregs of society, ranging from petty thieves to chronic drunks to con men to ladies of little or no virtue. There wasn't much money involved but the people he met and the places he went provided inspiration for many of the characters he eventually improvised. By the time he was seventeen he could handle a broad number of things as a performer.

Finally, around 1930, he got a chance to move up the ladder at the Gaiety Burlesque Theater in Kansas City. The "third banana" there got appendicitis and Red got the job for $75 a week, not bad at all for Depression days. It was here he met Edna Marie Stilwell, who eventually became his wife and guide for much of his later career.

But, that was later because she was only fifteen at the time. To top it off, she didn't think much of his act and told management he ought to be fired. At any rate, the Gaiety was raided several times, couldn't pay fines for its strippers and had to close, with Skelton then having to look for work again.

Once more, he was bailed out. Events that were really endurance contests known as Walkathons or Dance Marathons used a clown as part of the entertainment. Well, Red was indeed a clown and one was needed at the Civic Auditorium in Kansas City. For ten hours a day he'd do just about anything to get a laugh You name it, he did it...breaking plates, making faces, taking pratfalls, even swiped a mounted patrolman's horse to ride around the auditorium. No laughs, no job, so he did card tricks, rode a tricycle around the edge of the balcony, recited poetry, doused himself with soft drinks grabbed from customers, whatever it took.

Then, what do you know, one day Edna showed up as a contestant. She danced for two and a half months and won the championship $500. Exhausted, she slept for three days only to discover when she woke up that the money had been stolen. Red sympathized, took her to dinner and proposed three months later. In June of 1931, just four days after her 16$^{th}$ birthday, they got married and went on to work the Walkathons for two to three years.

After continuing ups and downs they finally met an agent who got them some vaudeville bookings, including one in Canada. That worked out well and word about the act spread south by early 1937 and Red got booked into the Capital Theater in Washington, D.C. Next came his first Broadway exposure at Loew's State in New York. He got to make his radio debut in Cincinnati on WLW on *The Red Foley Show*. It went well, but a shot at a variety show in Chicago with Tommy Dorsey fell through when the often irascible T.D. set aside his trombone long enough to say he wasn't going to split his billing "with some hillbilly comic out of the Midwest." They found another band and Red got do his own show sponsored by Raleigh Cigarettes on the NBC station. It wasn't a coast-to-coast hookup but it did lead to a 1938 gig on *The Fleischmann Hour*, one of the country's top-rated shows emceed by Rudy Vallee. Highly responsive audience reaction led to another appearance two weeks later, and still another in November. His own show went off at the end of summer and the agent got him a top comedy spot on *Avalon Time*, due to start in the fall. To say things were looking up would be putting it mildly because by now Skelton's asking price at top movie theaters was up to $2,500 a week and he appeared with such bands as Benny Goodman, Artie Shaw, Harry James, Glenn Miller and even one or the other of the Dorsey brothers. His vaudeville house price shot up to $4,300 a week by the beginning of 1940.

More recognition came with movies and the Raleigh cigarette people climbed aboard again for a 39-week run of *The Red Skelton Scrapbook of Satire*. You can bet Red's days of hunger were over for sure.

Many years later, your writer fondly recalls meeting Skelton at the famed Del Coronado Hotel in San Diego, where many of his exceptional clown paintings were for sale. He was very cordial and we had a pleasant chat. Next morning at brunch I introduced him to my wife, Carol, a big fan. As he was leaving, and at her behest, he screwed up that pliable face and gave her his memorable closing, "God bless."

A tortured, erratic man with many faults, but a gifted comedian and one of our great "clowns," who brought forth some of the finest pantomime pieces of business ever seen on any stage anywhere.

## She Had No Idea Who They Meant When They Said "Arthur Godfrey" But She Soon Learned

Your writer had the good luck to meet and chat with a person who is a living, breathing example of the word "charm." It's a fascinating trait and I only wish there was a way to put down on paper the delightful Irish accent of Carmel Quinn, who sang on the Godfrey show for six years. We wound up with an exclusive interview with the delightful lady.

TDOY: So you were born in Dublin, Ireland?

C.Q. That's right, good old Dublin.

TDOY: What are you up to these days?

C.Q. Lots of concerts, some radio and TV and speaking engagements, which is great fun. I really just do my show and chat about Ireland, coming to America, the Godfrey show, and in between I throw in a song.

TDOY: Tell us about getting together with the old red head.

C.Q. That was an accident, sort of; my whole life has been an accident. I had been over here for only a short time and was singing around the apartment. People said to me…the next door neighbors…why didn't I go in for the Godfrey show. The funny thing is, the night I arrived from Ireland, I wanted to see Broadway. I wanted to see the theaters, the names, the lights. I was so tired but I didn't care. I wanted to see it all that night before I went to sleep. I was taken to a pub at NBC…Connie Hurley's Pub. The man with me said Carmel sings a bit and Connie said what she should do is go in for *that* show. He pointed at the TV and it was the Godfrey program. I had never heard of him at all, didn't know who he was. But I looked up and thought, a television show, I wouldn't have a hope. Months later I was auditioning and it was that show. I went in just to ask for an audition and I sang without music.

TDOY: Do you remember what you sang?

C.Q. I did obscure songs first, sang one called *The Old Bog Road*…beautiful song. I sang a couple of others and then I threw in an American song. I thought I'd sing a real love song because they wouldn't go for those Irish songs. So, I went into *What Is This Thing Called Love*, and they said, "Oh, no, we hear that all the time. Don't do that!" So, I sang a few more and they said they were going to put me on Monday. There was supposed to be six-month wait. Well, anyway, I managed to win on *Talent Scouts* and Arthur asked me if I'd like to stay and I was there for six years.

TDOY: What was your background? What kind of training?

C.Q. Never had training to this day. I say to my children…my girls who sing and have voice and acting training…someday I must go in for training, you know? I always loved singing. It was all I ever wanted to do. I was able to express myself better in singing than in speaking.

TDOY: The tinge of accent is still there.

C.Q. I go back to Ireland about twice a year and sing a little over there…that probably accounts for it. Of course, I do concerts all over America and the audiences are just great.

TDOY: You had a radio show for a while.

C.Q. Oh, and I loved it. There's nothing, nothing, nothing like radio. I can wear flat heels. It's so personal. People hear you in their homes, their cars, everywhere. I did call-ins because I love to chat. My whole family was that way. You should have heard my father, he was so witty, and also my sisters and brother. We were always honing our skills with one another. But, anyway, the radio show, oh my, it was so much fun. Radio is so exciting. That's hard to explain to people who don't understand. You use your head to hear and picture everything. Well, anyway, my concert schedule got so heavy. I was taping the show a lot but it wasn't the same. I wanted to talk about things that were happening right now…you know, did you read in the paper this morning? So, I gave it up until such time as I stop concertizing.

TDOY: Did anyone else in your family have any kind of show biz leaning?

C.Q. Everyone. Everybody in Ireland is a bit of a ham. My father was a classical violinist and he couldn't bear when we'd be singing the pop songs. He'd say, "My God, you sound like you're in pain." My sister, oh, a lovely singer. My brother won a lot of medals for singing, classical, sort of. And, you know, all through this, I just loved Jo Stafford, the best singer in the world.

TDOY: Yes, I always felt she and Margaret Whiting were on a higher level than most.

C.Q. Oh, Margaret, I was talking with her and you know, her voice is still wonderful. You know, in Ireland we got a little on the radio but I always had my pencil and a piece of paper to jot down, "See the pyramids across the Nile," And my father would say, "What in the name of God is that…'pyramids across the Nile?' He'd tell us stories of the operas instead. But we had a great life. My sister was…still is…a better singer than I am.

TDOY: Did she do anything professionally?

C.Q. No, Bets wanted to stay home, marry, have children. She'd help me press my dress for going out to sing and she'd wait for me to come in. Now she says, "You're still on the go," because I send her things about what I'm doing. She worries about me. We're still very close. Now, she'd sing at parties and my brother was a bit of a ham. It's just that I was so lucky. Right place, right time.

TDOY: As a soloist did you find it difficult when you moved into musicals like *The Sound of Music* and *Finian's Rainbow*?

C.Q. Yes, and I got so alarmed. The first one I did, I went into *Finian's* in Chicago. I'll never forget seeing the cast, how talented they were, how great the girl singers, the boy singers, the chorus, the dancers, everyone was much better than I was and I knew it. But I was getting paid a lot of money and they were getting a pittance. It just wasn't fair.

TDOY: You mentioned there might be more radio ahead for you after you quit doing concerts. Does that imply some kind of stop date?

C.Q. I don't know. You know, everybody I worked with is retired. And I say, retired? Every show I do, I come off feeling like a million dollars. I just feel the love of the audience. I suppose I'm a person who needs that love. They tell me I bring them joy, so as long as God spares me and gives me my health and my voice holds out, I guess I'll just go on. I don't know. Did you ever say I don't know whatever possessed me to do that? I believe in my case it's fate or something nudging me this way and that way. Someone told me once that if you want to make God laugh, just tell him your plans. So, I just go along and whatever will be, will be…sounds like a song in there somewhere.

A memory concerning this very pleasant person came from Steven Hiss, a friend from down Florida way. He told us, "In the early 60s she and Arthur and the Geezenslaws came to our Music Tent in West Palm Beach for a concert. It clicked from the first joke through the last song. The entire crowd was exhausted from having such a good time. Afterwards, about twenty of us diehards surrounded Carmel and Arthur for questions, etc. After about twenty minutes, Arthur said he needed some tea (Lipton's, of course). So, we all went to a small restaurant, sat around and chatted for about an hour. Their handlers then said it was plane time and we adjourned."

When Carmel attended the Friends of Old Time Radio convention in Newark for a Salute to Godfrey presentation, I asked if she remembered that night. She said that was one of the best things about doing one-nighters. It's because people are hungry for entertainment in small towns and once or twice a year the audience becomes like family. She said those are the special nights that make the traveling worth it.

## A Whole Bunch of Charlies Even a Bald-headed One

It would be difficult for most people who knew and loved ventriloquist dummy, Charlie McCarthy, to visualize him with a face contorted with rage. Or, an old Charlie with vanished hair and graying at the temples. But, both of those Charlies existed, even if it was only in a storage area that few people ever saw.

In her book, *Knock Wood*, Candice Bergen (*Murphy Brown*), told of visiting her father, Edgar Bergen's office on Sunset Boulevard in Hollywood when she was seven years old. She remembered it was more like a shrine than an office. Out front there was a large portrait of Charlie with photographs on either side showing Charlie shaking hands with Eleanor Roosevelt, Winston Churchill, Mae West, Harry Truman, Sweden's King Gustav and others. Glass showcases had Charlie radios and watches, Charlie and Mortimer Snerd tin cars and Charlie's head on teaspoons, enameled compacts, cuff links, comics, etc. There was even a special wooden Oscar with a movable mouth.

But, the real treat came when it was time to leave. "Okay, Monstro, let's go home," Candy's father said. Can you imagine Murphy Brown being called 'Monstro?' She had never seen some of the offices off the dark tunnel leading to the garage. This day, however, her dad stopped at one of the doors, said he'd left something inside and let her in. Candice said there was a series of shapes suspended at eye level; shapes that became *bodies* when her dad switched on the light. All of them were Charlie's bodies; one in his traditional white tie and tails, another with the Sherlock Holmes' tweed suit and cape, one on Napoleon's full-dress uniform and yet another in monogrammed pajamas and silk dressing gown. Accompanying heads were in hooded bags on wooden stands above. She was dumbstruck, so her father took them down to show her. The first was friendly and familiar, the expected Charlie. But then, "A Charlie whose face was ugly with anger, the features twisted, contorted with rage...followed by a bleary-eyed, baldheaded Charlie, a face for whom time had not stood still. The skull was smooth, the forehead furrowed; the thick red hair had vanished, leaving only sparse grey patches that barely fringed the ears and failed to conceal the hearing aid now worn in one. The face was tired and flaccid, the expression weary, the eternal boy grown old."

Was this Bergen's way of recognizing his own advancing years? It may very well have been because it was apparent to many that he considered Charlie a sort of alter ego, the opposite side of a personality. It was almost as though at times he seemed to think of Charlie as a real person just as audiences did, that Charlie could say things he couldn't get by with if he said them himself. It was always amazing that a ventriloquist could be popular on radio since neither he nor the skill to operate him could be seen. Supposedly, there were three Charlies that survived, one in the Smithsonian Institution, another at the Museum of Broadcast Communications in Chicago and a third owned by magician David Copperfield who bought it at auction for $110,000.

It had all begun when Edgar was only eleven years old and ordered a book through the mail called *The Wizard's Manual* that gave him enough information to begin learning the art of ventriloquism. He eventually got a local carpenter, Theodore Mack, to carve his first dummy and that began a remarkable career. I've never heard what might have happened to the other (some grotesque) Charlies that Candice wrote about.

It doesn't matter, because as Candy put it so well about all those dummies in that garage area, "The eyes were dead and dark, the many faces lifeless, because they were nothing without my father."

Although nearing retirement, Edgar was active until the end. He opened at Caesar's Palace in Las Vegas for a two-week engagement with Andy Williams but didn't live to finish it. He died in early October, 1978 of apparent heart failure at the age of 75 before the show ended.

## Outstanding Versatility: Parley Baer Even Had a Wild Animal Act at One Time

Trying to cover everything the late Parley Baer did in show business would require virtually an entire volume. So, we'll condense it somewhat. Here's a partial list of OTR shows on which he appeared: *Gunsmoke, Lux Radio Theater, First Nighter, Escape, Those Websters, Count of Monte Cristo, Honest Harold, Screen Directors Playhouse, My Favorite Husband, Granby's Green Acres, CBS Radio Workshop, Rogers of the Gazette* and *The Adventures of Phillip Marlowe*. A sampling of TV and movie credits includes *The Young and the Restless, Dave,* and even a stint as mayor on *The Andy Griffith Show*. In addition, he was the voice of the Keebler Elf for something like twenty-eight years. Your writer had the great good fortune to work with Parley at the Old Time Radio and Nostalgia Convention in Cincinnati, the Friends of Old Time Radio convention in Newark and the SPERDVAC convention in L.A. It was an absolute delight just to be around him and hear his wonderful stories. We're pleased to pass along one of our interviews.

TDOY: Let's chat about your name first. Parley. Unusual name. I don't think I've heard it anywhere else.

P.B. Well, Salt Lake City was my home and Parley is an old Mormon name. One of Brigham Young's right-hand men coming into the Promised Valley had the unlikely name of Parley P. Pratt. My father's name was Charles…of course, Charley…and he had an abhorrence for juniors. He didn't like Big Charles, Little Charles. So, a friend of my mother's said to name me Parley, it rhymes with Charley. I've run into two people in my life with the name. One was a drummer in the university band, Parley Giles, and one other man I met just in passing. He couldn't believe it, saw my name on a piece of luggage and said that was his name, too, and that I was the only Parley he ever met.

TDOY: I got a kick out of it when Willard Waterman (*The Great Gildersleeve*) said, "I call him Barely Par."

P.B. (Chuckle) He never spoke a truer word.

TDOY: I bring that up because there seems to have been a real closeness among all the folks who were involved in the so-called Golden Age of Radio. There was a magic kind of chemistry.

P.B. Yes, we were more than co-workers, we were friends. Y'know, we saw each other frequently two or three times a week and if we didn't know someone was going to be on vacation or out of town or something, and they didn't show up, everyone was on the phone to find out what was the matter. We were solicitous of each other's husbands or wives, we were worried about the kids and whatnot. It was a much more closely-knit form of show business. I think the only thing close to it might have been a traveling company, a compatible group that would be together practically 24-hours a day. We developed some lifelong friendships.

TDOY: Since many of you did dozens of shows, you naturally kept running into one another.

P.B. Sure. Willard, of course, was part of the Chicago contingent. For a long time that city was the axis of everything.

TDOY: Do you think maybe *Amos 'n' Andy* beginning there shortly after origination of a network caused a proliferation of shows, or was it, perhaps, just a more central time zone?

P.B. I think time was probably it; it just kind of evolved there. A lot of the big local shows turned into network shows, some of the most successful began that way. *First Nighter* was local and the "soaps" all came from there at first.

TDOY: I have a copy of an original script of *The First Nighter* later on when it was done from the west coast and there's a notation at the bottom for the announcer to make absolutely no reference to the CBS Hollywood studios. Although it started in Chicago, throughout it was always called "The Little Theater Off Times Square" and they wanted to maintain that mythical aura.

P.B. Yeah, and they did. There were many through the years long after it was off the air would ask if the cast went back and forth to the east coast to do it. For a while, you know, we did two shows each time, one for the east and one for the rest of the country.

TDOY: Since the networks frowned on recordings.

P.B. Right. Recordings were only a means of air-checks.

TDOY: Bing Crosby is given most of the credit for changing that.

P.B. That was why he changed to ABC because that was the first net that said they'd let you tape.

TDOY: He helped the beginning of Ampex equipment that evolved from some German gear.

P.B. Uh-huh…probably had a piece of the company.

TDOY: When people talk about you, it's often about the most successful western show in history and many of the non-old time radio fans think of *Gunsmoke* as a TV creation, forgetting that it was three and a half years or so prior to that that it began on radio. With some of the finest writing, production, sound effects and acting, it was really a class act when William Conrad had the lead as Marshal Matt Dillon and you were there as Chester.

P.B. Good ol' Chester…y'know, that show had a lot of unity, a lot of camaraderie. The company that started out with Bill…nothing changed…it was the same till the end, and fortunately, when we recorded our last show we didn't know it was the final one. We were supposed to do some more. We were about 4 or 5 shows ahead as I recall and I was doing a *Petticoat Junction* when Norman Macdonnell called me, like on a Thursday and said, "I've got bad news. There'll be no *Gunsmoke* recording Saturday." I said, "Oh," not too concerned, and he added, "Or any other Saturday in the future." I asked what he meant and he said we'd gotten the axe. My first reaction was thank goodness we didn't know we were doing the last one when we did it because it would have been a sad, sad time.

TDOY: What a stunned feeling that must have been.

P.B. Well, it was like nine years of your life suddenly cut off. We had the same engineer, sound effects men, director, assistant director, script girl…all that time.

TDOY: Let's talk about Chester's last name.

P.B. Proudfoot.

TDOY: Yes, then in the move to TV because it was an Indian name and Dennis Weaver played the role with a limp I heard someone felt it might be considered a slur so it was changed to Chester Goode. Anything to that?

P.B. Perhaps. But the word got to me this way. The first show I did I was "townsman" but Bill said I had to have a name because he couldn't go around saying, "Townsman, come here, I want to talk to you." So, he named me Chester, as he had named "Doc" Dr. Charles Addams because Howard (McNear) played him with just a little blood-thirstiness and Bill got the name from the ghoulish cartoonist. One time, Bill just let me hang on a broken speech on purpose; we used to kid each other. I had a line something like, "As sure as my name is..." and he didn't come in and after a tiny pause, I added, "Chester Wesley Proudfoot." Proudfoot? Don't know where that came from. When it went to TV the story I heard was that Hal Hudson, a CBS exec who engineered the changeover, said they'd better change the name because Parley did the middle and last names and I might feel there was some ground for a plagiarism charge. That made me mad. I bumped into Hal in the lobby and told him that even though CBS didn't trust me, I didn't mistrust CBS and they could use the name Proudfoot if they wanted to; that it was public domain. I really don't know what prompted me to say the name Proudfoot in the first place. Bill hung me out to dry and I just had to come up with something.

TDOY: As you look back, are there any regrets or wonderings if there were other paths you might have taken?

P.B. I don't think so. I did what I wanted to do and I've been very, very lucky. I spent a lot of time with circuses, a branch of show business I'm very fond of; even once had a wild animal act. I did my first radio in 1933 on KSL in Salt Lake City; first network show I ever did was *The Whistler*. Fortunately, I was able to make the transition to TV and films. But, I remember Cantor's great line, "If radio is the theater of the mind, then (chuckle) television is the theater of the mindless." Y'know, just off hand I can't remember a show I *didn't* like to do. I think we all felt that way. You can't be any luckier than that."

I never ran into anyone who ever met or talked with Parley who didn't like him and I treasure the memories of his friendship. One of the biggest thrills I ever had in my own broadcasting career I tell about in my Kindle eBook, *Cat Whiskers and Talking Furniture: A Memoir of Radio and Television Broadcasting*. It happened at the

Cincinnati convention when I worked in a *Gunsmoke* re-creation getting to take the Conrad role as the Marshall while Parley did a reprise of Chester. A portion of the opening alone jump starts my memory bank, as I recall the announcer saying, "…the story of the violence that moved west with young America, and the story of a man who moved with it," and me getting to respond with the well-known Bill Conrad lines, "I'm that man…Matt Dillon, United States Marshal…the first man they look for and the last they want to meet. It's a chancy job, and it makes a man watchful…and a little lonely." Wow, what a kick that was! I still get goose bumps thinking about it.

## Cedric Adams Was a Down-to-Earth Communicator But He Still Had His Name in Neon on the Back of His Cadillac

A book once came out titled, *Poor Cedric's Almanac*, and it had an introduction by Arthur Godfrey. Here's what he had to say about the subject of the book:

"Here's a bird who wouldn't admit that the horse has passed out of American life, and he's been cleaning up ever since. Now, don't get the idea that's he's been following the horses. No sirree, not in any sense of the word.

What I mean is that my good friend out in Minneapolis, Cedric Adams…that's the guy I mean is making hay on the horse-and-buggy days. Let me tell you about this Adams.

He never forgets anything. Boy, what a memory! Anything he ever did or read about, he remembers. Anything his mother or even his grandparents ever told him, he remembers. How do I know his grandparents told him? Well, he remembers stuff that happened a hundred years ago. And I know he can't be that old and look at his secretary the way he does.

But, let's not forget the horses. Adams remembers how the hardware store used to sell buggy whips from a barrel on the sidewalk, and how the dray wagons used to squeak on winter days. He uses those memories to make items for his column in the *Minneapolis Star* and *Sunday Tribune*, or he talks about the old days over the radio on WCCO or the Columbia network. See what I mean when I say he wouldn't admit that the horse is a thing of the past?

Now, why should anybody want to share those memories you ask? Well, if you're an old duffer of eighty you'll read stuff that makes you feel forty years younger. If you're just turning fifty, Cedric has advice that will make you want to hang around until you're eighty yourself. At, thirty, some of Cedric's flashbacks will make your own memories seem like pretty hot stuff, and if you're fifteen this book will give you ideas on how to live."

Godfrey's comments concerned a man who had one of those great "folksy" programs, as well as the not-so-common ability to look at the news in a slightly different way. His ability began to surface when he was in college at the University of Minnesota. While on campus, it was only natural that this speech major, with an English minor, would gravitate into some master-of-ceremonies work. He had been the leading man in a play at Minneapolis Central High School and always admitted he was a ham at heart. He was variously billed as "campus entertainer of note," "Toastmaster without ceremony," and, "roastmaster." A publicity release noted that "Adams can be relied upon to add spice to any program on which he appears."

This stood him in good stead in a broadcast career that began in 1934. Press and radio were embroiled in a battle for the advertising dollar and in 1933, under pressure from newspapers, Associated Press, United Press and International News Service quit providing radio with news. Finally, though, in '34, newspapers, radio stations and networks reached agreement that created the Press-Radio Bureau. It was to provide a limited amount of headline news each day to broadcasters. It didn't take long for the news services to realize they were missing out on good income and that radio news could not and should not be impeded. That made way for people like Cedric Adams.

He was writing a *Shopping News* program that had caught on. He had a deep, authoritative voice, a news background, and an enthusiastic personality. Those were the factors that made him a logical newscaster choice for WCCO, the dominant radio voice in that part of the country. So, he was hired and did his first newscast on September 1, 1934 at 10:30 in the evening, later changed to 10:00.

From the outset he was sponsored on the *Nighttime News*, and eventually the Purity Baking Company signed on in 1939 and sponsored Cedric for nineteen years with tremendous results. Most broadcasters will let you know it's easier to get sponsors than it is to keep them, so Adams's longevity as a newscaster with sponsors was phenomenal.

Then, in December of 1949, he was able to write, "I've had a dream come true this last week. You may have heard – Ramona Gerhard and I have just been sold on a network show that starts January 3, and runs through next May over all the stations of CBS. We'll be on here at 2:55 to 3 p.m., following Art Linkletter's *House Party* and just ahead of Garry Moore's show. I told them I was strictly a corny guy and that all I could produce was corny stuff. They didn't squawk. It's going to be fun to see how a couple of Midwesterners will click on the national scene."

"Click" they did, big-time. The format was simple. Ramona furnished the music while Cedric gave little features and odd facts. The new CBS feature was mentioned by the staid *New York Times* and critic John Crosby wrote in the *Herald-Tribune*, "Adams comes to network radio with an awe-inspiring list of endorsements. He had the almost unlimited blessing of Pillsbury Mills, his sponsor; the best wishes of Arthur Godfrey, which is one of the aliases of the Columbia Broadcasting System; and the militant support of apparently all of Minneapolis."

On the third anniversary of Cedric's network radio feature, a CBS publicity release paid him a high compliment. "Adams, whose steadily growing network audience parallels his phenomenal regional following, adopted a new CBS Radio schedule in December to include a 5-minute Sunday afternoon program and a 10-minute series on Monday and Tuesday nights. On WCCO, Adams has built up an uncontested record of 16 programs a week, all sponsored."

Cedric Adams was one of a kind and we got an unusual story about him from Ted Meland, who once worked for Adams in a non-broadcast capacity. Here's what he said, "First, Cedric had a very distinctive signature. All you had to see was the "Cedric" part of it and you knew who it was. He had this signature made into a neon sign which was attached to the rear bumper of his car. It came on with the lights, a pinkish Cadillac with "Cedric" in neon across the back! Quite a sight!"

In spite of something that might seem a bit ostentatious, Adams never lost his very special way of communicating some down-home ideas and emotions. This man with the common touch died in 1961 just short of his 59th birthday.

## Parker Fennelly Used His Personal Background For a Radio Character He Played on the Fred Allen Show

The little island settlement of Northeast Harbor was located off the coast of Maine and that's where Parker Fennelly was born. This was a place where the environs prompted silence and where two words were considered an adequate answer, and four consecutive sentences could bring on a charge of loquacity.

That sort of regional attitude is why Parker was so perfect for the role of "Titus Moody" in the Allen's Alley segments of *The Fred Allen Show*. But Fennelly had done his fine-tuning on such a part long before, often paired with Arthur Allen, starting as far back as 1930. They appeared together on an NBC program that year called *Uncle Abe and Dave*. At one time or another they portrayed pretty much the same kind of rock-ribbed, taciturn Yankees on such shows as *Snow Village Sketches, The Stebbins Boys, Gibbs and Finney, General Delivery, The Simpson Boys of Sprucehead Bay* and *Four Corners, U.S.A.*

Fennelly had been a kind of so-so student in his home community until it came time for learning a part in a school play, then he became enthusiastic. He eventually decided Boston would be the place to launch a modest career in the legitimate theater. Luckily, one of his cousins had enough faith in Parker's ability to lend him part of the tuition fee for the Leland Powers School.

One of the courses required him to go out into the streets of Beacon Hill, the populous walks of the Common and the Public Gardens, the alleyways of Charlestown and the wharves of South Boston to study every character that came his way. Many Bostonians must have wondered about the slim, quiet young man with shrewd eyes who watched them, sometimes walked with them, and always studied them, jotting down notes and wandering off.

When he got his diploma he joined a Shakespearean company and toured the country playing in *Hamlet, Othello, The Merchant of Venice* and many others.

Parker was always highly interested in the everyday characters encountered around the pot-bellied stove in the general store on winter nights, the village handyman, the head of the local bank and all the other picturesque army of folks who became identified with the America of farmland and the small town.

In fact, the turning point in Parker's career was linked to the tiny barber shop in his home town. After his Shakespearean roles, he was offered a part with Walter Huston in *Mr. Pitt*. He accepted and was given the role of Buck Carbury, a youthful country boy. And there he found his niche. In Buck Carbury he suddenly recognized the identical image of a familiar lounger in the barbershop of his home town. He had spent many an hour listening to the village sages discussing local problems, studying their facial expressions, their gestures, their Yankee inflection. The result was complete success in his new role.

None of his performances, though, brought him as much attention as did that of his "Titus Moody" down in "Allen's Alley," starting in 1945. Here, he took the ingredients of all those previous characterizations and distilled them into one of the funniest of the "Alley" inhabitants. When Fred Allen would knock on his door, Fennelly's response of, "Howdy, Bub," never failed to draw laughter.

In the first week of April, 1948, the "Alley" question concerned truth in advertising, in particular Burma-Shave jingles seen on highway signs that were set up in sequence through many parts of the U.S. countryside. Titus claimed to have made some profit from what he termed the longest of such poems that went like this:

"John McGee
Had a long goatee.
When he combed it out
It hung down to his knee
Today, John's happy,
He married a Wave.
His goatee's gone
Thanks to Burma-Shave."

Fred: Say, that is long.
Titus: The poem starts a half mile down the road.

Fred: I see.

Titus: It comes in my gate – goes once around the house.

Fred: Uh-huh.

Titus: The last line is on my back door – on the inside.

Fred: You have to open the door to read the last line of the Burma-Shave poem?

Titus: That's the trick.

Fred: Trick?

Titus: As you open the back door, my wife's sittin' there sellin' the stuff!

One of his noted lines came when he was asked how he liked radio and he replied, "I don't hold with furniture that talks."

That was the source of part of the title of one of my Kindle eBooks, *Cat Whiskers and Talking Furniture: A Memoir of Radio and Television Broadcasting*. The first part of that title came from the thin wire used to make contact with the crystal in early radio's crystal sets that came to be known as a "cat whisker," with the second part stemming from the Titus Moody line.

## Kate Smith: A Song on Her Lips, But "Hurt" in Her Heart She Always Wanted to Sing

Kate Smith was nearly seventeen years old when she got a part in a show called *Honeymoon Lane* and it turned out to be a heartbreaker for her. The name of the character (Tiny Little) was, in itself, just another cruel way of poking fun at her size, although she was so happy at getting the part she didn't think about that at first. She wanted the job so much it just didn't matter, not until later.

The parents of Kathryn Elizabeth Smith, especially her father, had not been very much in favor of a show business career for their daughter, but she had the dream early and never wavered. She had won several five-dollar gold pieces at the Keith Theater in Washington, D.C. and was told by the manager he might be able to get her a week's engagement, probably going on the bill with a comedian.

Her father bristled at the thought and insisted she was going to nursing school when she finished high school. He went so far as to say, "Don't forget that you…well, you have a handicap."

Kathryn is said to have replied, "You mean I'm fat, don't you?" She had no way of knowing she was going to hear that same thing much more in the future.

First, though, she *did* go to nursing school and hated it. A fellow student persuaded her that if she felt she was good enough to earn a living singing that she should do it.

Kate won some more gold pieces at amateur nights and several months later gave up nursing when she got that belated week's engagement.

The job resulted in her being seen by producer Abe Erlanger and he offered her the "Tiny Little" role in *Honeymoon Lane* where she would do the Charleston and sing a few numbers.

She told her family and even her dad relented, saying, "It's obvious this is what you want, and I admire you for having stuck it out. You have my blessing."

## No Friends – No One to Talk to

She was going to need her father's words. Soon, she was staying in a sordid little hotel room in New York and having to put up with the cruelty of fellow cast members. No one ever invited her out to dinner with the others and in her mind she could hear a chorus boy greeting her with a snide remark as she arrived at the theater, "Hello, Fatty."

She had also heard someone say as they all bought coffee and doughnuts at a stand, "Betcha she buys a dozen doughnuts and a gallon of coffee." A photographer came to take cast pictures for the theater foyer and someone asked if they could get all of her in one picture. Even worse, the play's comedian used cruel adlibs on stage aimed at her size.

She suffered silently and kept trying. That first show of hers finally closed at the start of 1929 and she got a six-month part as a colored Mammy in the touring company of *Hit the Deck*. A year later she got into a new musical, *Flying High*, where she would sing a few numbers but also still have to act as a stooge for comedians, all because of her size. She was making good money and had her own apartment but she was disappointed that the public still thought of her as a fat girl who good-naturedly put up with funny remarks, and only second as a singer. But, there was even more bitterness ahead.

Just a few weeks after the opening of *Flying High*, Kate got a telegram saying her father was very ill. She called producer George White and told him her dad was probably dying, but he wouldn't let her off, saying she had a contract and he'd hold her responsible for any loss if she didn't show up. She was appalled by his inhumanity but was cowed by the threat because she didn't have enough experience to know it would never stand up in court, and there were no friends in the cast to advise her.

So, she did the show, dashed to Penn Station, caught a train home, and arrived in time for her taxi to pull up behind an undertaker's car.

When she returned to New York, she refused to acknowledge White and vowed that, from then on, she would give up everything to go to her family whenever they wanted her. She couldn't be blamed for the fact that "The show must go on" was meaningless to her.

Coupled with her sorrow was the fact that constant digs at her size multiplied the feelings of grief. Her mother thought it might cheer her up if her grandparents came to visit and see the show. She showed them the sights but was wondering what to do about what she knew would happen on the stage – more barbs about her size. Before the show, she went to one of the comedians to ask him to take it easy, but there was little hope. She tripped over a basket and he quipped he was glad she didn't fall on him because they'd have to scrape him up with a palette knife. Her plea for fewer adlibs got nowhere; the request actually made the comics that much worse. It was much later on before it was disclosed that one of the worst offenders was Bert Lahr, who later played the cowardly lion in the movie, *The Wizard of Oz*. Backstage, her Granny said to forget the terrible play and come home. Her grandfather asked if she didn't have more self-respect than to allow herself to be used as a butt for such cheap, nasty remarks evening after evening. She told them she had to stay because of her contract and insisted she still wanted to sing professionally.

Things were about to change. A couple of months later, a man who came backstage told her he was a recording manager for the Columbia Phonograph Company and he felt it was a shame that only people in the theater could hear her lovely voice.

His name was Ted Collins and the meeting led to a long and prosperous relationship. He did make a recording of her singing; it sold quite a few copies and more recordings followed. *Flying High* was going to close at the end of January, 1931. Kate wanted to sing more than ever but decided she would never be laughed at again in such a show. Ted told her not to worry, that he would become her manager and take care of everything – bookings, career, finances, etc. He told her, "We're going a long way together. We'll be millionaires before you know what to do with a million dollars."

They shook hands on it and that's the only contract they ever had, with no signed papers and no lawyers.

The stage show closed and she went home for a vacation, where she got a call from Collins in March, 1931, saying she was booked to sing (and only sing) five times a day at the Capitol Theater for a good many weeks.

Six weeks later, audiences were growing steadily and Ted told her she was going to be on the radio next. A funny story developed from that. When Kate told her Granny she might get to sing on this "new wireless system," her Granny said, "Oh, that's being foolish. That thing's just a novelty; they'll have forgotten all about it in a year or two."

At any rate, Ted arranged a 15-minute nightly show on CBS at 7:00 p.m. Whoops, it was opposite *Amos 'n' Andy*! How could she compete with that? Also, there was no sponsor and the pay was only ten dollars per show. It started on May 1st, her 21st birthday! The switchboard lit up after the show and within thirty days, Kate Smith was sponsored by La Palina Cigars and the pay was $1,500 a week, and inside of six months *Amos 'n' Andy* moved to a different time to avoid competing with her.

Within two years of the first program, Kate got an hour show on Thursday evenings and earnings went up to $5,000 a week. In the spring of 1938 she became a commentator on a noon program that became a regular daily feature of American life. November 11th, 1938 she launched Irving Berlin's *God Bless America*, and he gave her two-year exclusive rights to the song. She later did several war bond marathons, raising a hundred and ten million dollars on one of them. It was a climactic time for one who started so humbly and became one of the nation's most beloved performers on records, radio, TV and in person. Kate Smith had definitely put all those "fat" jokes far behind her.

## EVER WONDER HOW SOME OF RADIO'S BEST-KNOWN SPONSORS GOT THEIR NAME? THEY BECAME HOUSEHOLD WORDS

In the Golden Age of Radio, somebody had to eventually pick up the tab for all those actors, actresses, writers, musicians, singers, producers, directors, engineers, sound effects specialists, etc. Here are a few of the stories about famous clients.

### JELL-O

It was way back in 1845 when Peter Cooper got the first patent on a gelatin dessert, but he didn't do anything with it, most likely because he had other irons in the fire. For example, he invented the famous "Tom Thumb" locomotive and was a major patron of the arts and sciences. So, it was around a half century later when cough medicine manufacturer Pearl Wait began looking around for something new to try. He happened to come across the old Cooper notion and concocted an adaptation for the gelatin dessert in 1897. It was his wife, Mary, who suggested an intriguing name, *Jell-O* and there hasn't been much in the way of explanation as to what prompted the thought. There have been suggestions that this new jiggly stuff reminded her of jelly and "O" was a popular ending for various new food products. Others have felt that it might have been because the gelatin had to *jell* before serving but in a somewhat humorous vein, it could have been simply because she was inspired by the similar sound of gelatin itself and didn't know the main ingredient was spelled with a "g" instead of a "j." No matter, if the name hadn't been applied, just think that later on Jack Benny never would have said, "Jell-o, everybody," when his show was sponsored by the company.

No matter, though, back in the beginning, *Jell-O* didn't make much of an impression and after a couple of years of trying, Wait sold out to a neighbor, Francis Woodward. He didn't do much better the first year and, walking through his plant one day, he offered to see the whole deal to his superintendent for $35, The reply from A.S. Nico was, "Thanks a lot, but, no, thanks." When the product caught on finally at the turn of the century, you can bet Nico and his heirs-to-be, shed a lot of tears.

## WHEATIES

In 1921 in Minneapolis, a health clinician (couldn't find his name) declared that bran was a "fine regulator of the digestive tract." He did some testing by feeding some of it to his overweight patients every morning, with most of his early results being grumbles about how unappetizing the stuff was. However, fortuitous accidents can happen. One morning he was a bit careless and some of his bran concoction spilled onto the stove, forming wafers that were scraped off into flakes. He tried one himself and thought, "H-m-m, not bad," so he spilled some more on purpose to be sure his taste buds weren't playing tricks on him. That led him to tell James Bell of the Washburn Crosby Company what he had stumbled onto. Bell listened and gave it a try but the "flakes: crumbled to powder when they were swirled around in a box. Let's see now, the thinking went, what can we do about this? The head miller had a notion that wheat might work out better than bran and proceeded to try out around three dozen varieties before coming up with one that figured to fill the bill. Company board members tried some, liked it and gave a go-ahead. One of the executive's wives, Jane Bausman, thought nicknames were endearing and she's the one who came up with the name, *Wheaties*. Of course, you know what that led to, don't you? Lots of boxtops for eventual *Jack Armstrong* fans to send in for all those premium offers.

## CAMEL CIGARETTES

A man named Richard Joshua Reynolds was the one who began the first blended cigarette in the world. A lot of tobacco users had taken a fancy to Oriental names and Turkish tobaccos. So, a notion struck Reynolds that a camel would get across the idea of the exotic Orient and that his new brand would be named Camel. One of those coincidences that now and then happen occurred when the Barnum and Bailey Circus came to town. One of their attractions was a dromedary (a one-humped camel), called "Old Joe." The tobacco company proceeded to send out a photographer to get a picture of the beast, but the circus manager wasn't very cooperative until he was reminded the Reynolds factory had closed so its workers could go to the circus. That solved one problem, but "Joe" posed a bigger one. He proved to be very stubborn and also curious about what was going on and kept turning his head to watch. The handler would tug his head back in place. Patience was not one of "Joe's" attributes. The irked critter finally closed his eyes, lifted his tail and jerked his head as an indication of his wounded dignity. The camera clicked at just the right time and posterity was served. A drawing was made from the photo and the artist put in some palms and a pyramid in the background to bolster that strikingly foreign feel. The debut of the new symbol came in 1913 and "Old Joe" became the most pictured animal in the world with his image being seen on billions and billions of Camel Cigarette packages. For OTR fans, this all eventually led to quizmaster Bob Hawk singing out, "You're a L-E-M-A-C now," when contestants came up with right answers on his show.

## CHEVROLET

A fellow named William Durant was a kind of boy wonder in the new automotive industry in the early part of the 1900s and one day back of a plant he owned in Flint, Michigan he ran an auto race against a couple of daredevil young French brothers, Louis and Arthur Chevrolet. Louis won and Durant wound up hiring Arthur as his chauffeur because he was impressed by the fact the young Frenchman had taken no outlandish risks in the race. That was just a racing beginning for Louis and he went ahead to gain considerable renown. Finally, with backing from Durant, he designed an engine and directed assembly of a touring car. That set the stage for a name plate with an unusual shape that became almost as famous as an automobile itself. Durant had the notion that the young man's name had a sort of musical quality and decided to name his company and the new car, *Chevrolet*. The design of the name plate itself came from a small piece of wallpaper Durant had peeled off the wall in a French hotel several years before. He was quoted as thinking, "It appeared to be marching off into infinity." Coupled with the Chevy's long term success, he was obviously right. Every move made, though, didn't come off as well. The firm was sponsoring the Jack Benny program on radio, but the new Chevrolet president, M.E. Coyle, didn't like comedians and preferred soft music. So, this led to the agency handling the account being told to cut Benny's patter down to five minutes and let the orchestra offer more romantic melodies. Benny got his back up and told them if they did that he'd walk out. For the time being, Coyle backed down, deciding not to press the issue, right then, anyway. However, he did get in the last word and signed the Victor Young Orchestra to a 13-week deal that replaced Benny starting with the April 8th, 1934 NBC broadcast. That meant Jell-O became the new Benny sponsor as Chevrolet dealers all around the country became highly upset because they said the Benny show had been helping sales of their cars.

## MAXWELL HOUSE COFFEE

Way back in the dim, distant past, one of the most elegant hotels in the south was the Maxwell House in Nashville, Tennessee. Its reputation tied in with a notion conceived by a traveling salesman named Joel Cheek. He was selling some brands of coffee and he felt he could come up with a better blend than any of them. He got promoted to a partnership in his vendor company and that gave him time to work on his blending ideas. Cheek finally achieved something he really liked and took it to the Nashville hotel whose management agreed to give it a try. It wasn't long before guests were singing the praises of this coffee at the Maxwell House. Even better things were to come when some years later Teddy Roosevelt was a guest at the Hermitage at Nashville, Andrew Jackson's old home. At one point, the ol' Rough Rider was asked if he'd like another cup of *Maxwell House* coffee and supposedly replied, "Will I have another? Delighted! It's good to the last drop!" That brought on later remarks like, "What's wrong with the last drop?" From a semantics standpoint, nothing was wrong, according to an English professor from Columbia University. He resolved the whole controversy over use of the word "to" by saying it was accepted good usage and included "the last drop." Heck, even Gracie Allen knew that, as she always said about their sponsor on *The Burns and Allen Show*.

## A Poem Possibly Inspired By a Lack of Quality Programming on Modern Radio
## "I Will Arise and Go Now"

This appeared in *The New Yorker* magazine more than a half century ago. Written by wordsmith Ogden Nash in those bygone days, if refers to various radio personalities of the past and some of the advertisers of those times.

> In Far Tibet
> There live a lama,
> He got no poppa,
> Got no momma,
>
> He got no wife,
> He got no chillun,
> Got no use
> For penicillun,
>
> He got no soap,
> He got no opera,
> He don't know Irium
> From copra,
>
> He got no songs,
> He got no banter,
> Don't know Jolson,
> Don't know Cantor,
>
> He got no teeth,
> He got no gums,
> Don't eat no Spam,
> Don't need no Tums.

He love to nick him
When he shave;
He also got
No hair to save.

Got no distinction,
No clear head,
Don't call for Calvert;
Drink milk instead.

He use no lotions
For allurance,
He got no car
And no insurance,

He live just like
The lower mammals,
Got no sore throat
From not smoking Camels.

No Winchell warnings,
No Pearson rumor
For this self-centered
Non-consumer.

Indeed, the
Ignorant Have-not
Don't even know
What he don't got.

If you will mind
The box-tops, comma
I think I'll go
And join that lama.

## Three Notes From the Famed NBC Chimes
## Did You Know About a "Fourth Chime?"

The well-known NBC chimes originated on radio but a variation stuck around to be used on television as well. Those with a musical "ear" know the notes are "G-E-C," a kind of subliminal reminder about the **G**eneral **E**lectric **C**orporation, one of the network's early owners forced to divest itself of the holding in an anti-trust ruling. Now, tell me truthfully, how many know about the "fourth chime?" There *was* one and here's the way I hear the story.

The excellent efforts of Edward R. Murrow and his "boys" on CBS at the beginning of and during World War II received a lot of credit for the maturation of radio news broadcasting. Of course, that's justified because their work was exceptional. However, NBC was also there and wanted to be sure they got some attention by publishing a book in 1944 that pointed out their efforts. I came across Copy #72 of a limited edition of one thousand copies called *The Fourth Chime*. In their story, they stated there was no question as to the fitness of the title.

"The Fourth Chime, a note added to the familiar NBC three-chime signal, is the exclusive property of the Newsroom of the National Broadcasting Company; rings out from the NBC newsroom only when events of major historical importance occur."

Contrived originally as a confidential "alert" to summon an immediate gathering of those members of the NBC news staffs, engineers and other operating personnel responsible for broadcasting the news to the people, NBC's Fourth Chime has come to be significantly identified with every major news break of the past seven years.

The Fourth Chime was first used by NBC news and Special Events in 1937, when the Hindenburg exploded at Lakehurst; again in 1938, when it became apparent that the political artifices leading to the Munich crisis were making news affecting the future of every American citizen. Its dramatic notes were sounded the day news came of the Pearl Harbor attack. They were heard again on that early D-Day morning when word flashed that the first wave of the Allied assault had beached on the Normandy coast of France."

Your writer has a set of manual chimes used by an NBC station in the 1930s. It has four notes on it and in addition to the recognizable G-E-C, the fourth note is "G" up an octave. Is that the one used as the *fourth chime*? How many remember hearing it? I don't, having unfortunately missed it!

## "Coming, Mother"
### An Interview with Ezra Stone ("Henry Aldrich" of *The Aldrich Family*)

I had been scheduled to appear with Ezra at the 8th annual Old Time Radio and Nostalgia Convention in Cincinnati when tragic word came that he had been killed in an automobile accident. Veteran actor Bob Hastings volunteered to fill in and did his usual terrific job, including a re-creation of another teenager with problems, *Archie Andrews*. Ezra first played Henry on stage in 1938. At the time of his death at age 76, he was serving as director of the David Library of the American Revolution at Washington Crossing, Pennsylvania. It was founded by his father, Solomon Feinstone, and it was one of the subjects we discussed during an interview on my Old Time Radio program in Denver in April of 1993.

TDOY: Clifford Goldsmith came up with the idea of the Aldrich Family, originally a Broadway play.

E.S. Yes, the play was *What a Life* in which I created the role of Henry Aldrich. That was after being in *Brother Rat* and working in the George Abbott office as a "gopher" and then production assistant. Mr. Abbott produced and directed *What a Life*.

TDOY: In radio's early days, many programs featured vaudevillians and as a result Rudy Vallee's show was one of the few variety programs on; it probably introduced more people and sketches than anyone else. And, of course, the Aldriches were originally a sketch there.

E.S. Yes, and bless him. He did have a policy...personal or agency I'm not sure...of doing scenes from current Broadway plays. They did all the big hits first but when summer came they ran out of hits and it was our turn at bat. It caught on. A young agent, Sam Weisbord, who later became president of the William Morris Agency, got the notion that a spin-off for a series might work. The story that Clifford (Goldsmith) loved to tell was that he was approached and asked if he could write a special sketch involving Henry Aldrich. Clifford's response was, "Well, I wrote a three-act play about him; I think I can, yes." And, of course, it then ran on radio for 15 years.

TDOY: When I do my OTR stage presentation, I use a montage of old shows to stir up memory banks and the opening of the Aldrich program gets one of the biggest reactions.

E.S. It was…for good or evil…the progenitor of what we all know as the domestic situation comedy on TV and radio. Until that time on radio, there was never a half-hour comedy family show with a beginning, middle and end in the half hour. Y'know, *One Man's Family* was a continuing series and Clifford devised a way of telling a story and wrapping it up in twenty-three minutes. Very frequently, he'd have at least one and sometimes two sub-plots woven into that half-hour episode.

TDOY: There was an interim period after the sketches on the Vallee program when you were picked up and appeared on the *Kate Smith Show* for quite a while.

E.S. Yes, we became hot and agency bidding wound up with the best deal on CBS with Kate Smith. We did 39 weeks with an 8 to 10-minute sketch with her.

TDOY: Then, you went on the Blue Network for a while.

E.S. I've forgotten whether we were Red or Blue or even black (chuckle). It was more black-and-blue than Red or Blue. General Foods sponsored Kate and they felt we were ready for a half-hour for one of their products. What really clinched the success of the half-hour was that Jack Benny turned over his 1939 summer time and our debut was as his replacement…pretty lucky when you get right down to it. Jack flew me out and I appeared as a guest on his last show of the season.

TDOY: As was often the case in the Golden Age, there were many changes in casts. That was certainly true on your show as well as others and there were different actresses who played Mrs. Aldrich. Who did you work with most?

E.S. Kay (Katharine) Raht. Kay played Mrs. Aldrich for the longest period of time and to the very end of the series. The first Mrs. Aldrich was Leah Penman, who created the character in the stage play. She was a wonderful actress but she was part British and they didn't feel her speech pattern would apply itself to a non-regional feeling of Centerville, U.S.A.

TDOY: Was it a disappointment for you when a decision was made for a movie version of *The Aldrich Family* and someone else got the part?

E.S. Yes and no. Actually, Jackie Cooper got it. I tested for it in New York and they decided to go with Jack. After they made the film of *What a Life* then had second thoughts. So, Paramount gave me a one picture deal co-starring with Bill Holden in a movie called *Those Were the Days*. It was the Old Siwash stories of Knoxville College and the picture was really a bomb. They held the picture and released me. By then, they were pretty sure they wouldn't get enough out of me at my advanced age…I must have been around 20…playing a *16*-year old and that's when Jimmy Lydon came on board. He did, I believe, 7 or 8 of the Aldrich movies.

TDOY: What are you up to these days, Ezra?

E.S. I've got a job for the rest of my life…there aren't too many who can say that in this era of downsizing major corporations. It's not the way I planned to spend the rest of my life. Theoretically, I'm retired but I'm working harder now than I did when I was working. I promised my dad that I would do everything I could to see that his foundation continued to do the work that he'd planned for it. It's a very complex operation. Our key enterprise is the David Library of the American Revolution in Bucks County at Washington Crossing, Pennsylvania. He founded the library and turned over his collection of over 2,500 manuscripts of the American Revolution, the core collection of the library. He created an endowment for which we're responsible for trying to make it run.

TDOY: Sounds as though you're helping continue nostalgia in yet another way.

E.S. I guess it's more than nostalgia. We have become a very respected research institution. We give fellowships and have residence scholars going ahead with their work in the library. We have a very aggressive acquisitions program, mostly from microfilm and mostly from public records offices in England, West Germany, France and Canada. We have a lecture series that takes a good bit of time. It has elements of showmanship in it.

TDOY: Are these lectures only at the library?

E.S. Yes, but my father did endow several annual lectures at the Military Academy at West Point and other places and also scholarship awards to all the universities he attended or fell in love with.

It was obvious that Ezra was proud of the David Library and in spite of his protestations about working hard, he was pleased with the project.

He mentioned appearing in *Brother Rat* in 1936. Actually, he appeared before that in a George Abbott farce, *Three Men On a Horse*, after getting his diploma from the American Academy of Dramatic Arts in 1935. He was producer, director and actor with the Army's Special Services during World War II helping stage a number of productions, including *This Is the Army* by Irving Berlin.

Following that, there was a considerable amount of work producing and directing on both Broadway and in television. Just to give you an idea of the broad range of his talents, the Broadway shows he directed included *January Thaw*, *See My Lawyer*, *At War With the Army* and *Me and Molly*. On television, he handled such programs as *Lassie*, *The Munsters*, *The Debbie Reynolds Show*, *The Flying Nun*, *Lost in Space* and *Love American Style*. At one time, he was director of program development at CBS-TV.

He was a quiet man with a delightful sense of humor and when I first met him I thought he was a trifle stand-offish. However, as I got to know him better and had an opportunity to visit at greater length I came away with the feeling that part of the original impression may have stemmed from what I assessed as an innate shyness. After all his successes and uninhibited approach to the Henry Aldrich role, this would seem to be an incongruous facet of his personality. I readily admit my feeling may not have been entirely accurate. All I know is, I grew to like him very much, He had a built-in natural rapport with audiences and that's why those reactions I mentioned in the interview persisted when people with good memories would hear the call, "Hen-REE...Henry Aldrich," followed by the inevitable cracked voice, "Coming, mother." This was a man with a big talent and a big heart who contributed much to family entertainment.

## "Kissin' a feller with a beard is like a picnic. You don't mind goin' through a little brush to get there."

That's not the kind of line you'd expect from a gracious, cultured and sensitive lady like Sarah Ophelia Colley Cannon. But, it sure did fit the happy and somewhat hopeless Cousin Minnie Pearl, a character that Sarah made up from a composite of a number of women she'd known in her younger days, a character who became an integral part of the *Grand Ole Opry*.

Sarah ("Minnie") passed away at the age of 83. She hadn't performed since 1991 after suffering a stroke. Before that she'd had a double mastectomy in 1985, but bounced back to do her act and also some volunteer work for the American Cancer Society. President Reagan presented her with the ACS Courage Award in 1987.

Nowadays, the *Grand Ole Opry* has its own fancy Opryland but the program was originating out of the famed Ryman Auditorium in downtown Nashville when Minnie first appeared on the show in 1940. It really wasn't much of a place but that didn't make much difference to the 3,300 fans who packed it for every performance. There were stars like Uncle Dave Macon ("The Dixie Dewdrop"), who could really plink-plunk a banjo;; Roy Acuff and his "Great Speckled Bird;" the "Tennessee Plowboy," Eddie Arnold; the Duke of Paducah ("I'm headin' back to the wagon – these shoes are killin' me."); Ernest Tubb, Bill Monroe and a flock of others. But none of them left a more indelible impression than Cousin Minnie's special opening line, "<u>How-dee</u>…I'm just so proud to be here," and her calico and gingham dresses, a great big toothy grin and, of course, her flowered straw hat with the $1.98 price tag dangling from it.

Those were trademarks that were recognized for more than a half century on the *Opry* and for a couple of decades on the syndicated show, *Hee Haw*.

It's difficult to think of her in any persona other than Minnie Pearl and that's the name the headlines used when she died. I remember her being on one of my radio programs one morning and me asking whether I should call her "Minnie" or "Sarah." She gently replied, "I 'spect I wouldn't be on this program if it wasn't for 'Minnie' so we probably better stick with that." Mostly we did. But, some "Sarah" also crept in and we discovered what a delightful lady she was. There's more about that visit in my Kindle book, *Cat Whiskers and Talking Furniture: A Memoir of Radio and Television Broadcasting* that you might enjoy.

Minnie was voted into the Country Music Hall of Fame in 1975 and the Country Music Association named her Woman of the Year in 1966. A commemorative LP album featuring the stars of the *Grand Ole Opry* said of this native of Centerville, Tennessee that she was "one of the most gracious ladies ever to appear in any medium. Her charm and wit made her a friend of everyone. She was a philanthropist who worked unstintingly for many worthy causes."

It's for sure there'll never be another like her. One of those dresses and that hat with the price tag belong in the Smithsonian as a treasured part of our national heritage and as a fond remembrance of an icon of the country music world.

## Egos on Parade

With some early radio performers, there was considerable ego involved, but often it merely took the form of a healthy, natural human conceit that makes a small boy boast, "I can lick any kid on the block." Of course, there were times when it could be a bit on the obnoxious side.

For instance, many considered Ted Husing to be the most cheerfully arrogant man in the world, in or out of radio. He didn't wait for the world to tell him he was good – he just admitted it. Whenever he would show up at any event of importance, his favorite greeting was, "Okay, you can start the parade now, *Husing's here!*"

Husing was once almost the object of a lynch party by members of the CBS press department. It was the morning of a big affair to launch the Blue Eagle of the National Recovery Administration in 1933. It was set to be a gigantic demonstration lasting for hours and Husing was scheduled to describe the goings-on and explain the intricate setup of the NRA. A network group of trained workers spent all night putting together a 24-page pamphlet on the NRA to aid Husing in his coverage. They knew he was no political expert and would need help. It was a good piece of work and all those who labored all night on it were proud of it. The information was handed over to Husing and he was told the carefully indexed material would provide him with the answers for every possible question about NRA.

Terrible Ted took it, glanced at it quickly and grumped, "It would make a swell broadcast for Edwin C. Hill. The great Husing doesn't need it."

One story of hatband swelling had to do with someone considered by some to be an unlikely candidate for such didoes. Actually, it turned out that a colorful Italian with an English name – Frank Parker – thought he was the greatest singer around. In private he called himself "The Incredible Wop."

Well, it seems he had a burning ambition. He wanted to sing in *Pagliacci* at the renowned La Scala opera house in the heart of the ancient city of Milan, Italy, the center of the world's greatest opera.

Fresh from U.S. radio success he headed for Milan, fully confident they would greet him with open arms. They didn't though and he was turned down when he finally got an audition. Parker apparently brooded about it and when time came that *Pagliacci* was scheduled for a performance he was in the audience. On stage the heartbroken clown, Canio, sang of his faithless wife and his shattered heart and there was hardly a dry eye in the house.

But suddenly, two Canios were singing!

Determined to sing at La Scala even if he had to buy a seat to get in, Parker was standing in the audience singing at the top of his voice. He was matching the on-stage singer note for doleful note, but not for long!

The excitable Italians, outraged at this vocal intrusion, rose and roared their disapproval. The show stopped, but Frank Parker sang on. A flying wedge of ushers came down the aisle and "The Incredible Wop" was borne aloft, but not in triumph. Instead, he was carried to jail.

Parker languished there for two days but apparently it bothered him not because all he wanted was to be able to say, truthfully, for the rest of his life, that he had, indeed, sung at La Scala.

Another story concerning operas and egos had to do with a pair of singers – Rosa Ponselle and Grete Stueckgold, the latter who was on the Chesterfield radio series in 1933. They each decided they should be the one to sing the leading role in an opera being cast at the Metropolitan. Unfortunately, both of the ladies headed for the casting director's office at the same time. They met at the Met in a head-on collision and there was spontaneous combustion! Before anyone could stop them the two beautiful, gracious ladies were very much in each other's hair.

Was that the artistic thing to do? No! Was it the human thing to do?" Yes! – and let her who has never pulled hair cast the first stone.

So, radio people had their share of egotism. But, who doesn't? Some psychologists have given the opinion that the greater a person's talent, the stronger the ego is bound to be. However, I would be derelict if I didn't add at this point that the many participants in Old Time Radio that I've had the privilege to meet generally do not fall into that category. I believe the reason is that although they were exceptional performers the public didn't really know the majority of them. They knew them only by their voices and not their appearance. Therefore, the various cast members could go just about anywhere without being recognized and there was no reason for ego to come into play. That, plus the fact that they were often members of on-going casts for long-running programs and they became more like members of a family, instead of just professional friends. Obviously, television eventually came along and changed all that.

## Try This Tongue-Tangler Three Times

A bit of trivia for you before we get to the tongue twister referred to above. Scout's honor now, how many of you are aware that the real address of Fibber McGee and Molly was #81 Wistful Vista and not #79? It's true! In the book, *Heavenly Days*, by Charles Stumpf and Tom Price, it is pointed out that McGees visited the little town of Wistful Vista on their program of August 26th, 1935. There was sales promotion going on by the Hagglemeyer Realty Development Company, with a house being given away in a raffle. Fibber bought a two-dollar ticket and Miss Susie Glotz pulled out number 13-13-13. It was Fibber's and he fainted when he found out the house at 79 Wistful Vista was his. Ah, but wait, on the show of February 15, 1939, they discovered the real house number (81) had been hidden for years behind an old lilac bush. They didn't change, though, and 79 remained as the address for the McGees.

Now, for that tongue twister, a bit of verbal carrying-on that Fibber did quite often on the program. It was generally alliteration of the highest order and he would breeze right through it. Here's a very difficult one in McGee's own words.

"The Bakersfield Bakery used big batches of batter for bakin' and they liked their batter beat with butter. Now, some of the batter beaters beat some awful bitter batter, but the batter I beat made better beaten batches – and baby, I beat batter by the barrel! We had about as beat-up bunch of bakers as ever balled up a bunch of batter, but the reason my batter baked better was because I beat my batter in a platter – which made a better batter, splattered the platter, scattered the batter, sputtered the butter, buttered the platter and beat the Be-Junior out of the butter..."

Jim Jordan, as Fibber, rarely messed one of those up but during the one above, on November 16, 1948, he accidentally did the last part in a different way, "...but the reason my batter baked better was because I beat my batter in a platter – which made a better batter, splattered the bladder and..."

Needless to say, the audience cracked up.

If you really tried to say the "twister" you discovered how tough it could be. A publicity release came out in 1937 that purportedly explained how Jim Jordan did it.

*"McGee has a unique formula for his non-stumble success. The first time he reads his lines he balances a loaded laundry basket on his head and is so concerned with his uppermost difficulty that he has no time to worry over enunciation."*

Oh, sure! All those who buy that can muster in the nearest phone booth. Sounds like another zany concoction by writer Don Quinn, if you ask us. Of course, it really doesn't matter because Fibber (Jordan) would roll them out with great speed and darn few flubs over the years.

Quinn, by the way, was out of work as a cartoonist and gag-writer when he first encountered Jordan while Jim was looking for some funny material he had to have right away. It is said that Quinn quickly introduced himself and suggested he might be able to write something. That DID it! First came Marian and Jim in *Smackout – The Crossroads of the Air*. It began on WMAQ, Chicago, March 2, 1931. NBC bought the station and eventually around a dozen of the *Smackout* shows originated in New York. At the end of May, 1933 the network took it off, claiming a lack of listeners. Stacks of protesting mail started coming in and the show went back on in September. It ran for 948 broadcasts and went off for good the first part of August, 1935, and that was almost <u>four months</u> after the *Fibber McGee and Molly* series had gotten started. At the peak of his time with the Jordans, Quinn was making $3,000 a week and was, at that time, the highest paid comedy writer in radio. He left in 1950 to create and write *Halls of Ivy* for Ronald Colman and his wife, Benita Hume. Quinn won a Peabody Award for that show. It truly demonstrated his versatility as he moved from the cornball humor of the McGees to the sophistication of the Colmans.

One added note about the McGees. The famous hall closet routine started in March of 1940. Charles Stumpf wrote it was on the 5th, but a copy of the show in our collection indicates it was the 12th. Sound effects man Manny Segal did it first with a broad array of "stuff" piled on some steps so they could be knocked off when the door of the closet opened. A couple of times the closet was really cleaned to help wartime scrap drive efforts. One of the funnier incidents was in March of 1947 when Doc Gamble (Arthur Q. Bryan) opened the door and there was absolute <u>silence</u>. A long pause…then Fibber proudly proclaimed, "<u>I cleaned out the hall closet!</u>" It got as big a laugh as when all the junk came spilling out in the usual routine!

## The Voyage of the "Seth Parker"
### (It was a radio show AND a sailing ship)

The story begins with Phillips H. Lord. He was born in Vermont, the son of a minister. He was graduated from Bowdoin College in Maine in 1925. Much of his life was passed in Maine towns among characters such as he portrayed in his radio programs. He moved to New York, determined to break into magazine writing. One night he heard a radio program with a country setting and the unreality of the characters and the situations disturbed him. So, he wrote some scripts himself. The result was gratifying to millions of listeners. Churchmen described Lord, in the role of *Seth Parker*, as the outstanding evangelist in America, all because of the remarkable manner in which he captured the imagination of his hearers with his semi-religious drama.

(**Note:** The above information stemmed from a book called *Radio Round-Ups*, published in 1932. *Seth Parker* began as a sustaining feature in 1929 and went on to become an eminent Sunday night component for NBC by 1933. Then, the story took on an additional aspect. A 1934 booklet put out by the sponsor, Frigidaire, told of an unusual adventure.)

"Although his father's farm was many miles from the coast, there was inbred in this lad all the lusty lore of the sea – so dear to the hearts of New Englanders. It so happened that two of Phillip's most cherished friends were grizzled old salts who had spent many blustery years before the mast on sailing ships. Their hands were gnarled by hundreds of hard tasks, but their alert minds were weathered by the breath of many winds – their minds and clear eyes could recall and see the strange sights of countless distant ports. They loved to regale young Lord with stories of their high adventures and he loved to listen.

"Some day," he told himself, I shall sail the Seven Seas, just like good old Dan and Jed. Not in any shiny boat with engines and whistles – but in a really-truly sailing ship with lots of masts and sails. And I'll go to all the strange places they've told about, and have *adventure!*"

Well, as his program achieved success, Lord was able to do just that. He bought a rugged 4-masted schooner as he remembered his boyhood promises to himself. He fitted her out for a two-year cruise on which he planned to circle the entire globe, and he renamed her the "Seth Parker." Soon, it was announced that weekly broadcasts would come from the ship as it made its way down the Atlantic coast. They would put into port and the main cabin would become a radio room each week. It was a delightful old-world cabin that included a pot-bellied stove and a studio piano. In that era it was probably the world's most unusual radio entertainment as it came direct from the old sailing ship. There was just one major problem. In early 1935, a storm in the South Seas wrecked the schooner. An SOS went out and everyone was saved but newspapers thought it was phony-baloney hype and the bad publicity caused the program to go off the air by 1936. But, Phillips Lord wasn't through!

Instead of sailing a ship that may or may not have gotten into legitimate trouble, Phillips Lord fought crime…sort of. In *Don't Touch That Dial*, J. Fred MacDonald wrote, "All Lord's shows were, as stated so often in the introduction of *Gangbusters*, presented in conjunction with 'America's crusade against crime."

That held true on *Policewoman*, based on real events in the career of Sergeant Mary Sullivan, who had a 35-year career in the New York police department. It was true on *G-Men* that lasted only 26 weeks because of a personality clash with J. Edgar Hoover of the FBI. No matter, he switched to city police files and that naturally brought about *Gangbusters*, which we can safely say lasted considerably longer. Here, it was a case of dramatizing actual police cases. A police officer would get a small amount of cash for telling his story to a scriptwriter. Long ago CBS Radio vice-president and WCBS general manager, Sam Slate, used to write up some of the "cases." In a co-authored book, *It Sounds Impossible*, he told of one such incident.

"I was in an eastern city interviewing a detective who was credited with breaking up a counterfeit money ring which had been all over the papers. We were sitting in a local bar having a few orange flips when I finally asked him, 'What's the real story?'

"You wanna know what really happened?"

"Sure."

"Well, what really happened was that I used to play poker a lot. I was crazy about poker. Some days I'd play poker far into the night – and a couple of times I was late for work. Well, the chief didn't like this. He told me either I quit playing poker or I was through. He really bawled me out. Well, three days later, I was late again. I didn't crawl out of bed until about noon. I had to think up something to tell the chief. Boy, was I worried! Because anything I told him he wouldn't believe. He'd just yell some more about my playing poker, and I knew that this time he'd really fire me."

The detective took a long pull on his orange flip.

"On the way to work I saw a real seedy-looking character standing on the curb looking very suspicious. I hadn't seen him around town before, but he looked like a terrible guy. After all those years you can spot 'em. Now, you know that cops don't go around putting the arm on just anybody. This was definitely a criminal type. Of course, if he wasn't there's still nothing to prevent me from giving the guy the onceover. And this guy was seedy. I'd hauled in a hundred of 'em. So, I took him in. The Chief would know I was working. Just imagine how surprised I was to find out that the FBI had been looking for him for three years. There was a $3,000 reward – and I broke up the biggest counterfeit ring in the country. Boy, was the Chief proud of me!"

Can't you just hear how a scriptwriter would turn <u>that</u> one into a radio show?

Back to Lord. He acted on *The Story of Mary Marlin* (NBC) in 1935. He created and produced a show that started as a segment of the Rudy Vallee program. That was the 1936 *We, The People*. Long-time narrator of that human interest story format was newsman Gabriel Heatter ("Ah, yes, there's good news tonight.") Lord produced *By Kathleen Norris* on CBS in 1939. That was also the year of the start of the famous *Mr. District Attorney*. Edward Bynom created and directed it, but Lord came up with the title and was the producer. That same year he produced and wrote *Sky Blazers*, which featured ace aviator, Colonel Roscoe Turner, as narrator. It lasted only one season. Lord acted on the 1941 Mutual comedy, *Great Gunns*, which didn't amount to much but a great cast – Bret Morrison, Barbara Luddy and Marvin Miller, who was announcer and handled three roles. Lord created, produced and wrote some of *Counterspy* on the Blue Network in 1942 and produced *Treasury Agent*, which starred Raymond Edward Johnson, the most noted host on *Inner Sanctum*.

Putting all this work together, it's easy to say that Phillips H. Lord had quite a career and made some unique contributions to the medium. But, it should be noted that one report said some of the parties back on board the "*Seth Parker*" after broadcasts were not exactly the type one expected from a radio personality who proclaimed, "Just have faith in God, and by His grace you'll reach the promised land." A true character in the history of Old Time Radio.

## Tots in Clover

One of the natural winners in radio history was what was an unlikely hit show of 1940, *Quiz Kids* (Wed. NBC) A report in February of 1941 mentioned that although the show had only been on the air eight months, it had probably garnered more unsolicited nationwide publicity than any radio program ever over a comparable period. In one week, the "Quiz Kids" rated five big national magazines. They were publicly toasted by Eleanor Roosevelt, Walter Winchell, numerous radio personalities, even columnist "Bugs" Baer. Then, they were on the verge of appearing soon in Paramount short subjects. There was a nationally syndicated column, "Beat the Quiz Kids." Their stamp was appearing on toys and kids clothing. In those first eight months about fifty children between the ages of seven and fifteen appeared on the show, earning a total of $17,000 in government bonds. At that time almost all the earnings were being saved for future education, although nearly all the children were from families in moderate or even poor circumstances.

One ironic aspect of the show was that the quizmaster for these extremely bright youngsters was a guy who dropped out of school after third grade. Joe Kelly had once emceed *The National Barn Dance* out of Chicago and was called "The Man in Overalls." But producers tried out a lot of people ranging from professors to other broadcasters and Kelly seemed to fit better than any of them. He knew his educational shortcomings and didn't let his ignorance of a lot of subjects get in the way. He admitted he was scared at first but managed to work it out.

## A Slip of the Lip

Most announcers discover that over a period of time there'll be days they can pronounce just about anything, no matter how polysyllabic – and then, next day, find it difficult to say their own name. I know, I've been there and I'm convinced it may be tied in with phases of the moon. It can happen to anybody.

For example, noted sportscaster Bill Stern once wrapped up a show with, "This is Bill Stine, serning off."

Don McNeill of *Breakfast Club* fame once had Nelson Eddy on as a guest and he was supposed to sing a "Nelson Eddy medley" of some of his hits. Well, what emerged from McNeill's mouth was a "Nelson Eddily medley…uh, I mean Nelly Edison melody!" Eddy went ahead and sang anyway.

This isn't exactly the same thing and I'm not sure if an Einstein could have resolved a question once posed on KOSI, a station in Aurora, Colorado. The announcer reeled off this beaut, "Here's something to think about; if a man's wife is his better half and he gets married a second time, what happens to him mathematically?"

## IT...IS...LATER...THAN...YOU...THINK!

That statement delivered in ominous measured tones introduced one of the most successful of Old Time Radio's frightening shows.

Arch Oboler gets justifiable credit for making *Lights Out,* one of the best of the spine-tingling radio presentations. However, he wasn't the originator of the program concept. Instead, that honor goes to a man by the name of Willis (sometimes spelled "Wyllis") Cooper.

It started as a novelty – an experiment. In the early part of 1934, Cooper figured a great many listeners might welcome a dramatic show late at night as a change from a glut of dance bands. He was an avid reader of mystery and horror stories and decided that midnight and ghastly stories might make a great combination for night-owl listeners. So, instead of just <u>reading</u> tales of horror he spent some time <u>writing</u> them. His scripts and suggestions were presented to NBC's program board and it was decided to give the notion a trial. Without any kind of ballyhoo, *Lights Out* went on the air as a 15-minute presentation on WENR in Chicago on a Wednesday at midnight early in January, 1934.

Studio personnel, accustomed to all types of programs and therefore generally indifferent to all, started staying up on Wednesday nights. A few radio editors paid tribute to something new on the air. Letters from listeners started coming in, slowly but surely increasing in number each week. It was a successful experiment but nobody imagined it was a sensation until a few months later. Cooper was continuity editor and decided he didn't have time for the show and all of his other work. In January, 1935 the show announcer signed off with, "This is the last of the series of *Lights Out* programs."

Then came the deluge. Letters, phone calls, telegrams, petitions – all poured in. Radio editors were swamped with protesting mail. The dominant theme was, "Put *Lights Out* back on!" Just three weeks later, the show resumed on WENR. Shortly afterward, the program was scheduled for the entire network (NBC Red).

Cooper wrote and Ted Sherdeman produced, as watching the show became an experience in itself. For promotional value, as opening words were spoken, all studio lights were extinguished. Working in utter darkness except for a few pinpoints of light enabling actors to see their scripts, and another in the control room so the producer could be seen, the studio became a perfect setting for the eeriness to follow. In spite of the effect, no audiences were permitted but, unlike many programs, no listener illusions would have been spoiled if they had been let in.

Cooper decided to spread his wings and moved to the west coast in 1936. That's when Oboler came into the picture. He did his first program in May of that year and continued for, two years before leaving. NBC staffers kept on with the show until mid-August of '39. It came back when Oboler breathed new life into it on CBS in the fall of '42. That lasted for not quite a year. In 1945 and '46, NBC gave it a go during summertime. In mid-year of '47, who came back but Cooper to try the whole thing again on Mutual with horror actor Boris Karloff, but a month was the extent of the run and that was that; for radio, that is. It was tried on TV and had a decent run but never achieved the following it had on "imagination" radio.

## Orson & the Mercury Theater Players Didn't Cause Nearly As Much Fuss As Some Copycats Did in Quito, Ecuador

It wasn't quite ten years and four months after Orson Welles and Company terrified thousands with their famous dramatization of *War of the Worlds*, on October 30, 1938 that a couple of guys at a radio station in Ecuador thought it would be exciting to try pretty much the same thing. The program director and dramatic director at Radio Quito had heard of the famous "War" show and decided to put together a similar script adapted for their part of the world.

The station was owned by the city's top newspaper, *El Comercio*, and both the paper and station were in the same downtown building. Saturday, February 12, 1949 turned out to be a momentous evening for both businesses.

After the usual evening newscast, a music show was aired and just like Orson's *War*, a song was interrupted by a news bulletin – an announcement that captured listener attention in a big way. The announcer said invaders from Mars had landed and destroyed a village about 20 miles south of Quito (shades of Grover's Mill, New Jersey, huh?). These outer space terrorists were heading for the capitol in the form of some sort of menacing cloud. This was followed by another bulletin that an air base had been obliterated with a great many victims.

The script then called for several actors to emulate some recognizable public authorities, somewhat akin to the acting done on the dramatized *March of Time* in the U.S. An "Interior Minister" called for calm and requested help in "defense and evacuation" of the city. The "Mayor" (another actor) told women and children to head for the hills so the men could fight the enemy unimpeded. Recorded church bells rang out as a priest pleaded for mercy. Frightened "residents" of a nearby village phoned in to say they were under attack. An announcer supposedly sent to the city's tallest building tremulously reported a monster surrounded by smoke and fire was headed toward the city.

Much like the chaos caused by the Mercury Theater Players, thousands of Ecuadorans fled into the streets, some wearing their nightclothes. The actors in the studio heard the wild noises in the street and realized for the first time what their program had caused. An announcer departed from the script to tell listeners it was just a fictional program. But that didn't help. The mobs not only didn't calm down but became angrier and angrier when they found out a hoax had been perpetrated.

The *El Comercio* building became a target as thousands of outraged citizens converged and began throwing rocks. Most of the hundred or so people in the building had managed to escape out a back door but dozens were trapped on the third floor. Their plight became more serious when the rioters brought gasoline and lighted copies of the newspaper to throw. The building was filled with flames that spread to surrounding structures and many of the trapped workers jumped or fell. Police and army units were summoned but they were on the way to help the first village that had reportedly been attacked by aliens. They did finally arrive and the crowds were dispersed but it was too late for the building and people in it. Only the front was left standing and twenty people died, with fifteen others injured.

Radio station and newspaper equipment were destroyed and the following day the two who started it all, the program director and dramatic director, were indicted.

Bitter memories were left and when the newspaper did a story in 1980 about the radio station's 40$^{th}$ anniversary, not one word was mentioned about any "Martians."

## The Ad Read, "Put a Mirror Near Every Radio...and There Would Be a New Philco in Every Home!"

By the time 1938 rolled around, most radios sounded pretty much the same, so an advertising guy got the bright idea of having people think how they <u>looked</u> when they changed stations. Prior to that time, cabinet model radios required a lot of bending to see the dial and do the tuning. So, what did they do but come up with a slightly tilted face on the cabinet and provide a large dial for tuning that brought a famous slogan into being. The ad read "No squat, no stoop, no squint," and that slogan caught on in a big way and the first thing you knew it was being used by comedians, in headlines and even in political speeches. Naturally, Philco thoroughly enjoyed all the extra and <u>free</u> attention.

More of the ad copy read, "Give tuner-inners a chance to see themselves as others see them – and it would be only a question of which Automatic Tuning Philco they would choose! The call letters of <u>all</u> your favorite stations appear on the lighted windows of the Philco Automatic Tuning Dial. One glance – a flick of your fingers – there's the station you want, tuned with the accuracy that assures full perfection of Philco High-Fidelity reception."

And you thought "hi-fi" was a more modern term. It is to be hoped the adman who thought up the successful campaign got a big raise!

## Nowhere in the Pages of History....

There were several different announcer-narrators on *The Lone Ranger* over the years, including Harold True, Harold Golder, Charles Woods, Bob Hite, even Brace Beemer, who also played the title role in two separate stints. However, none of the announcers measured up to the superb interpretation by Fred Foy. It was a pleasure to meet and chat with Fred.

TDOY: In your booklet, *Fred Foy from XYZ to ABC*, you talked about being a "ham" most of your life. Was there anything in your family background concerning show biz? How'd it come about?

F.F. I was the only one. My parents and grandparents on both sides had no background in show business of any kind. But, my interest as far back as I can remember was in acting and dramatic elements. I may have been blessed by previous genes but no one close.

TDOY: You've mentioned how lucky you were to get involved with the George Trendle organization at WXYZ in Detroit. How did you get there?

F.F. I started out in Detroit working at a little 25-watt station where they had a production gropup that would audition would-be actors. If they thought you had potential they'd ask you to join them and, of course, you'd work for experience but no money. I began there and worked on a couple of their shows. I did some part time announcing on Sundays...again for free.

TDOY: How old were you?

F.F. That would be right after graduation from high school, so let's see...1938...I was about 17-18 years old. As time went on, one of their men left and they asked if I wanted the job. At the time I was running elevators at Kearn's Department Store in downtown Detroit, making $14.95 a week. They offered me the staggering amount of $25 and I jumped...I was in show biz! And that's where I learned – by doing! At a small station in those days you did everything – even swept the floors occasionally. As time went on – before the war – I auditioned at WXYZ and I went on staff before going into service. When I came back in 1948, they auditioned for

Harold Golder as narrator of *The Lone Ranger*. He was going out to L.A. and they auditioned a goodly amount of people. I was lucky enough to have my number picked out of a hat and suddenly I was working with people who were wonderful actors, marvelous talents. The sound department was great – every element was top drawer.

TDOY: You referred in your booklet to the meticulous approach and the rehearsal schedule. Give us a rundown on how *The Lone Ranger* was put together for air.

F.F. Many people think you just walked in maybe an hour before, grabbed a script and just did it. Not so. We started every Monday, Wednesday and Friday at 3:00 o'clock in the afternoon, at which time director Chuck Livingston would cast the roles. We'd do a run-through for a rough timing and this would end at 4:00 o'clock. We'd take an hour break and then from 5:00 to 6:00 was production rehearsal in which all the elements were put together. We'd start at the top of the script – add the music, sound effects and so on. If there were difficult sections, they'd be worked on to smooth them out. We did this for the hour and then from 6:00 to 6:15, I would time the General Mills commercials. They had to be accurate because of the overall show timing. Then, 6:15 to 6:45, dress rehearsal as it would go on the air. If it was short, the writer was always there to knock out an added scene. Cuts would be made if it was long. We'd go on at 7:00 o'clock with the show, minus commercials, and feed Chicago for recording. At 7:29:30, with 30 seconds to go, we'd get ready to hit the network with the full show, commercials and all – pretty involved.

**Note:** This intense attention to broadcast management of time is referred to in my Kindle book, *I'm Not Resting, I'm Creating: The Power of POSITIVE Procrastination*.

TDOY: You said, "I went in the service," and sort of passed over that. A lot of great things happened to you with Armed Forces radio.

F.F. Yes, they did. I was very fortunate. I wound up briefly in Cairo, Egypt and had the opportunity of working on Egyptian state broadcasting. When I arrived, our radio section was just being set up, and because I'd been in radio they pulled me out on special service. They felt there should be an American voice in there with the British who controlled the Egyptian operation. I did some news and got to work with a lot of USO people who came in – like Andre Kostelanetz, Lily Pons, Nelson Eddy – it was a fortunate time of my life.

TDOY: Let's get back to *The Lone Ranger* and the situation with Brace Beemer. You would sometimes play the Ranger in early rehearsals but actually only did the Ranger on the air <u>one</u> time.

F.F. That's right. I was contracted as understudy for Brace by Trendle but never went on. When Brace made a trip the writers would turn out short scenes for shows he'd miss and record them on 16-inch discs – little bits the sound men would drop in when the show was on the air. There never was a foul-up and it <u>could</u> have happened easily. One day, Brace came in with laryngitis. There was no way he could go on so it was my day in the sun. I played the ranger and Jay Michael (announcer on the *Sergeant Preston* series) did my narration.

TDOY: More about Brace and you. Trendle tried to play you off against one another – perhaps a contract argument with Brace. Brace thought you were trying to get his job.

F.F. It was strange. Writer Fran Striker got me in the hall one day and said Mr. Trendle would like to see me start taking riding lessons. He told me to do it – that it could be good for me. It was kind of a mystery and, unfortunately, horses and I don't get along. I went to a riding stable and got a horse that went wherever he pleased. I sort of forgot about it and heard no more. After the program, we'd often go to a club down the street and rehash the show. One night Brace came in, sat next to me and asked, "Are you trying to get my job?" He said he knew what was going on. I explained all I knew and said there was no way I wanted to take his job. After that, we became very close friends. I think Mr. Trendle liked to cause those little waves to keep Brace in line from the money standpoint.

TDOY: You wound up being announcer on the Dick Cavett TV show for half a decade or so. What was that like?

F.F. It was a delight working with him and he was a *Lone Ranger* fan which made it great. There were many instances when he would work it into some part of the show and have me do the famous opening lines. Dick was a great person to work with and a brilliant guy and I enjoyed the years I spent with him. I still think he's one of the top interviewers around. I remember one *Lone Ranger* bit. Zubin Mehta, the famous conductor, was on the show and the whole thing had been set up. I was in white tie and tails. Mehta came out and Dick told him we were going to have a very special presentation and asked if he'd conduct the orchestra. So, Mehta took his place and the orchestra took off on the *William Tell Overture*. I walked up in white tie and tails and did the opening – a wonderful bit.

TDOY: Let's get to another show from the Trendle stable. First, it was *Challenge of the Yukon* and later *Sergeant Preston of the Yukon* – maybe should have been *Yukon King* because of the dog's importance. Paul Sutton was the sergeant, Jay Michael the announcer. Eventually, though, Brace Beemer became Preston and you were announcer toward the end of that series.

F.F. Yes, when the Ranger finally went off as a long show and Preston was still running, they made the switch.

TDOY: John Todd moved from Tonto to the Inspector. Stories about Todd - an octogenarian at the end – indicate he'd occasionally fall asleep in the studio.

F.F. Oh, definitely. We were always told to be alert about John, If he didn't have too many scenes with the Ranger he had a special chair in one corner of the studio and he'd doze off. Once I did an intro to a scene between the Ranger and Tonto. Brace started off and we looked over and John was snoozing. We tried to get him and he dropped his script so Brace had to do a monologue. But John was a wonderful man, a delight to know and a good actor too – had some Shakespearean training.

TDOY: You can learn how to use your voice but the basics – the essence of it is always there, I guess you were blessed with those dulcet tones.

F.F. I really was. People ask what did I do to train my voice. I can only say – nothing. It was just there.

A terrific guy, and speaking of dulcet tones, I wish there could be a way for you to hear Fred Foy in print – the way he delivered on our interview tape those wonderful opening lines for *The Lone*

*Ranger*. But, since you can't and for those who don't have a copy of the famous phrases we'll have them right here next. Fred could, and did, give it that extra <u>something</u> in his 70's at the time. I still get goosebumps. I guess it's true – once a fan, always a fan.

You'll have to imagine your own *William Tell Overture*:

"A fiery horse with the speed of light, a cloud of dust and a hearty, 'Hi-yo, Silver,' the Lone Ranger. With his faithful Indian companion, Tonto, the daring and resourceful masked rider of the plains led the fight for law and order in the early western United States. Nowhere in the pages of history can one find a greater champion of justice. Return with us now to those thrilling days of yesteryear. From out of the past come the thundering hoofbeats of the great horse, Silver. The Lone Ranger rides again!"

'Easy – steady big fellow – Hi-yo, Silver, awa-a-ay!'

## That Masked Man Was…John Barrett!!!

That headline is correct! George Stenius (later Seaton) may have been one of the first Lone Rangers on WXYZ in Detroit, but there was another "first" as well. At the time when Fran Striker submitted his initial scripts to the George Trendle station in Detroit, it was not yet on an exclusive basis. He also tested the scripts for a few weeks before the Detroit debut on station WEBR in Buffalo, New York. There, the Ranger was portrayed by a man named John Barrett whose sister, Mary, directed the broadcasts. Ironically, she later joined WXYZ as an actress and played the part of Mustang Meg on the Lone Ranger series.

## Some Other Things You May Not Know About the Lone Ranger

The part of Tonto was not crated until the 11$^{th}$ show when it was determined the Ranger had to be able to talk to someone. It's relatively well known that Tonto was always played by John Todd for the entire run of the radio version but you might not know he was on the very first program even though Tonto didn't exist yet. Todd played the sheriff on that one.

Incidentally, Striker got the name out of an atlas where he noted the Tonto Basin in Arizona. There is also a Tonto National Forest, a Tonto National Monument, Tonto Creek and, yes, a village called Tonto Basin, all in Gila County north and east of Phoenix. When Striker submitted the script he said Tonto might not be as good as some other name if they wanted to change it, but no one did. Perhaps they would have if they had known the true meaning of the word. I spoke with the Arizona State Historian, Marshall Trimble of Scottsdale Community College, and he told me it's a Spanish word meaning "fool," not a name you would have knowingly selected for your trusted companion.

More about the first "Ranger" in Detroit. Except for a brief stint by a Jack Deeds, the initial acting job was done by George Stenius, who later changed his name to Seaton and did extremely well on the Hollywood scene. He became president of the Academy of Motion Picture Arts and Sciences (the "Oscar" people) and directed the final takes of Marlon Brando's version of *Mutiny on the Bounty*.

Earle Graser, who succeeded him and became the Ranger until his death in an auto accident on April 8, 1941, was slight and didn't physically look the part. Therefore, all early promotional pictures were of Brace Beemer, who took over the role upon Graser's death. One of the pictures showed Beemer and John Todd ("Tonto") both riding "Silver." Animal lovers sent in complaints so a script provided Tonto with his own horse, "White Feller." When a movie version came along in 1938, an assistant director said that wouldn't work – that two white horses didn't provide enough contrast. Instead, he suggested a paint – "You know, piebald – calico –mottled – black and white."

So, Striker wrote a radio script where "White Feller" injured a leg and Tonto borrowed a horse named "Scout." It stayed that way from then on.

Who knows? Fran Striker might never have been associated with the Lone Ranger if it hadn't been for Phillips Lord. That's right – the same man associated with *Gangbusters, Mr. District Attorney, Seth Parker*, etc. When Striker was at WEBR he got mail from Phillips Lord offering a script for broadcast at a nominal royalty fee. It isn't known for sure if the station bought it but the submission gave Striker the idea of trying the same thing. He started a one-man syndicate, "Fran Striker Continuities," and that led him to placing some shows (including one called *Manhunter*) on WXYZ.

In a letter dated December 28, 1932, the station asked for some wild-west scripts. Striker had a series called *Covered Wagon Days* and he decided to recycle some of those scripts in answer to the request. That, of course, led to *The Lone Ranger*.

What's that old line about, "you can fool some of the people some of the time...?" Well, a young listener once proved the point. He pointed out to the program department that whenever the Lone Ranger cocked his pistol it made two clicks. He informed them that in those days there were only single action revolvers and that they made <u>four</u> clicks when cocked. I have no record of whether the sound effect was altered as a result.

## Death-Dealing, Space-Cleaving, Time-Dissolving Devices of the 25th Century
### Can such things be?

E.R. "Jack" Johnstone never had any scholastic training in science, yet he was the mastermind who dreamed up every rocket ship, disintegrator and gyro-cosmic relativator used on *Buck Rogers in the 25th Century*.

Of course, credit on the show from 1931 to 1939 went to the character of "Dr. Huer," who also supposedly invented gadgets like the teleradioscope; a mechanical mole for digging deep into the earth, and such things as psychic restriction ray.

Fans would hurry home to twist the dial for the CBS program and their ages ranged from four to what have you as they offered living proof that the inventions seemed convincing.

Jack Johnstone may not have had formal training but he was a practical scientific inventor even as a boy. His early experiments with electricity and chemistry went on in a den on the third floor of the Johnstone homestead.

He contrived a secret automatic door opener which nobody else could operate. He knew just where a little thread in the wall was concealed, and after wiggling that he pressed a button and the door would open silently and mysteriously. Anyone else who tried to enter thought it was a simple matter of pushing the button, but when *they* did, nothing happened.

Another early Johnstone device was an electric signal which announced the approach of anyone climbing the stairs. That was a mere matter of a loosened board on one of the steps, under which were hidden wires that made a contact when someone stepped on the board.

His inquiring mind kept him busy tearing apart and putting together again anything mechanical, from an alarm clock to an automobile, right on up until age seventeen. That's when he enrolled at Rutgers and left the den behind. He wasn't at the college long, though, before he left to attend a school of institutional administration. It's difficult to see how that helped him very much for the vocation that was ahead of him, unless it gave him some insight in how to cope with all the ins-and-outs of that marvel known as radio.

In any case, he eventually put his youthful background to work as producer/writer/director of the futuristic Buck Rogers program. He claimed that all his ideas emerged from his typewriter and pipe smoke. But, he studied scientific publications and was abreast of all recent discoveries. He had to maintain accuracy because listeners were quick to call attention to any slip. In 1935, the program made mention of ten moons around Saturn and a critic wrote in at once to say there were only nine. Johnstone referred the writer to the *World Almanac*, which listed a recent addition of a previously unknown Saturnian moon.

Another bit of legitimate knowledge at the time that was passed along via the script was the fact it had been discovered not long before that a red spot on Jupiter, formerly regarded as volcanic, was really a frozen island of ammonia, floating on a cloud of hydrocarbon.

Like many a science fiction writer to follow in years to come, Johnstone firmly believed that the things he was creating would someday come to pass. The death ray he predicted had been used in similar form by the French for killing mosquitoes at a distance of ten miles. Why shouldn't rocket guns and rocket ships, vibro-destructor rays, paralysis rays and others of the weird-sounding devices become matters of reality some day? After all, they sounded plausible in helping Buck and his aide, Wilma Deering, make their way through the complexities of the 25$^{th}$ century.

Johnstone did his best to see to it that all of the seemingly wild notions were more than just figments of an active imagination. They were planned to be within the realm of possibility, if not probability. That was the one major element that made the program convincing even though it dealt with the world of imagination.

The whole idea of the show originated with a comic strip in 1929 but it was the magic of radio that brought it all to life. When Jules Verne released his *Twenty Thousand Leagues Under the Sea* and *Around the World in Eighty Days*, they were received incredulously. Imagine, said the wise ones, a boat that could travel under the water! What nonsense! Once again, the imagination factor that made radio such a stellar factor built a world that couldn't be, or so it was said.

The role played by Adele Ronson that is likely more remembered than any of her other characterizations is that of Wilma Deering on the Buck Rogers program. But, to limit this actress' credits to just that, would be doing her a great disservice.

She appeared on *Emo Crime Club*, *The Gibson Family* (one of the first drama shows to have music written specifically for it), *John's Other Wife*, *Meyer the Buyer* (with Harry Hirschfield, later to be on *Can You Top This?*, and Teddy Bergman, later to change his name to Alan Reed), *The Coty Playgirl* (as hostess), and *We Love and Learn* (as announcer).

All this from a girl who wanted desperately to join the Glee Club in high school in Tulsa, but was turned down because, primarily, she just didn't sing very well. So, she went out for the Dramatic Society where the director told her to study the part of Ophelia in the school production of *Hamlet* – that she could have the part if she read lines better than anyone else. Adele was thirteen at the time and went to the elocution teacher's house each night to study the Shakespearean role. She got it down pat but when the time came for selection she was told she didn't look the part of the melancholy Ophelia and that an older girl seemed more suitable.

Adele eventually got roles in school and local amateur theatricals and became convinced she wanted to become a professional actress. Miss Ronson headed for New York and got a chance to join the cast of *All for Love* at the Greenwich Village Theater. She read for the part but her old nemesis – singing – got in the way and she lost out. She did manage some understudy jobs but none of the stars dropped out.

A part as a slave in *Road to Rome* was at least some encouragement and when it closed she got an opportunity to try for the role of a French vamp. But, the director took one look and said, "You don't look like a vamp and never will." Perseverance pays, though, and she got a small part on *Court of Human Relations*. Then came an audition for *Buck Rogers* and her career made a big jump forward. She was chosen the very next day and became Wilma! She had learned to profit from her disappointments rather than being defeated by them.

## Bits 'n' Pieces About Comedy

A year after Fred Allen graduated from high school, he started getting booked at "amateur nights." It was part-time stuff and after a year, he finally got a chance at a vaudeville date, filling in for a professional juggler. He did it as "Paul Huckle, European Entertainer," and got a booking out of it, taking the professional name of Freddy St. James. That didn't work out very well but he knew show biz was the thing for him. He started switching from juggling to comedy patter and was then just plain Freddie James, the "world's worst juggler."

He eventually got a route on the Loew circuit and a round of some bigger cities around the country got him a sixteen week tour in Australia. He made about $125 a week and he stayed there a year. When he finally came home, he was afraid he'd be offered the same money he was making before he went Down Under if he tried for bookings as Freddie James. His agent was Edgar Allen, who suggested the comedian take his name. So, from then on, the man who had been born John Florence Sullivan, became Fred Allen for good.

In 1922, he made his first appearance on the legitimate stage and alternated between musicals and vaudeville for a few years. His last stage show was *Three's a Crowd* and when it closed in 1932, he worked out a sample radio program and did his first broadcast on October 23, 1932.

It was not a particularly auspicious start with his voice seemingly a detriment. The best description of it came from columnist O.O. McIntyre. He wrote that Allen's voice sounded like, "a man with false teeth chewing on slate pencils." Thank goodness, history denotes that Allen succeeded in spite of it.

Another comedian of the times, Eddie Cantor, got a lot of comedy mileage out of his "banjo eyes," but his audiences never seemed to get tired of hearing his gags about being the father of five girls and no boys. So, we offer a bit of trivia. What were his daughters' names? They were Marjorie, Natalie, Edna, Marilyn and Janet.

Eddie and his wife, Ida, became grandparents in 1939 when Natalie and Joseph Metzger had a child – and finally, the Cantor "jinx," if you could call it that, was broken. It was a boy!

There is no 100% certification, but odds are that the first real comedy program on radio came about as the result of something that happened October 18, 1921.

It was a red brick factory building belonging to Westinghouse where Ernie Hare and Billy Jones walked into a room with tarpaulins hung on the walls. It was unfamiliar territory and they were somewhat apprehensive but went ahead in that makeshift studio with songs and jokes on Radiophone Station WJZ. People listening in crystal sets liked it and it wasn't long before Jones and Hare had a regular show for Happiness Candy Stores on WEAF. It was supposed to be a five-week deal but the *Happiness Boys* wound up being on for that sponsor for five and a half years, helping pave the way for the many comedy shows to follow.

## A Gift of Improvisation
## Or:
## If You're Not Sure, Fake It!

Character actor Hans Conreid had a great knack of being perfectly able to make something up if he didn't really know the subject. Hans had particular capability along these lines when it came to subjects of Oriental nature because he had served in the Army in Japan. But, one day he really got his comeuppance from Jess Oppenheimer, the creator of *I Love Lucy*.

They were walking along a street in L.A. and passed by the Temple Baptist Church. It so happened that some of the lights in the church sign weren't working and Oppenheimer noticed it. The sign was reading, sans the bulbs, "Temple Ba Chu." Jess couldn't resist the chance to test Conreid's mental reflexes and asked, "Have you ever heard of Temple Ba Chu?"

Conreid wrinkled his brow as they kept walking and then answered in fully confident fashion, "Certainly. Temple Ba Chu is one of the more beautiful, but obscure, Oriental temples. It's located somewhere in Southeast Asia, in Laos, I believe – or is it South Viet Nam? It's a Shinto Temple, I think, or perhaps Zen."

As he finished his little discourse, he happened to look up and see the broken church sign spelling out "Temple Ba Chu."

Oppenheimer recalled that Hans proceeded to chase him down the street.

Conreid had credits on such shows as *Burns and Allen, The Great Gildersleeve, The Judy Canova Show, My Friend Irma, Life With Luigi* and *The Mel Blanc Show*. He was also a frequent guest later on TV's *Tonight Show* with Jack Paar. Paar had a story about him in his book, *I Kid You Not*.

"On one occasion when Hans was a guest, I was talking with Virginia DeLuce, a voluptuous actress known for her interest in astrology and her vital measurements, not necessarily in that order. We spoke of astrology and she said that I was a Taurus and she had ties to Venus. "I've been checking my horoscope,' she said, 'and your Taurus touched my Venus.'

Hans raised an eyebrow, looked from the curvesome Virginia to me, and beamed, 'Congratulations!'

He was one of my favorite guests – a tall, flowing-maned actor, whose Shakesperean flair and gentle wit made him sort of an Elizabethan Good Humor man."

## Another Star Interview

Your writer had the very pleasant assignment of sitting and chatting with Florence Williams, a delightful lady. Among her radio credits were the female leads on *Front Page Farrell* and *Barry Cameron*, with roles on *The Light of the World* and *Roses and Drums*, among others. Here's the way our conversation went.

TDOY: One of the many shows on which you appeared was *Front Page Farrell*. Over the years, the male lead was played by Richard Widmark, Carleton Young and Staats Cotsworth. Who did you work with?

F.W. First, Richard Widmark. Then, an interim when a young man came in but was taken into the Army. That brought in Costworth...Staats and I worked the rest of the time with him.

TDOY: What a delightful talent he had; he could use his voice in so many different ways.

F.W. Oh, yes, and he was a nice person. I enjoyed him very much.

TDOY: There was one show – and speaking of fine voices, Bret Morrison (who portrayed *The Shadow*), was in this as the speaker and you did a thing called *The Light of the World*, which had Bible dramatizations. Tell us about that.

F.W. Well, I did several things on it but the one I liked most was playing Ruth in the *Book of Ruth*. I enjoyed that very, very much.

TDOY: What kind of reaction on the program did you get from the general public? Anything specific?

F.W. I believe they appreciated it a great deal and it was very well presented. It was exceptionally well done and I was proud to do it.

TDOY: Many of the folks I talk with, Florence, had no one else in the family that was ever in show business. What about you and your background?

F.W. (Chuckle) The closest was my father, who was a lawyer. (Laugh) He would have been a good actor, I think.

TDOY: What got you started?

F.W. From the time I was about eight years old, I was trained to be a pianist and I was working very hard at it because that was what was expected of me. That was until I was about sixteen or seventeen when I fell in love with the theater. I was, by that time, in St. Louis during the summer. There was a magnificent open-air theater with big oak trees as a proscenium arch – a little pond in front they could cover up – and they did Shakespeare. Other classics and there were a great many people (very good actors) from Carnegie Tech. Also, excellent directors and I was just absolutely fascinated. I decided I wanted to be an actress but I didn't dare tell anyone. My sister (about four years older) caught on, though. One night at the garden theater, one young actor was Will Geer (later on TV's *The Waltons*). Somebody knew him and I was introduced. My sister – I could have wished the earth would open up and swallow me – said, "I think my sister wants to be an actress." Oh, I could have died.

TDOY: How old were you?

F.W. About sixteen or seventeen. Anyway, Will Geer said, "Well, why don't you?" I told him I'd never know what to do with my hands. He picked one of them up, looked at it and said, "Looks like a perfectly ordinary hand to me. I think you might learn." Many years later, I got to tell Will, "It's your fault. You did it." I never would have had the courage.

TDOY: Why wouldn't you tell anyone in the family? Were you afraid people would laugh at you?

F.W. Oh, yes, and I feel in those days people thought going into the theater was very frivolous and not the proper thing for a young woman to do. But, my father was very understanding. I confided to him that I wanted to go to this theater colony that I'd heard about from someone (actually someone from the touring company of George Arliss's *Merchant of Venice*). It was in Peterborough, New Hampshire and they took apprentices. I wanted very much to go and in those days it cost $400, a good bit then. My father said I better get it out of my system, so he let me go with the notion I'd come back to music and forget all about the theater, But, he was wrong. He'd also agreed before I went that if I wasn't so thoroughly disgusted with it that he'd let me go to some sort of training school. Of course, I was far from disgusted; I was more enchanted than ever. The colony was right next door to the MacDowell Colony, where Thornton Wilder happened to be. He would come over to see our productions. I did the balcony scene from *Romeo and Juliet* and he came backstage afterwards and said, "Miss Williams, I do believe that if you want to get into the professional theater, you might make it – if you get rid of your white mice." I knew exactly what he meant. My mother had a very high-pitched voice – melodious and sweet – but very high-pitched. I, of course, had copied it so I took Mr. Wilder quite seriously and worked very hard to get rid of my "white mice." I also took my father up, before he had a chance to say no – went to New York on my way home and took the entrance exams for the American Academy. What could a poor father do?

TDOY: He was stuck with an actress daughter.

F.W. That's right. I went to the Academy for a year, enjoyed it and I think it did quite a bit of good.

TDOY: Did you ever pursue the music at all?

F.W. I used it in plays on Broadway a couple of times but as far as doing it professionally, I just teach any child who comes within range, for fun.

TDOY: What was the very first role you did on radio?

F.W. I was working in *The Old Maid* on Broadway with Judith Anderson and Helen Mencken and I got a call. A lady who did casting for radio said there was something she wanted me to do. I think the first thing was Sigmund Romberg's music program where they didn't feel the singers could act. I would double for the singers' speaking parts. Later, the same people called again and said that *Roses and Drums* needed a Quaker girl, a replacement for someone leaving. It never dawned on me I was being auditioned. Such a thing I'd never heard of. When I got up to the mike (they had the old-fashioned ones), without looking at it much I auditioned into the dead side, I thought sure I was doomed but they turned me around and I got the part anyway. I tell you, another of the first people I auditioned for was a charming lady who was doing the casting for Ivory Soap commercials. She listened, was very kind, but said, "I can't use you." I asked why not. She replied, "Because you don't sound as though you ever do dishes." I assured her I did do dishes and floors and windows, too. But, she told me, "I can't help it, Florence. This is radio. It's not what you do or how you look, but how you sound.

TDOY: No question, the essence of radio. I admit to not knowing anything about one show you were on, *Barry Cameron*.

F.W. It was short-lived. It was a daily soap kind of thing and was also called by another name, *The Soldier That Came Home*. I was the young wife when the soldier returned. I had just had the experience <u>my</u> soldier <u>not</u> coming home and it was kind of traumatic.

TDOY: Were directors a big enough part of shows that could make a difference in performance?

F.W. There was a wonderful director and actor, Joe Bell, who decided for some reason to help me. He booked me on several things and helped me understand the difference in the mediums. On radio, you often <u>under</u>played vocally but you <u>over</u>played emotionally. You did the opposite for theater.

TDOY When you were talking about the "white mice" – the higher pitched voice – did you rid yourself through on-going practice or training?

F.W. I just worked with myself because once I was truly conscious of it, I decided I could work out of it and I did.

TDY: Time and again, I've observed that people who worked in old time radio had an almost mysterious camaraderie – an affection for one another.

F.W. It was like a big family. They were all so gracious. I enjoyed working with them all. I must say it was nice to play the same character like on *Front Page Farrell* – I was on it for eleven years. And it was quite a challenge if you got to be a villainess. I often did that on *Mr.Keen, Tracer of Lost Persons*. I tell you, I am so grateful for my time in radio. It meant so much to me. And the people who still like it, even though many of them never heard the original, I love them all.

## It Was a Case of Turning Imagination Into Money!

Dave Elman had lost his young son and was not only out of work but heavily in debt. In addition to having to work those things out, he realized he'd better create a diversion, a hobby, or the financial pressures and grief were going to cause him to crack. He looked into several possibilities and found his interest was growing in *all* of them.

As he thought more and more about it, Elman decided it would be a great idea to set up a radio meeting place for hobbyists from all over everywhere. That way they could let people with troubles know that you could help knock gloom out of the way by using spare time to better effect.

With solid belief in his idea, Elman sold his car and borrowed himself deeper into debt so he could pay for his first broadcasts. For a while, he lost $100 a week, but then got a sponsor. The idea came along in March of 1937 and by 1939, Dave Elman was head of the biggest proving ground in the country for hobbies and his program, *Hobby Lobby*, was one of the most popular on the 155 stations that carried it nationally.

For a guy who fingered the after-hours pulse of the nation, it was easy for Elman to answer an often asked question, "What kind of hobbies give people the most solid pleasure?" Actually, there had been similar answers from psychologists for years but Elman's newfound authority emphasized the concept. "Hobbies that, while giving us fun in themselves, have the added importance and human interest of helping others at the same time."

He suggested that if you wanted to have an inner glow that would grow over the years, you should ask yourself:

What injustices around me make me mad?
Which human problems arouse my greatest sympathy?
What unanswered need in my community could I help to meet?

As an example, in the late '30s in the heart of the Great Depression, a Massachusetts truck driver got a great idea going. He built some swings in the back yard for his five kids but invited other youngster in when they looked on wistfully. The idea grew from there as John Nickerson built small replicas of popular amusement park attractions – like a merry-go-round, a four-child Ferris wheel, shoot-the-chute, even a home-made microphone so the kids could sing and act. Four neighbors liked the notion so much they took down their fences and as many as 500 kids could and did crowd in to have fun. We might not have as many "street" problems today if people bothered to do something like that.

There were a great many other wonderful projects spurred on my Dave Elman's *Hobby Lobby* radio creation, just another reason for fondly remembering the Golden Age of radio.

## Gloom Chasers

They got to be a team in a rather unusual way, to say the least. The story has it that Wilbur Budd Hulick was at work at WMAK, Buffalo on the morning of October 10, 1930 and suddenly found himself having to fill in a lengthy slot on the air. He dashed frantically to the continuity department and found scriptwriter Frederick Chase Taylor banging away on a typewriter, The two of them headed into the studio and Hulick, who had had his own band, played the organ. Taylor responded in comic style as Hulick kept calling him "Colonel Stoopnagel" – no particular reason, it just popped out. The response was so good they wound up with a trial on CBS on a show called *Gloom Chasers*. They were called "Stoopnagel and Budd," with the former eventually becoming Colonel Lemuel Q. Stoopnagel. One of the tools as they progressed was the use of "spoonerisms" by the Colonel. For the uninitiated that means" a transposition, especially a ludicrous one, of the beginnings of two or more words. Your writer is currently the world's foremost practitioner of the art form. It was Taylor, as Stoopnagel, though, who popularized the garbled grammar in story form with many of his works appearing in print in the *Post Scripts* section of the long-ago editions of the *Saturday Evening Post*. And, yes, an example of his lunacy is about to be inflicted upon you.

**The Loose That Gaid the Olden Geggs**

Back in the not too pastant dist, a carried mupple were nortunate efuff to possoose a gess which laid an olden gegg every dingle way of the seek. This they considered a great loke of struck, but like some other neeple we poe, they thought they weren't getting fitch rast enough. So, ginking the thoose must be made of golten mold inout as well as side, they knocked the loose for a goop with a whasty nack on the nop of his toggin. Goor little poose! Anyway, they expected to set at the goarse of all this meshuss prettle. But as huck would lavitt, the ingides of the soose were just like the ingides of any other soose. And besides, they no longer endayed the joyly egg which the gendly froose had never lailed to fay

And the storal to this mory is: Remember what Shake-sed speared in *The Verchant of Menace*: "All that golders is not glit!"

So, now, you've been exposed. Be careful, it's contagious. You should see what such material does to the Spellcheck on my computer.

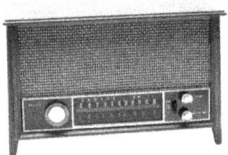

## Why British Broadcasting Became Non-commercial

Actress Grace Hayes was credited with telling the story of why there was no advertising on England's radio programs. It seems they once tried it and the announcer devoted two minutes to tell what a grand kind of tea somebody or other was selling. "Why," he exclaimed, "the King drinks it!" And immediately the band played, "God Save the King!" So, commercial broadcasting died that night in London.

## Good Evening, Mr. and Mrs. North America, and All the Ships at Sea

The latter part of a certain newscaster's opening once got some extra attention. A year before Pearl Harbor the very wordy broadcaster/columnist Walter Winchell wangled a Navy commission as Lieutenant Commander and was assigned to raise money for Navy relief. He staged a benefit at Madison Square Garden and raised a quarter of a million dollars, big money for the time. That was enough to impress some Navy bigwigs and they requested Winchell to put out an appeal for private boat owners to loan their vessels to be used for patrolling the nation's territorial waters just in case there might be a threat from German U-boats. Good ol' Walter complied and a few days following the radio plea, the Navy called him and said, in effect, "Stop. Don't say anything else. We got offers of more than 2,000 boats and we can't handle any more!"

## The Mystic Voice of the Ether

Your writer found a delightful piece about the meaning of radio. It was in a 1930 publication and it's something that should be shared.

<u>Voices</u>
By Robert Davis

I am Radio. Distance nor barrier oppose me.
Through all space I fling my mysterious reverberations.

I am the whisper that leaps the hemisphere; the
song that echoes around the world;
the cadence that rides the ether in a thousand tongues.

I am the wisdom of the ages revived in a single breath;
the lullaby of the cradle; the thunder of war;
the voice of the state.

I am the litany and the surplice choir;
The trumpet and the reed;
The bow and the string; the singer and the song,
in key with the cosmic chords

I am the rhythm to dancing feet. I sway the world in
rhapsody to the measure of beating hearts.
I am the universal orchestra in tune with the carnival.

I am the life of the market place; the thrill of the bourse;
the roar of the ring; the cheers of the coliseum.

I am the comrade of the sick; the courier to the lonely;
the ally that knows no frontier.

I am all the voices of the earth and the murmur
of the multitude merged in one vast articulation.

I am the message from the microphone.
I am the conqueror of the void.
I am the triumph of the centuries.
I AM RADIO.

As stated, that was from 1930. How times, and radio, have changed. What a shame!

Lum and Abner became an early radio success beginning in 1931, with Chet Lauck and Norris Goff portraying the bucolic duo. The program ran in one form or another into the early 1950s, with a syndicated version finally ending in 1954.

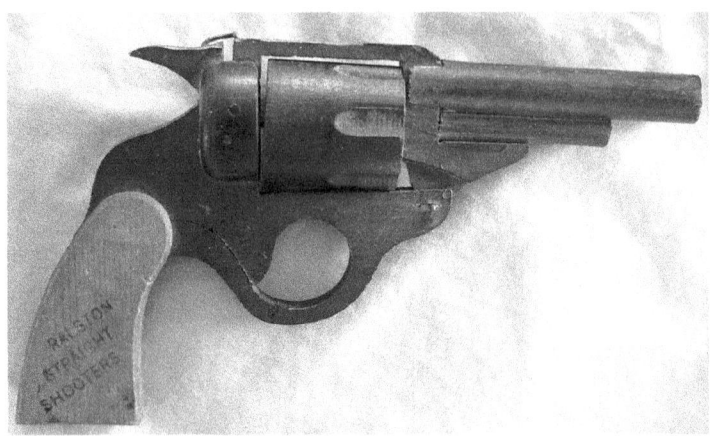

*Youth oriented programs such as Tom Mix in the 1930s attracted additional following by offering premiums usually for box tops from the sponsor's product. One such was this wooden Tom Mix pistol for the Ralston Straight Shooters.*

*"Who's that little chatterbox? The one with pretty auburn locks?..." was part of the theme introducing Little Orphan Annie in the 1930s. Among the show premiums offered were an Ovaltine shake-up mug and a decoder badge (1937 vintage).*

*After the author interview with radio/TV performer Durward Kirby he sent along a picture of the first microphone he ever used, back on February 19, 1932, at WBAA, West Lafayette, Indiana.*

*An integral part of radio-TV shows were the sound effects men and one of the foremost practitioners was Bob Mott (right). He worked such programs as Gangbusters, Perry Mason, The Garry Moore Show (eight years) and Captain Kangaroo. We did numerous skits together at various Old Time Radio Conventions in the 1990s.*

*One of broadcasting's busiest and most versatile actresses was Lurene Tuttle (with the author) who also had scores of movie supporting roles. She portrayed Harriet Nelson's mother on The Adventures of Ozzie and Harriet, a nurse on Dr. Christian and worked other programs such as Duffy's Tavern, The Great Gildersleeve and The Red Skelton Show.*

*An Old Time Radio convention in Newark gave the author (left) a part in a script reenactment with Lon Clark (next to me), who created the lead role on* Nick Carter, Master Detective. *Far right is Herb Ellis, who appeared on such shows as* The Adventure of Nero Wolfe, Broadway Is My Beat, *and* Escape. *Partially hidden behind Herb's script is Harry Bartell, who had many different roles on* Gunsmoke *and appeared in approximately 10,000 different program roles.*

*A Denver Old Time Radio gathering gave the author (left) a chance to work with (left of me to right) Sam Edwards (Meet Corliss Archer, Gunsmoke, Escape, One Man's Family and scores of others), Pete Smythe, dominant Denver radio personality, Hal Stone ("Jughead" of Archie Andrews) and (hidden in front behind a script), Dick Beals, versatile actor and decades-long voice of "Speedy Alka-Seltzer."*

The author (right front microphone) announced a gathering of many former cast members of One Man's Family at a Los Angeles Old Time Radio Convention. In the middle on the back row is Sam Edwards of wide-ranging roles of virtually every description and at back on far right is Tyler McVey who gained credits on One Man's Family, Lux Radio Theater and countless other shows.

*The author was privileged to play the father in a reenactment of Archie Andrews with virtually the entire original NBC cast. That included Bob Hastings ("Archie"), second from left in the back row. Rosemary Rice ("Betty"), second from right in back row, and Hal Stone ("Jughead"), down left front with the author. Far right at back is great sound effects specialist, Ray Erlenborn, who worked with Red Skelton for ten years.*

*Singer, actress, speaker, Carmel Quinn, was born in Dublin, Ireland and had never heard of Arthur Godfrey when she came to the U.S. in the 1950s. However, she won a contest on Arthur Godfrey's Talent Scouts, and was part of his daily show for six years.*

## It Was a "First" and It Lasted For an Hour and a Half

November 27, 1921: A ninety minute music show that became the first "live" broadcast by a well-known orchestra. It was the Vincent Lopez band from a WJZ studio in a converted cloakroom of a Westinghouse factory building in New Jersey. There was available space of about 10 feet by 18 feet but somehow they managed to jam everyone in. Tommy Cowan had been taken from a Westinghouse factory department and made WJZ's first announcer and he introduced Lopez to announce the music. Lopez related that he stepped up to the ugly thing called a microphone and said, "Hello, everybody – Lopez speaking." That's all he said and Cowan had to do all the rest. It was certainly an inauspicious forerunner for all the band remotes to come. By the way, the band played (among other things) *Anitra's Dance, Celeste Aida* and Lopez himself played *Canadian Capers* as a piano solo. The band usually played in the Grill Room of the Hotel Pennsylvania in New York and Lopez had suggested putting in a speaker so people there could hear the broadcast and dance. It went over well, so Lopez asked Cowan if a mike could be put in the Grill so the band could send music down wires – or something – to the station in New Jersey. The phone company said it wasn't feasible but Western Union figured out a way after a month of study and on the Thursday before Christmas of 1921, Vincent Lopez did the first remote dance band pickup. Response was so good that phone calls knocked out one of the mid-Manhattan telephone exchanges. Obviously, no one knew at the time that many years later, the airwaves would be filled with the sound of bands coming from the top venues all around the nation. Your writer once had the pleasure of doing a dance band "remote" with the renowned Tommy Dorsey orchestra. I had a bit of trepidation because of all the stories about the temper of the sometimes irascible T.D., but he treated me with graciousness and the broadcast was a success. I mention this incident in my Kindle e-Book, *Cat Whiskers and Talking Furniture: A Memoir of Radio and Television Broadcasting*.

## Pompous! Arrogant! Pretentious! Windbag! Supercilious! Blowhard!
Those descriptions fit the characters he played, but not the man!

One of the entertainment world's finest character actors succumbed to cancer in a health center in Escondido, California in mid-year 1995. Gale Gordon died at age 89, a few weeks after the death of his wife, Virginia. As usual with long-time radio performers, the wire services devoted most of the story to his work on TV. For the most part, they overlooked a truly remarkable radio career. Of course, his best known TV work was on *I Love Lucy*, but long before that he was featured with Lucille ball and Richard Denning on *My Favorite Husband*, the radio forerunner of *Lucy*. Gordon and Bea Benadaret were the original choices for the Fred and Ethel Mertz roles on *Lucy* but contractual obligations got in the way and the parts went to William Frawley and Vivian Vance.

Many Old Time Radio fans will remember Gordon most as Osgood Conklin, the principal of Madison High on the classic *Our Miss Brooks* with Eve Arden. Others will say he was great as Mayor La Trivia on *Fibber McGee and Molly*, where he also had the lesser role of weatherman Foggy Williams. However, even those memorable performances just scratch the surface of his career. He was the D.A. on *Big Town* when it starred Edward G. Robinson and Claire Trevor. He was one of the many leads on *The Case Book of Gregory Hood*, others being Elliott Lewis, Jackson Beck, Paul McGrath, Martin Gabel and George Petrie – talk about a stellar group! He appeared on *Burns and Allen*, *The Judy Canova Show*, *Junior Miss*, *Tarzan*, *The Penny Singleton Show* and *Johnny Madero, Pier 13* with Jack Webb. He was Father Leahy on that one. He and Sheldon Leonard were on *Mr. and Mrs. Blanding* with Cary Grant and his wife, Betsy Drake. Gordon appeared with Bea Benadaret on *Granby's Green Acres*, the show that led to TV's *Green Acres*. Gale was the harried sponsor (Rexall) on the *Phil Harris-Alice Faye Show*. He portrayed Flash Gordon in 1935, a year before Buster Crabbe did it in a movie serial. The lead was his on *Jonathan Trimble, Esq.* with Irene Tedrow and he was on Mutual with Joan Blondell in 1942 in *Miss Pinkerton, Inc.* He was a well-to-do, obnoxious neighbor, Rumson Bullard, on *The Great Gildersleeve* and when *The Shadow of Fu Manchu* was syndicated in 1939, Gordon was Dr. Petrie to Hanley Stafford's Nayland Smith role. Incidentally, Stafford, who was daddy Higgins on *Baby Snooks*, took his acting name from his home town of Hanley in Staffordshire, England. His real name was John Austin. Oh, and lest we forget, Gordon was Weary Willie the Stork on the children's Christmas classic, *The Cinnamon Bear*. Even with this extensive list we've covered only part of his career. He personally estimated he had done at least 5,000 radio shows and it's likely there were more than that. Add to that the fact that he had a walk-on part on Broadway when he was just a teenager, had a role in a silent movie with Greta Garbo, and performed in a stock company in Denver for a year, and it makes up a fantastic list of credits. And to think that TV covered mostly just his TV career.

**The amazing thing is that he started with a terrible handicap!**

Gale Gordon was born with a double cleft-palate and his parents were told by doctors that he might never be able to speak. He had to have more than a dozen operations and during all the rehabilitation he came up with the exceptional deliberate style of speaking that was his and his alone. If it can be said that comic pomposity became an art form, then it must be added that Gale Gordon was the one who made it so.

Some friends, John and Larry Gassman and Randy Skredvet of the SPERDVAC old time radio organization in L.A., had an extensive conversation with the man about his incredible career, and passed along the result to *Thrilling Days of Yesteryear*. The talk led off with a question about a 1926 radio debut as a budding ukulele player.

G.G. I almost killed radio in its tracks. There was a little studio at the base of a tower on Sunset Boulevard at the Warner Brothers Studios. They had a little room at the bottom where they broadcast radio – quite a novelty in those days. Someone told me once that if you had anything to say or do just go in and they'd be happy to put you on the air, It sounded interesting because I was between jobs looking desperately for work, So, I went down and they asked what I did. I had learned three or four chords on the ukulele and I'd written some words to *It Ain't Gonna Rain No More*. They said the mike was mine and I sang the song with those lousy chords. Nobody much heard it I'm sure, because they only had about 50 listeners at the best of times.

The first time I went on and got paid, I was cast (miscast, as it happened) on the telephone. It was a show written by Kay Van Riper (*English Coronets*). I had just done a play or something that failed in San Francisco so I called radio and was told to come in next morning. I was only 27 but Miss Van Riper thought from my voice I was a middle-aged Englishman and had cast me that way. I got the job anyway at $3.00 a show and 10% went to Warner Brothers for hiring you. That was in the early 30s.

TDOY: Was radio something you were sort of gravitating toward?

G.G. Oh, radio was a make-shift, a fill-in, because nobody really took it seriously. It was a new fad then. I remember in my teens trying to make a radio by buying a little crystal, cat's whisker, etc. If you got sound it was a triumph. That was all, it was a toy, but it caught on, didn't it? It stimulated the imagination and that's where television dropped out completely. In radio you see what you want to see, you create the characters. In the old days when radio was important it was so powerful that families gathered round to hear.

In that first series, I was finally making $5.00 a show and in the second season I asked for $7.50, which they reluctantly gave me. For the third series I asked for $10.00 and they wouldn't hire me because I was too expensive. By the way, Kay Van Riper was a brilliant writer but also a terrifying one because very often she was printing the pages of the script as we were on the air doing the show. The old, hand-cranked jelly machines turned out purple print which tried to disappear under the lights. Many episodes would come to the last scene and an assistant would hand you the next page just in time – no read-throughs on those.

TDOY: There was quite a stock company with many going on to great successes, weren't there?

G.G. Yes. Barbara Luddy was one, Bea Benadaret, Bret Morrison, Michael Fitzmaurice, Mary Jane Higby, Hanley Stafford. Hanley and I auditioned to play opposite Mary Pickford and finally she selected me just on voice quality. She wouldn't look at us, just sat in a booth and listened. It was on the *Mary Pickford Show*, not *Parties at Pickfair*, but we did rehearse at the estate for her convenience.

TDOY: We've heard she suffered tremendous mike fright and had to have the mike camouflaged as a lamp or something. True?

G.G. Not in the series I did with her. But, she <u>would</u> change her clothes for every scene to be in character. She'd do it on breaks – didn't mean anything, there was no audience.

TDOY: Was mike fright fairly common, though?

G.G. Oh, yes, I'll tell you one case. I did a show in New York and they had a character actor with 40 years on the stage. We started rehearsing and he was charming. Then, he took one look at that big square carbon mike and he turned white. It was long before the show; it was just rehearsal. I imagine he saw millions of ears all clustered on top of that little pole. He trembled, perspiration flowed off his brow and his script rattled. The engineers said it sounded like a high wind in a dry forest. When show time came he was almost a dithering idiot. We all got together, sat him down, told him it was just a radio show – just relax. Then, we went on the air, somebody pushed him to the mike when it was his turn and he read his part very well. Everything was going fine – until we came to page 9. He had a long scene with one sentence at the bottom of that page that was continued on page 10. He got to the bottom, turned to the next page <u>and it was number 14</u>! He'd messed it up. There was this long pause as the actor stared at the mike, unable to speak, until he finally muttered, "Oh, Jesus Christ," turned and left the studio. Somebody else had to finish the part and I never saw the man again.

TDOY: Isn't that the sort of thing that led to "doubling" in roles?

G.G. Yes, you had to in order to get roles. You had to do at least two dialects to get any job on radio because a cast of 15 would often be done by an actual cast of 5 people, just to save money.

TDOY: One of your 1933-'34 jobs was on *Tarzan*.

G.G. And it was directed by the story creator, Edgar Rice Burroughs. His daughter, Joan, was Jane and her husband, James Pierce, was Tarzan. I played one of the English lords and I always doubled as a dying native because I could scream louder than anyone else, So, every scream when a native got speared, that was me. Burroughs, of course, had no radio background, he just directed for a little extra money and mostly left us to our own devices.

TDOY: Any other director stories?

G.G. Well, there was one, Bill Bacher, who came to California from back east somewhere. He was a great self-promoter and came billed as a genius director of radio – had his little coterie of "gofers" around him. He had a shock of red hair that stood straight up and he was terribly dramatic when he directed because of the studio audience. He put on more of an act than any of the actors. While you were trying to read lines he'd gesticulate to bring out more fervor or to tone it down. People would start to laugh during dramatic moments. Unfortunately, he was one assigned to direct John Barrymore in something. And Barry was not one to be outacted by anybody – not *anybody! Ever!* He treated a microphone as something that was personally antagonistic to him and he'd grab the neck of the mike as though he was going to throttle it. The poor engineers would go crazy because he'd practically swallow it. So, they decided to literally put a guardrail fence around his mike so he couldn't smother it to death. Barrymore would come up to the railing that was bolted down and Bacher would get on his knees just outside the railing and raise his hands pleading and making wild gestures. Barrymore was so busy looking at the mike and snarling at it he didn't notice at first. He suddenly looked down and saw this man with the unruly shock of red hair making all kinds of overdrawn gestures and without a moment's hesitation, Barrymore reared back on one foot, put the other foot in Bacher's face, shoved him back into the audience and continued to speak. Needless to say, Bacher never directed Barrymore again!

In the course of the conversation, Gale mentioned that his mother, Gloria Gordon, played the landlady, Mrs. O'Reilly, on *My Friend Irma* with Marie Wilson. And that his wife was the original Mrs. Conklin on *Our Miss Brooks*. However, she was in an auto accident, suffered whiplash and had to quit.

One of the few people to make an adverse remark about Gale Gordon was the late, generally amiable Mel Blanc. He once stated, "There were several other voice actors in Hollywood and over time we became as close as the CBS and NBC studios in which we worked together, The little circle included Bea Benadaret, Joe Kearns, Mary Jane Higby, Sheldon Leonard, Verna Felton, Hans Conreid, and Gale Gordon. If ever there was an example of typecasting, Gordon as Theodore J. Mooney and Harrison Otis Carter (essentially a reprise of the same role) was it.

I ran into him a few days after Noel was born and announced proudly, 'Gale, guess what, I'm a father!'

His eyes narrowed, his mouth puckered – the same sourpuss expression for which he'd later be paid exorbitantly – and he sneered, 'Big deal!' Not only didn't I receive his good wishes, Gordon went into a tirade about never wanting children because they 'pester you to death.' I thought to myself, *'you schmuck!'* From that day on, I steered clear of him."

## The Sound Effects Specialists Were the Unsung Heroes of Old Time Radio

If you are a big fan of OTR, there's a book that might be of great interest for you. It's by Robert L. Mott and the title is *Radio Sound Effects: Who Did It, and How in the ERA of Live Broadcasting*. It was published several years ago but fortunately McFarland Publishers keeps material around for longer shelf life and last I saw, it's still available. Bob did an outstanding job of research and writing and the contents are considerably more than just sound effects. Of course, that's the main focus but the book is liberally sprinkled with some wonderful anecdotes and philosophies.

The latter comes into play immediately in the Preface where Bob says, in part, "Sound effects are to our ears what pulling rabbits out of a hat is to our eyes. It's the art of deception. It's the art of painting pictures for the imagination – involvement – that's what made radio magic, the involvement of sound and imagination. Little wonder radio was called the theater of the mind."

He goes on to get your attention early by stating at the opening of the first chapter, "Listening to the radio today, it is difficult to imagine how important radio once was and what a tremendous influence it had. But back in 1942, at the height of its heyday, it was different. Radio, unlike films or newspapers or even a good book, could both inform and entertain with no more effort on your part than simply listening, all in the comfort of your easy chair or bed, or while doing the housework, or in the evening gathered in the living room with your family."

I should say that Bob Mott is a friend of mine and that makes it an extra pleasure to be able to extol the virtues of his book. Sound effects, yes, but so much more.

For example, he tells the story of Ora Nichols and her husband, Arthur. He was a violinist and she played piano and they got their start in vaudeville. Getting jobs got tougher when silent movies hit the scene, but they wound up doing music to go along with the films, and also some sound effects to heighten the effect. Then, oh-oh, sound movies put the quietus to that way of making a living. Fortunately for them, radio came along with the realization that sound effects made shows more believable and exciting and they were first hired as freelancers by CBS in 1928 and used their talents for them and for NBC for several years. As a result, Ora and Arthur Nichols are given the lion's share of credit for making sound effects an integral part of radio.

As to the anecdotes in the book, my favorite concerns a happening on the *Jack Benny Show*. The sound effects man was Virgil Reimer and he had taken all the pre-show precautions for checking batteries on his equipment. However, for some reason or other, when the script called for a telephone to ring, Virgil pushed the button and nothing happened. In a desperation move to save the joke, he yelled out, "Ding-a-ling-a-ling!" The studio audience cracked up and Benny, trying not to do the same, turned around to Reiman and said incredulously, "*Ding-a-ling-a-ling??!*" The audience howled louder. In an effort to help, cast member Phil Harris chimed in with, "That's some phone call you got there, Jackson." Benny, still struggling to control himself, adlibbed (something rare for him), "I know – it's *person-to-person!*" To Benny's credit, after the show he went to Reimer, thanked him for the fast thinking and admitted it was one of the biggest laughs of the season.

So, you see, this is a book crammed with all kinds of background information and excellent pictures of some of the devices used to picture sounds.

One thing wrong is that Bob Mott doesn't give himself enough credit. In the final chapter, he lists all the sound effects people and the shows on which they worked, but under his own name he merely puts CBS, New York and NBC, Hollywood. Call it a case of modesty, but this overlooks the fact that he provided sound effects on both radio and television for such shows as *Gangbusters, Philip Morris Playhouse, Perry Mason, The Web, The Garry Moore Show* (8 years), and *Captain Kangaroo*. Some of the anecdotes about the latter show are, alone, enough to make the book worthwhile. After the credits, Bob includes some short profiles on several of these great specialists. He writes, "As you read their stories, perhaps you'll come away with a better understanding of not just sound effects but, more importantly, what it was like to live and work during the live days of radio."

If you happen to be just a collector of old shows, this would be a good beginning for a print collection. If you already have such, this is sure enough a great addition. I hope you find a copy.

## The Story Behind a Song

Ruth Lowe was a pretty Canadian girl who turned the grief of losing a husband, with whom she was very much in love, into words and music that became one of the biggest hits to ever appear on the musical horizon. Ruth played piano with Ina Ray Hutton's all-girl orchestra and stayed until a blind date resulted in meeting Harold Cohen, who later became her husband. Tragically, he died a short time later during surgery and the effect on Ruth was tremendous. She would sit and stare at her husband's picture for hours at a time and once said to the picture, "Darling, I'll never smile again." From that phrase came a musical masterpiece that became one of Tommy Dorsey's biggest hits, the one with Frank Sinatra and the Pied Pipers that established vocal groups forever. In 1940, the recording topped the charts for twelve weeks.

Just as a side note, in George Simon's 1967 book, *The Big Bands*, Sinatra listed an unusual aid for his singing success.

He forthrightly stated, "I've said this many times, but it can never be said too often; a singer can learn – should learn – by listening to musicians. My greatest teacher was not a vocal coach, not the work of other singers, but the way Tommy Dorsey breathed and phrased on the trombone."

In a *Metronome* interview in the mid-forties, Sinatra elaborated a bit more. "There's a guy (again referring to T.D.) who was a real education to me in every possible way. I learned about dynamics and phrasing and style from the way he played his horn, and I enjoyed my work because he saw to it that a singer was always given a perfect setting.

Interestingly, veteran broadcaster Fred Hall once asked singer Jo Stafford what Sinatra was like to work with back in the Dorsey days. Her reply was, "Great, great. He was a talent that you seldom run across with a solo singer. He's primarily a solo singer, but when we would do the group things he had a marvelous discipline. I mean, he never went off on his own – he blended right in with the group and you don't find that very often."

Judging by some of the stories about Sinatra in later days, this was pleasant to hear because he didn't always feel he was Chairman of the Board and have his later "Rat Pack" attitude.

## In the Early 1920s, a Lot of Copper Wire Was Wrapped Around Oat Boxes

That became the thing to do for a great many people anxious to hear this new thing called radio. They would wrap the copper wire in order to form a coil so they could make their own crystal radio sets. The Quaker Oats Company took advantage of the fad and early in that decade gave away more than a million crystal radio sets designed to be mounted on top of empty Quaker Oats containers. Talk about a marketing ploy! It happened as a post-World War I boom overtook the country and the mysterious whirrs, whines and screeches of early radio were first being introduced into many American homes.

An article in the *Persimmon Hill* magazine helped spread the word and they kindly gave me permission to reprint part of an article titled, *Cerealizing America: The Unsweetened Story of American Breakfast Cereals*.

Writers Scott Bruce and Bill Crawford told that, in addition to providing hardware, Quaker Oats and the other cereal companies quickly became leading producers of radio programming, exerting a powerful influence on the American imagination and the medium. And, some of the most popular characters they chose to ride across the electromagnetic spectrum were cowboys. In 1932, the St. Louis based Gardner Agency lost its lucrative Hot Ralston account to Batten, Barton, Durstine and Osborn, Inc. in New York. Gardner assigned a couple of young writers, Charles Claggett and Margaret O'Reilly (both in their 20s) to come up with a scheme to lure the account back home. Claggett described Hot Ralston as a "hot cereal which kids hated," but decided to make an effort to sell parents through their kids.

The two youthful writers interviewed school children and discovered the hero among seven to twelve year-olds was Tom Mix, "The King of the Silent Film Cowboys." Anyone who met Mix knew why silent was the operative word in his title. The cowboy hero spoke in a high, squeaky Oklahoma drawl, completely unsuitable for a he-man in talking pictures.

By the time Ralston ad man Claggett met him, the handsome stunt man with the great name was broke. While kids remembered his silent movie appearances, Mix, who was the highest paid man in Hollywood, had burned through his money and could get no work. The silent film star was thrilled to have a cereal endorsement deal land in his lap. He agreed to a five-year stint as the Hot Ralston pitchman and signed his name to a contract written on the back of an envelope.

In 1933, Tom Mix rode onto the breakfast table and stayed there for seventeen years. "First, you had to get a kid's attention, then you had to get his loyalty," recalled writer Claggett on the magic of the Mix program.

"And once their hero tells them to do something, they do it. It's that simple." A full-page Tom Mix comic strip ad promoting the Ralston Straight Shooters Club drew a quarter of a million responses to Checkerboard Square and "broke the record for returns from a single advertisement," said Claggett, who wrote the Straight Shooter's manual while nursing a bottle of brandy.

"The more I sipped, the more I wrote, confessed the author of the slogan, "Straight shooters always win, law breakers always lose. It pays to shoot straight."

The Straight Shooters Club print campaign was a hit with everyone but William H. Danforth, the president of Ralston Purina. The founder of the "I Dare You" program railed against spending so much money on advertising until, "we literally buried him in boxtops," remembered Claggett. "We took a picture of him with his head sticking out of a pile of boxtops and then he was all for it."

Once Danforth found Straight Shooter religion, he became convinced that Tom Mix and Hot Ralston could save the health of American children. By the end of 1933, Danforth agreed to spread the word by radio.

In exchange for regular checks, Tom Mix happily agreed to sign away all control over the content of the radio show that bore his name. The 15-minute *Tom Mix Ralston Straight Shooters* show won a huge and loyal following with tales of Mix's exploits in the Boxer

Rebellion, the Boer War and the Spanish American War, some of which were even true.

(**Note:** It should be noted that the radio "Tom" was portrayed over the years by Artells Dickson, Russell Thorson, Jack Holden and Curley Bradley and that Ralston picked up the tab all the way except in 1939 when the sponsor was Kellogg.)

Millions of kids found only one drawback to collecting Hot Ralston boxtops for rodeo ropes, comic books, decoder badges, branding irons, face masks, spurs, cowboy hats and other Tom Mix Paraphernalia. Once Mom had shelled out a quarter to buy the steaming paste, "the little monsters had to eat it," laughed Claggett.

The death of Tom Mix in a 1940 car accident did nothing to check the popularity of the Tom Mix radio show. "Even though Tom Mix has gone to the Great Beyond," wrote Claggett for the program the day after the accident, "the spirit of Tom Mix rides on."

Dozens of other cereal-pitching heroes rode across the American airwaves during the 1930s and 1940s, following in the footprints and hoofprints of Tom Mix and his horse, Tony.

Bobby Benson of the H-Bar-O pitched cereals for H-O Oats, dispatching 1,200 cowboys with stage coaches and chuck wagons to appear at schools and playgrounds in 1932 to sign up H-Bar-O Rangers. That show came back eventually as *Bobby Benson and the B-Bar-B Riders*.

Rancher Steve Adams disappeared in times of trouble to re-emerge as a Comanche warrior on *Straight Arrow*, screaming his personal war cry, "Kennah!," in order to promote sales of Nabisco Shredded Wheat.

The original singing cowboy, Gene Autry, crooned for Quaker on his CBS radio series, *Melody Ranch*, while Buck Jones, a retired rodeo champion turn B-western star, appeared in the series *Hoofbeats* for Grape Nuts Flakes.

"When it comes to grub for breakfast," announced that cowboy, who died a real hero's death trying to rescue victims of a nightclub fire at the famed Coconut Grove, "nothing hits the spot with me like a heapin' bowl of Grape Nuts Flakes."

## Harry Bartell Appeared on at Least 181 Different Radio Series, Just Between the Years of 1943-'57

It's difficult to say who was the busiest actor in the great days of radio, but Harry Bartell would have to be high on the list. His daughter found some of his old engagement books and discovered that in the period of 1943-1957, he was on at least 181 different series. And the shows were "biggies" more often than not – the likes of *Gunsmoke, Lux Radio Theater, My Friend Irma, Dragnet, Suspense, The Man Called X, Meet Corliss Archer* and *Escape*, to name just a few. And that was just part of his career that actually got started in 1930. In total, Harry appeared on more than 10,000 programs. We had the privilege of chatting about it.

TDOY: Let's start with a little bit of word association. KPRC. 1930.

H.B. Houston, Texas, when I first started in radio. I knew an announcer who thought he was Arch Oboler and he started a series of midnight horror shows. Since everyone worked cheap, I was in the cast. Prior to that time he had done a show that was 15-minute versions of movies. The studios sent out scripts for the condensed version of pictures they were showing. They were broadcast for free and all the actors and producer got tickets to the show – 25-cents worth – that was my first professional wage.

TDOY: You were born in New Orleans. How did you get to Houston?

H.B. My daddy took me, (chuckle) he was a merchant and moved his business.

TDOY: Nothing to do with show business?

H.B. Nobody in my family did anything remotely connected with entertainment.

TDOY: You were a disc jockey back when a deejay was really a deejay, unlike today's automatons.

H.B. Yes, on KFWB, the Warner Brothers station from 1941 throuugh 1943.

TDOY: You did some plays at the Pasadena Playhouse.

H.B. 40-45 of them.

TDOY: I noted some big name shows you were on and I want to get into some of the good but lesser publicized productions. Here's one I didn't know about. Of course, I know you can't remember every show you were on – no possible way – but I don't recall hearing this program – assume it was a comedy because of who it was named after, the *Charlotte Greenwood Show*.

H.B. Charlotte had a show that ran a season or so and I believe it was on NBC and ABC at one time or another. I can't remember much about the format but she was a lovely lady, a wonderful person to work with.

TDOY: You were one of several Archie Goodwins when Sydney Greenstreet was doing the lead on *The Adventures of Nero Wolfe*.

H.B. I did a 13-week stint and NBC couldn't sell the show. Mr. Greenstreet, I remember, moved very little. He sat while everybody else stood – just sat – rarely looked up from his script, but was wonderfully effective.

TDOY: A show that was really classy simply because of the talented people involved with putting it together – a production by Cathy and Elliott Lewis. In 1953-'54 they did a show called *On Stage*.

H.B. And I remember absolutely nothing about it. Obviously, I was on it but I cannot recall anything I did on that show. I remember doing other shows with Cathy and Elliott but that one escapes me – am I a big help?

TDOY: Hey, 10,000 shows – you can't be expected to remember them all!

H.B. I've discovered after all those programs I've become what I never intended – an historical artifact – a talking dinosaur – a radiosaurus!

TDOY: During World War II a great many programs were done for the military to help keep up morale but in 1945 you were on the *Sherlock Holmes* program and I was listening to one – here's the show, here's Harry, the whole bit and it was coming from a military base. I didn't realize a show like *Holmes* went on location.

H.B. Oh, yes, we were at Camp Roberts and we also took some Eddie Cantor shows to veteran's hospitals – had to keep up morale at home, too. We always played to a great house, captive audiences, you know. Of course, the comedy and variety programs went out frequently. Bob Hope did more overseas but the whole industry chipped in with some needed divertissement at home as well.

TDOY: A lot of OTR fans are unaware that the *Yours Truly, Johnny Dollar* audition program featured Dick Powell, who wound up doing *Richard Diamond* instead. We mostly remember Edmund O'Brien, John Lund, Bob Bailey, Robert Readick and Mandel Kramer in the Dollar role. Which did you work with?

H.B. I worked with three of them – O'Brien, Lund and Bailey.

TDOY: Which did you think did the best job?

H.B. They were totally different characters. Their individual styles varied a great deal. John Lund was probably the lowest key. He was not a flamboyant type. Eddie O'Brien was very hard-hitting and Bob Bailey sort of fell in between.

TDOY: Bailey, of course, had an extensive background in many of the soap operas, particularly out of Chicago.

H.B. Bob told a story which I hope I can tell without offending anyone. He was doing a show called *Bachelor's Children* and the announcer, a rather pompous sort, had a closing question he delivered in stentorian tones that was supposed to read, "Will the District Attorney find Art guilty?" One of the versions of what happened is that the line came out this way, "Will the District Attorney 'ind Fart …eh…fart…uh…guilty?" People fell out of the booth and there was nothing, nothing at all, until they finally went to the network system cue. Bob was present at all that – and he was very happy about it, still laughing.

TDOY: What about you? Did you ever goof like that?

H.B. (Chuckle) Not quite that. I think my worst problem was sometimes forgetting to read a line. I was playing a scene one day and I <u>knew</u> I had read my line and the other actor knew he had read his. I stood there waiting for him to say something and finally he read <u>my</u> line which I had <u>not</u> said. That's not as bad as Bill Conrad did once, though, on *Hollywood Star Playhouse*. He had the tagline of the show that finished off the entire performance and he just walked away from the microphone. The music came in and people wrote from all over the country wanting to know how the show ended. Ever after he swore he <u>had</u> read it!

TDOY: There was a classy program that I don't feel got as much acclaim as it deserved – from 1947-'60 – some very fine things on it – *Romance*.

H.B. Oh, that was a lovely show and you're right – it had class. It was done by my favorite producer, Norman Macdonnell. Anything he did was high quality.

TDOY: Tell me more about him.

H.B. I don't know quite how to begin. Norm started as an usher at CBS. At that time there were big audience shows, tremendous lines of people to get in to see free radio shows. Getting tickets was very difficult and fans often had to write months in advance to get in. Anyway, Norm became an assistant director, essentially a timekeeper. Usually what happened on a radio script, you'd be given a bunch of pages that most people marked one way or another where their lines were, You'd read around the table, then stand up and work on the mike with sound effects and music cues, Then dress rehearsal, corrections and finally, broadcast, a pretty involved process. The assistant director would use a stopwatch and put a check mark every 15 seconds. Any changes dealt literally with split seconds. That's how Norm learned the art – he was clever at giving signals so a changed reading could shorten or stretch the material. He became a director of local shows, then regional, etc., a gradual upward progression. He was a man of artistic integrity with great taste and warmth. That's what made working with him on *Gunsmoke* such an enjoyable experience. We worked with many of the same people and that made things easier. You knew if you made a mistake it was going to be covered some way. It could get pretty precarious on "live" shows so that trust was important. Norm cast people with capabilities he knew they had. There was great artistic integrity in working with him.

TDOY: April 26, 1952, the first airing of that series with Dick Beals as Billy the Kid. You were in that original cast. Did you think you had something already?

H.B. I thought I was in there for a whole career. I doubled (two parts). I played the role of Mr. Hightower, who was the newspaper editor and telegrapher and another role I can't remember. I figured Hightower had to be a member of the community and I'd have myself a running part that would be in every week. But he didn't show up again in a script until one year later. So much for high hopes.

TDOY: Although you didn't have an on-going role, in looking through the cast files of *Gunsmoke* you certainly played a myriad of different characters.

H.B. One of the surprising things to people listening to the program was that the actors alternated between the "heavies" and the "good guys." That was one of the grand wonders of radio that you could make that kind of switch and be efficient and have fun at the same time.

TDOY: Parley Baer ("Chester") once told us he felt the whole cast could have been told, "Here's the story line for today," and all of you could probably have adlibbed a whole show without a script.

H.B. That's absolutely correct and it would have run long, too!

TDOY: Of all the shows you worked on, did you have a particular favorite?

H.B. *Escape*! The show had such quality and good writing done with such care and dedication – still had a full orchestra for bridge music, etc. and it was a pleasure. I got some of my best parts there. By the way, before I forget, when the final *Gunsmoke* show was done on radio, the cast wasn't told it was the last show until they were through – they figured everyone would have had a tough time getting through it had they known – and that was probably true.

TDOY: Parley told me that story and he agreed it was best not to know until it was over. Speaking of parts, how did you go about getting them in those days, with agents or how?

H.B. There was a wonderful thing about radio, different from any other medium. Anybody could audition for radio. You had access to directors, producers and you could go there on a certain day at the studio, read for them, do short selections of various kinds. If they liked your work they might call you. It was open and clean.

TDOY: That whole era of broadcasting seemed that way.

H.B. It was and I have nothing but the warmest feelings about it.

TDOY: A great period of time.

H.B. Oh, yes, and, of course, there was the wonderful magic of what radio acting was all about, making those words on the page come along. It required fertile imagination and quick responses. It was such a joy and I'm thankful I had the opportunity to be a part of it.

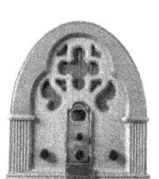

## "It might be...it could be...it IS...a home run! Holy Cow!"

For anyone suffering under the oft-repeated delusion that New York Yankee broadcaster, Phil Rizzuto, originated the on-air expression shown in the headline, as it regarded something unusual or outstanding during a game, forget it!

The credit more properly goes to one, Harry Christopher Carabina, or as listeners around the nation knew him – Harry Caray, whose first major league broadcasting job was with the St. Louis Cardinals, starting in 1945.

Harry first used "Holy Cow!," when he was with station WKZO in Kalamazoo, Michigan in 1941, He was sent to Battle Creek to broadcast games from a semipro tournament and it was the first baseball play-by-play he ever did. It's where he initially used the above build-up for a home run and he was fairly certain that was also his first time to air, Holy Cow!" It became part of his professional persona and he most certainly used it from the outset of his major-league coverage. I know that for a fact, because my beginning job in radio was in 1946, a year after Caray began with the Redbirds and I was on duty and had to lead into the games every evening. Rizzuto, of course, continued his playing career with the Yankees through 1956 so there's no way he could have been first. Or, as Caray put it, "If the "Scooter" did say it, it must have been to his infield mate, Jerry Priddy." Harry described it as an expression that conveyed excitement and wouldn't offend anybody and it was the only exclamation he could think of that wasn't profanity. His were on the streets and he says the kids he knew sure didn't say, "Holy Cow," when they got excited but he couldn't use what they did say!

Harry was a prime example of using personal initiative to get ahead. As a brash young man with no broadcasting experience, he found out the home address of Merle Jones, the man who ran the biggest station in St. Louis, KMOX, and told him he wanted to broadcast baseball. Jones was impressed by the effort, gave him an audition and eventually recommended him for a job at WCLS, a 250-watter in Joliet, Illinois. Station manager Bob Holt was the one who suggested changing his name from Carabina to Caray. Harry complied, making it a legal change, and spent about a year and a half in Joliet before moving to Kalamazoo. There, he worked with a news director named Paul Harvey, who was also just getting an illustrious career underway. Harvey also did some sports in that half-century ago period and Caray said he has a photo of him doing a football game in 1941. Harry said a couple of others who moved through the station at about the same time were Roy Rowan, who announced scads of network radio shows later and was the CBS-TV announcer for *I Love Lucy* and *Rawhide*, and Ralph Story, who later hosted quiz shows in California and became a news anchor there. Years later it was delight meeting Rowan at an OTR convention and reminiscing about the "good old days."

Finally, Caray got back to St. Louis with a staff job on KXOK, did some sports, moved to WIL and handled his first St. Louis play-by-play on that station with games of the St. Louis Flyers hockey team. The next year, 1945, Griesedieck Brothers Brewery decided to broadcast home games of both city baseball teams, the Cardinals and Browns. Harry talked his way into the job and worked with old time player, Gabby Street. They did some re-creations in 1946 but times they were a'changing and in 1947 Harry and Gabby not only wound up with all the Cardinal games, home and away, but they now traveled with the team. No more ticker descriptions – now it was the real thing and it became even more so when, as Harry said, "That year, 1947, was the year baseball started to change America." That was the year of Jackie Robinson. It should be pointed out that Harry came full circle and wound up airing the games on KMOX, the first station he had ever contacted.

Harry left the Cardinals and did games for the Oakland A's in 1970, then moved to the Chicago White Sox in 1971 and finally to the Cubs, replacing the retiring Jack Brickhouse on WGN-TV in 1982. He became a national cult figure because of the superstation coverage and his colorful descriptions, including his singing of *Take Me Out to the Ballgame* during the $7^{th}$ inning stretch. He had a stroke in 1986, but bounced back and kept on working. He passed away just before his 84th birthday in 1998 after decades and decades behind the mike, on the road for much of the time. Hall of Fame credentials for sure, and Harry Caray is, indeed a member of the Baseball Hall of Fame. *"Holy Cow!"*

## A Gallon Jug of Milk Played a Part in Getting a Career Started!

The young man graduated from high school in 1938 and went to Bluffton College in Ohio. He came home to Lima, Ohio after his freshman year and his dad told him it was time to go out and find a job. He tried but nothing happened and he was about ready to leave at the age of eighteen. However, one day in May of 1939 his mother sent him on an errand. It was more economical to buy a gallon of milk at a downtown milk depot, especially if you took along your own jug.

So, off the young man went on his assigned chore, still fretting over being turned down earlier that day for a job with a roofing company. When he arrived at the milk depot, he noticed radio station WLOK located next to it and figured there might be a job possibility of some kind there. Carrying the empty milk jug with him he went inside and blithely asked for an announcer's audition. He was told the manager was on the air so he went back out and bought the milk he'd been sent for in the first place, returning to the studio afterwards. The manager first thought he was selling milk but gave him some copy off the teletype, a couple of commercials and told him to read. The teenager did and it wasn't very good but the manager felt there might be some possibilities. A part-time job three hours a day at $7.50 a week was offered beginning the next Monday, along with a promise that it might result in a full-time announcer's job down the line. The young guy headed home to report that he was now employed, at least part time. The father didn't think it was such a big deal and told his son to spend the rest of the week looking for something better and if that didn't work out, on Monday he could report for duty at the radio station.

Nothing else developed and a career was underway. In 1940 there was quite a break as the young announcer moved from WLOK in Lima to WWJ in Detroit, where he also put in some time at Wayne University as a part-time student. He went into the Army from there in 1942 – got out of the service in '43 and joined WMAQ,

Chicago. All this, of course led to **Hugh Downs** having an exceptional broadcasting career on radio and TV that lasted for a great many years.

I'll never forget a comment Hugh made to me during an interview when he was the announcer on Jack Paar's *Tonight Show* on NBC. It was in response to an often-asked question, "What is Jack Paar really like?"

Downs answered, "If we happened to be on the set and a sand bag holding a stage "flat" broke loose and fell onto the stage, everyone but Jack would immediately react and wonder if anyone was hurt. Paar, though, would in somewhat panicky fashion, ask, "Who's trying to get me now?"

## A Pre-Med Course Gave Way to Radio!

Bill Cullen contracted polio when he was only a year and a half old and he wound up with a limp. As a teenager, he was in a hospital for nine months after being hurt in an auto accident and while there made up his mind to be a doctor. He became a pre-med student at the University of Pittsburgh after his high school graduation. A lack of money forced him to quit so he worked for a while as a mechanic and tow truck driver in his dad's garage, He would provide some laughs for fellow workers by imitating radio announcers and this led to the thought that maybe he ought to try being one himself. He auditioned at a "coffee pot" operation – WWSW, a 250-watter in Pittsburgh and got a job working nights for no money. Finally, though, he was put on the payroll after a couple of months and went on from there, remarking that, "radio was a place where a ham like me could limp and still have a job." In 1941 he moved to the history-laden KDKA. He was still there in '43, making a quite good $250 a week emceeing a variety show. He went back to college and got a B.A. degree and did some flying as a patrol pilot for the *Civil Air Defense.*

In 1944, Cullen headed for the Big Apple and within a week had a job on CBS pretty much as a result of wartime staff shortages. He never looked back as he fell into a kind of type-casting on quiz shows. He worked with Arlene Francis on a Saturday afternoon variety show called *Fun for All*, but quizzes were his bread and butter as he was on *Hit the Jackpot, Quick as a Flash, Hollywood Jackpot* and *Winner Take All*, as well as announcing on the soap opera, *This is Nora Drake.*

That's quite a list, but it's just a small part of his career that spanned five decades. Altogether, Bill hosted 23 different game shows over the years, more than anyone else in broadcasting history. He hosted the original version of *The Price is Right*, served as a panelist on the popular programs *I've Got a Secret* and *To Tell the Truth*. Not too bad for someone who once considered being a doctor.

## Perhaps You Should Call Me, "Mrs. Quiz"

Her voice was never heard by the radio audience and the studio audience didn't have any idea who she was. Nevertheless, she was a very important member of the weekly battle of wits featuring *Professor Quiz*. She sat at a small table during the program and helped the Professor's manager, Bill Gernant, keep score. At the halfway point in the show the pair would pass along the names and scores of the contestants in first and second place and do the same thing with the final figures.

Actually, Betty, as she was known to intimates, was "Mrs. Quiz."

As she would laughingly explain, "I think you'd better introduce me that way when we're out in public together; otherwise people will wonder why Professor Quiz is traveling around with Mrs. Earl."

And that's the way it often worked out, too. The professor's wife was generally known as "Mrs. Quiz," just as he was "Professor," or "Professor Quiz," even though his professional name was Dr. Craig Earl. He, by the way, had been a magician in vaudeville days and took over the show after the original emcee, Jim McWilliams, was dropped for some reason or other. The whole thing had started on WJSV in Washington, D.C. when the promotion manager came up with the notion. The station (later WTOP) did so well with it that CBS took the show into New York in March of 1937. The commercials were done at first by a WJSV announcer named Arthur Godfrey,

Getting back to Betty Earl, in addition to acting as scorekeeper on the show, she also supervised the secretarial staff that handled the Professor's mail. Thousands of letters came in every week and small wonder. It was smack-dab in the middle of the Great Depression and in 1939, the winner on the show got 25 silver dollars and the runner-up got 15. That was quite a bit more than a lot of folks made in a week. So, naturally, many of the letters were from people who wanted to get on the show. You could also win money by submitting questions – 25 of those silver dollars if your list was picked. One guy wrote it was nice to win the money but he was just as glad to hear his name pronounced correctly. Phillip Lopatnikov wrote, "Even among teachers and college professors, my Russian name is frequently mispronounced."

It was said that Dr. Earl spoke many languages, had traveled extensively and had been a practicing physician and psychiatrist. Of course, that didn't explain how he managed all those different things and still had time to be a vaudevillian. To say that a lot of the information fell into the "hokey" category would be putting it mildly.

It appears that "Mrs. Quiz" helped smooth his path in more ways than one. For example, she saw to it that he had a white carnation for his lapel every day, which brings up the question, when's the last time your wife did that for you. She was a constant, devoted companion in virtually all of her husband's activities, except one in particular. She wouldn't go with him to prize fights. Instead, when he wanted to take in pugilistic displays, she'd head to the theater.

During the first four years of the show, $65,000 was given away to contestants and those who provided questions. The director of the show had finally made a deal with a bank to supply the coins that were getting more scarce all the time. Even though that was quite a bit of loot for the times, Bob Trout, the show announcer, took considerable pleasure in telling that the "Professor" had to borrow twenty-five dollars from him to award as first prize to the first successful contender in 1936. He further disclosed that the Professor never paid back the 25 smackers.

He related, "When I mention it, he says something about the statute of limitations, or maybe it's the law of gravity or something like that. The Professor knows everything."

Incidentally, that's the same Bob Trout who became such a distinguished newsman and who was credited in most quarters for having coined the phrase "Fireside Chat" for the messages that President Franklin D. Roosevelt gave to the nation during the Great Depression and World War II.

A final note: It is said that agent Lew Wasserman heard *Professor Quiz* while on the way to a meeting with young band leader, Kay Kyser. He asked why they couldn't do a show like music. So, the *Kollege of Musical Knowledge* was born soon after.

## Creative Energy

A law school degree helped Himan Brown acquire the rights to several fictional characters. Programs that he managed to gather included *Dick Tracy, Flash Gordon, Bulldog Drummond, Nero Wolfe, The Thin Man* et al. One of Brown's first big hits was an anthology program, *Grand Central Station* – remember that opening – "the crossroads of a million private lives, a gigantic stage on which are played a thousand dramas daily." He once estimated that with his producing, directing or just taking part in one way or another that he participated in more than 30,000 programs during the 1930s and 1940s. With all that work, though, his program that comes to mind more than any other is *Inner Sanctum Mysteries* that got its start in 1941 and ran until 1952. One of the most famous sound effects radio ever had was used to open the program – an eerie sounding creaking door accompanied by the chilling introduction of, "Your host, Raymond," portrayed at the beginning by Raymond Edward Johnson. The program featured his gruesome puns that led up to the drawn-out closing, "Pleasant dreaaaams, hmmm-mmm?" Johnson joined the Army in 1945 and Paul McGrath hosted the program the rest of the way. In an interview with Himan Brown, he once voiced some displeasure with Johnson saying, in effect, "He got to the point he thought it was *his* show, but it wasn't, it was *mine!*"

Just as a side note, I recall chatting with Raymond at an Old Time Radio convention in Newark. He had developed multiple sclerosis in his 40's and had to attend in a portable bed. He would still perform a reading, needing help to turn the pages of the script. He recalled for me his delight in knowing that his birthplace of Kenosha, Wisconsin was also the hometown of Orson Welles, Don Ameche, and his younger brother, Jim, who played the original *Jack Armstrong, All-American Boy* for five years. Don was on that show for a while, but his voice was so similar to Jim's that it caused confusion and he moved on. Don, by the way, was born Dominic Felix Amici but so many folks pronounced it A-mee-cee that the spelling was changed to Ameche so it would be said as A-mee'-chee in the original Italian way.

Three decades after that initial success of Inner Sanctum, Brown resurrected the basic theme on *CBS Radio Mystery Theater*. He had never stopped believing in the form right up until his death in 2010 at the age of 99. His enthusiasm for the medium never waned as he stated, "I am firmly convinced that nothing visual can touch audio."

## Time Marches On

*The March of Time* was an amazing program, telling it the way it was in the 1930s.

Here's the way it was described in mid-1936.

"With a blare of trumpets Time marches, sonorous and dramatic, out of your loudspeaker. For fifteen minutes the significance of today rumbles majestically through your home. The day's news comes alive.

Twenty-three floors above New York's busy Madison Avenue sit six people, tense as death watchers in the dark. Forbidden cigarettes glow behind concealing hands. Ears strain for nuances. Exasperation sighs. Fatigue titters nervously. Heads nod with satisfaction. Here, too, Time Marches On. A day's work of 240 hours is ending. Lights in the sub-control room flash. Chatter breaks the listening hush. Writers and researchers for the March of Time yawn and gather their papers. It is almost eleven now. Tomorrow, at ten-thirty, work begins again.

For fifteen minutes on the air, seven writers, one editor, two researchers have worked twelve hours each; two directors have worked eight hours; ten actors have worked five hours; orchestra and leader have worked three hours and a half. Two hundred forty hours is a conservative estimate of that day's work. Five days a week, they do it. The fifteen minute news broadcast is radio's most elaborate program, the most difficult on the air to produce. It is two jobs in one. It is newspaper business. And it is show business. It must be "good theater" because it is show business. Yet, no fact may be distorted for theatrical effect. "Accuracy always" is the newsman's creed. Dramatic, it must be, as life, shorn of its tedium, is dramatic; the truth as good reporters see it, without cynicism or sentiment.

Dress rehearsal jitters clash with deadline nerves. Actors hunched over scripts pace the studio, mumble and grimace their lines. During fifteen short minutes, they must dramatize the whole gamut of life's emotions; flash from comedy to tragedy; from pomposity to terror. They must be trigger quick, ready for spot news, five minutes before air time. This is a newspaper, eager as any to scoop the town.

Nerve tension stretches rubber-thin as 10:30 nears. Head bent before the one desk light in the sub-control room, William Geer, managing editor of this strange newspaper, works against time, against the deadline. There are no presses here to hold for last minute news flashes. The show must go on. Newspaper business and show business. Proudly, these Time-Marchers call it a madhouse, a three-ring circus out of a nightmare.

During five years on the air (until last fall (1935) as a weekly half hour program, it has attained international importance. It is banned in Germany, disapproved in Italy. No Hearst paper lists the program on its radio page. Publisher Hearst had branded it as Communist propaganda. Communists scream that it is fascist!! The March of Time is under no political banner, proud of its impartial presentation of fact. President Roosevelt asked the Time program to stop impersonating him. March of Time's impersonator was stealing his political thunder. During the winter of 1934, the President had planned five fireside chats, psychologically times to quiet a nervous nation. The sound of what many thought was his voice each Friday night on March of Time was ruining his effective plan. Bill Johnstone was President Roosevelt, is also King Edward VIII and Cordell Hull; is Scots, Irish and German when needed. For two years, Dwight Weist, Time's mimic-extraordinary, played Bruno Richard Hauptman. He is Hitler, George Arliss, Bernard Shaw, Hearst, Father Coughlin, Fred Allen and all three Barrymores, including Ethel! Ted de Corsia is Mussolini, Laval, Herbert Hoover and gangsters. They study newsreels, radio speeches, recordings of all famous voices, all dialects. Sound effects must be accurate to the last echo. Mrs. Ora Nichols, the only woman sound expert in radio, works her imagination at top speed. The regular acting staff members work at a fixed salary of $150 a week, but if they sound like actors, they're fired. Their efforts blend with the Voice of Fate, Westbrook Van Voorhis, and <u>Time Marches On</u>!"

## Apocryphal o' Wry
### Also known as a classic "Shaggy Dog"

Back in the heyday of radio, when you could still hear a great deal of live classical music on many radio stations, it is said that the following MAY have happened.

An orchestra was giving its rendition of the famed Ninth Symphony by Beethoven. There was a prolonged break between parts for the bass section so the conductor indicated that those musicians should leave the stage during that portion.

So, the basses made their early contribution and left the stage as told. One of them suggested going across the street for a beer in the meantime. They did so and one beer became a couple, then three. Keeping a careful eye on the clock, one thought maybe they should be starting back to the concert hall. However, the head bassist assured them there was no need for worry – "Before the concert, I took some string and tied together the last pages of the conductor's score. He'll have to slow down the symphony while he uses his free hand to try to untie the pages."

That left time to hoist some more "suds" before the basses finally went back to the hall, a bit the worse for wear. As they sort of wobbled back to their places, with the leader working away at the string, he gave them the dirtiest of dirty looks. And, could you blame him?

After all, it was the bottom of the Ninth, the score was tied, and the basses were loaded.

Or, at least that's the way *we* heard it!

## Who Was Mrs. Calabash?

Jimmy Durante began saying goodbye to the mysterious Mrs. Calabash while he did his show with Garry Moore and, in a way, she became one of the popular women in the country. At the outset, Jimmy would say goodnight to Garry but it gradually turned into, "Goodnight, Mrs. Calabash, wherever you are." No one ever knew for sure just who or what was meant. There was a great deal of speculation though, such as the lady was his former wife, or perhaps a secret love, possibly just a mixed-up name seen on a sign over a railroad depot. Somehow, it didn't matter. His wife once said it was Jimmy's way of reaching out to everyone in an effort to give back some of the warmth that millions of people had extended to him. Writer William Chan sort of echoed that when he penned, "When Jimmy says, 'Goodnight, Mrs. Calabash,' he is expressing a sad clown's bond of friendship and sympathy with members of the human family everywhere. He is saying good night not only to Mrs. Calabash, but to you and me."

Incidentally, Durante has often been referred to as "Schnozzola," but that wasn't the way he used it when he applied to the U.S. Patent Office in July of 1933 to register his trademark. The paper included a caricature, Jimmy's signature and the name, "Schnozzle," and to our knowledge, represents the only time a living person copyrighted his nose and name.

Durante received countless thousands of fan letters and some were known to reach him without having his name on them – just a drawing featuring the nose and 'Hollywood, California.' Naturally, the postmen knew where they were supposed to go. Just try that today with the modern USPS!

Before achieving added fame on radio and later television, Jimmy had some wild successes in his own club, in vaudeville, and on stage. Walter Winchell wrote about him. So did Ed Sullivan. Even noted humorist Robert Benchley was a fan after Club Durant and many other clubs were closed by Prohibition. Clayton, Jackson and Durante resurfaced at the Parody Club.

Benchley wrote, in part, "I do not take the responsibility of recommending Jimmy Durante to you. A great many people are at first mystified and then irritated by his annihilation of the unities. If you like things that are just like other things in their class, you won't like Durante, because there never was, and probably never will be, another entertainer like him. He is quite mad, not in the literary sense of the word, but rough-hewn out of the madness of childhood. The fact that there is a fine satire running through his madness should not be seized upon to elevate him to the rostrum among the cognoscenti. The satire is there because anything which distorts our modern orderly arrangement of clichés becomes satire automatically. We think so badly nowadays that merely to shuffle our thoughts around in a different order is to show them up as ridiculous."

The article prompted Jimmy to proclaim, "Me old partner Clayton had to get a translator to read us what it said."

Once, after Jimmy had finished a number in the club, the "Great Profile," John Barrymore, called him over to his table and told him he should play Hamlet. The Schnoz answered, "I don't wanna play dem small towns. New York's good enough for me!"

Barrymore was probably right, though – Jimmy would have been "collosial!"

## The Witch's Tale

It may not have been the scariest of radio's various macabre programs but it was certainly the first of the genre that amounted to anything. *The Witch's Tale* first came along at the end of May in 1931 on station WOR. Later it was on CBS for a while, then Mutual. It was a virtual one-man setup with Alonzo Deen Cole writing, directing and hosting the program. But that wasn't the unusual facet of the presentation. The part of "Old Nancy" was originally played by Adelaide Fitz-Allen, a veteran 78-year old actress. When she died in February, 1935, Cole auditioned nearly a hundred actresses for the part, finally selecting Mildred Holland, another veteran of over 70 years, who had retired from the stage several years before. Then, starting in 1936, the role went to an 11-year old girl named Miriam Wolff. Cole consistently refused to publicize the fact that she was a child, probably feeling it would destroy the illusion when the weird, hoarse, cackling voice sounded in eerie fashion from loudspeakers.

And you couldn't blame him. When Old Nancy would rasp, "hunnerd and three year old I be today…heh, heh, heh!" and have her "wise black cat, Satan," yowl for the listeners to be sure to douse the lights, it just wouldn't have seemed right to know a child was narrating the chilling stories.

## Another Young Performer

When Bea Wain was six years old, she sang on a WJZ children's program and got $2.00. In high school they didn't think she was good enough to join the glee club. After that turndown, a small New York station offered her a job. She continued with school and sang, too. The station soon got her a sponsored show but she wanted to graduate and said no, So, they saved the sponsor for her until after graduation.

In 1934, she joined three boys and became *Bea and the Bachelors*. One of the guys was Al Rinker, ex-*Rhythm Boy* with Harry Barris and Bing Crosby. Just for the record, the others were Ken Lane and Johnny Smedburg. They sang on WOR and Bea said later that she learned all she knew about rhythm and swing from her confreres.

The four joined the Kay Thompson choir in '36. That lasted for a year and a half. Then, accidentally, they teamed up with the *Modernaires* and became the *V-8 Octet* on Fred Waring's show – a maid and seven men. She met Andre Baruch during the run of that program and pretty much ignored him.

Pneumonia forced her retirement until September, 1937, when she joined Ted Straeter's chorus on the Kate Smith program. Baruch was announcer on that show. A photographer wanted a picture of a girl on a man's shoulder. He picked Andre and Bea. That started something!

She had sung exactly four weeks with Straeter when she got a call from a new band leader. He had a recording date at Victor the next day. Would she come and ask for Larry Clinton? He heard her sing for the first time when she made a recording of *True Confession* with his orchestra, He asked her to join his band and sing on a Thursday night NBC program competing with her own show. It was a big gamble. Should she leave Straeter and Baruch and take a chance on an unknown? She took the chance. She didn't lose. She married Baruch in May of 1938. And, of course, Larry Clinton didn't stay an unknown for long. His recordings with Bea of *My*

*Reverie* and *Deep Purple* were major hits. They played frequently at the famed Glen Island Casino in New Rochelle, New York.

As for Bea and Andre they later shared a disc jockey show in Florida and co-hosted a modern syndicated version of *Your Hit Parade*. She didn't continue after his death September 15th, 1991 at the age of 83, telling your writer in a conversation, "It just wouldn't be the same."

## "Bowes No. 1 Money Man"

The above headline from *Variety* on September 18, 1935 provides an answer to what could be one of the toughest Old Time radio trivia questions ever posed. Be honest now, if someone had asked you who the number one money maker in all of show business at the time, would you have unhesitatingly answered, "Major Edward Bowes?" I certainly wouldn't have.

That period of the Great Depression was when a lot of folks were working for maybe two dollars a day, if they were working at all. The story went on to say, "Major Edward Bowes is the new No. 1 money man of show business with a current weekly income that, if maintained, will place him in the $1,000,000-a-year class. About 98% of the total comes from his amateur shows on the radio, screen (shorts) and in theaters (units)."

The lion's share of his weekly $19,000 take came from the various road versions of his amateur program. People desperately hoped that his programs would somehow provide them with a way out of their dire financial straits. It was mostly wishful thinking and many of the losers didn't have enough money for bus fare home.

Ah yes, the good old days, huh? I recall hearing someone say once, "The thing most responsible for the good old days is a lousy memory!"

Among those who did survive the sounding of a gong to terminate the appearance of untalented individuals were opera stars-to-be Lily Pons, Robert Merrill and Beverly Sills, pop singer Teresa Brewer and a lead singer for a quartet called the Hoboken Four by name of Frank Sinatra.

## "Who's that little chatter box? The one with pretty auburn locks?"

That was the opening for the radio version of Harold Gray's well-known comic strip, *Little Orphan Annie*, a show that became one of the first on-air juvenile serial dramas. The program got started on WGN in Chicago in 1930 and in 1931 it became a national sensation on the Blue Network of NBC. The chief participants were Annie, her dog, Sandy, and buddy, Joe Corntassel. The latter was once played by young singer, Mel Tormé, with most of that role handled by Allan Baruck. Much of the program featured the ringing tones of announcer Pierre Andre singing the praises of the sponsor, Ovaltine. Premiums were a big part of the show and Andre gave the chocolate drink and the premiums exuberant pitches. He also provided the "Arf" for Sandy. I don't know if the plaque is still there but at one time WGN had a door marked "Pierre Andre Memorial Studio."

As to those sought-after giveaways serendipity can be a wonderful experience and your writer has physical evidence of that fact. First, though, what is the full meaning of the word? Well, dictionaries describe it as, "the faculty of finding valuable or agreeable things by accident." In that case, one of my discoveries truly fills the bill.

Like many Old Time Radio advocates, my tie-ins with the Golden Age cover a broad range; everything from collecting the programs to finding old radios, microphones, wire recorders and memorabilia such as those show premiums. Harking back to my childhood I had been on the alert for an Ovaltine shake-up mug from the *Little Orphan Annie* show. I happened to mention my search during a live, three hour, once-a-week OTR broadcast. After the show, a lady was waiting for me in the station parking lot. She told me that her late mother had saved the lid from a shake-up mug because its rounded top made it ideal to slip inside socks while darning them. She added that I could have it if I wanted it – which I did, of course, and for a very special reason. Just the day before

I had taken a jaunt along our city's Antique Row and had found a mug without a top, something that was of no particular use to me. Naturally, when I became the recipient of the top. I immediately headed back to the shop and got the mug and they were a perfect match – the original "Beetleware" made, as they said, "exclusively for the Wander Co., Chicago, makers of Ovaltine." My new acquisitions were the model from the 1930's with a light-cream-colored bottom and orange top.

To make it even better, a friend, Steven Hiss of Alachua, Florida sent me a jar of the original formula drink of my youth. It was the import version from Switzerland with more malt and not as much sugar as the U.S. variety. I keep a supply of Ovaltine on the kitchen shelves to this very day.

## In Show Biz – at age 4?

That's right, according to singer, Mel Tormé. The orchestra led by Carlton Coon and Joe Sanders was appearing at the famous Blackhawk Restaurant in Chicago, Numerous network "remotes" attracted attention throughout the Midwest and Tormé said he would listen to the Coon-Sanders band on the radio until it was coming out of his ears. One night in 1929 his parents took him to the Blackhawk for dinner and to hear the band. He knew all their numbers by heart and was singing along with them. Some of the dancers noticed this and pointed him out to Sanders ("The Ol' Left-hander").

Sanders came over to their table and asked Mel's folks about him, then, before the next set, they played a drum roll and it was announced that the band's youngest fan, Melvin Howard Tormé (he pronounced it Tormee) was present and knew all the songs. "Whaddya say we give him the chance to prove it?"

Little Melvin went to the bandstand, told them what he'd like to sing and a career was begun. The song was "You're Driving Me Crazy," and before the night was over the band's co-leaders had invited him back to sing a couple of numbers every Monday evening as a special feature. The offer was $15 and a dinner for the three of them. It was accepted and Mel was there for six months. As a side note, "You're Driving Me Crazy" became a hit record for Tormé in early 1947 (on Musicraft) – the first record he ever made as a solo singer.

In spite of all the later successes, Mel's original aim was to be an actor – a movie star. He wound up doing a lot of things on radio and personally felt he was probably one of the five busiest child actors in the country from 1933 to around 1941. He appeared on *Jack Armstrong* with Jim Ameche when he was about 10-12 years old. When he was only 8 there was a role on *Song of the City*, a soap opera done at the Merchandise Mart. Mel was on *Stepmother; Mary Noble, Backstage Wife; First Nighter; It Can Be Done*, (the Edgar Guest program) and as mentioned before, *Little Orphan Annie*.

## Big Band "Remotes"

Speaking of the band "remotes" in the Tormé story brings to mind the countless hours of enjoyment listening to bands all around the nation. No one who ever heard them can forget

"…coming to you from the beautiful Frank Dailey's Meadowbrook just off the Pompton Turnpike near Cedar Grove, New Jersey."

Or:

"…emanating from the famed Glen Island Casino, off the Shore Drive in New Rochelle, New York,"

The bands that would be playing on the "remote" broadcasts generally were not touted in advance so you didn't know for sure who you might hear that evening or how long you might hear them. The better known orchestras would get probably half hour exposure with many of the lesser bands gratefully settling for fifteen minutes of valuable air time.

From the outset of any broadcast you immediately knew what band would be featured because of the highly recognizable theme songs. When the sound of "Redskin Rhumba" came out of the speaker it couldn't be anyone but Charlie Barnet.

Arguably the best known of all the themes was "Moonlight Serenade" by Glenn Miller. They even added lyrics to that one for use other than a theme. Frank Sinatra recorded it later with a studio band.

"I stand at your gate and the song I sing is of moonlight,
I stand and I wait for the touch of your hand in the June night.
     The roses are sighing a moonlight serenade."

The instrumental theme song version was better. For a while during an ASCAP ban Miller used "Slumber Song" as an aptly titled number when it came time to finish a broadcast or to close down for the night.

Most bands used the opener also for closing but many had a different closing theme. Barnet had one that didn't take a lot of imagination in deciding what to call it. It was merely, "Closing Theme." Benny Goodman did better than that after opening with "Let's

Dance," he closed with a simply titled, "Goodbye." There were no lyrics for that one.

Getting your immediate attention were such highly swinging numbers as Count Basie's "One O'Clock Jump," that he also used to close, as did Tommy Dorsey and that ultra-smooth trombone sound on "I'm Getting Sentimental Over You." I always thought a number recorded with the band by singer Jack Leonard would have made a good finale, "I'll See You in My Dreams."

Brother Jimmy put his clarinet to good use on "Contrasts," used on both ends of broadcasts or personal appearances. Duke Ellington once began with "East St. Louis Toodle-oo," but that gave way when Billy Strayhorn joined the band and produced "Take the 'A' Train." Bob Crosby had George Gershwin's "Summertime," with no stated reason other than a strong liking for the song. Their biggest hit, "South Rampart Street Parade," might have been better but they well knew they'd have to play that at least once during an evening's performance. Les Brown used a rollicking "Leap Frog" to open but settled for one of the band hits to shut down for the evening, "Sentimental Journey," those times with no Doris Day vocal.

A quick listing would show:
"Artistry in Rhythm" – Stan Kenton
Wayne King's – "The Waltz You Saved for Me."
"Sugar Blues" – Clyde McCoy
Freddy Martin's classics-based "Tonight We Love."
"Nightmare" that sometimes fit the mood of leader Artie Shaw.
An expected "Bubbles in the Wine" – Lawrence Welk
Pianist Teddy Wilson's group, "Jumpin' on the Blacks and Whites," (the keyboard's 88)

Rudy Vallee with his megaphone and "My Time is Your Time"

One of the most unusual titles of all was the original opener used by drummer Gene Krupa. It was called "Apurksody," with the first part being Krupa spelled backwards, accompanied by part of "rhapsody" for the rest.

An unusual approach was taken by Ray McKinley in "Howdy, Friends," as he used it for introducing his top sidemen with very brief solos. A couple of bands using two themes found Henry Busse with "Hot Lips," and "When Day is Done," and Eddy Howard using "Careless," with an appropriate, "So Long for Now" to finish the evening.

Others best known included:

"Ciribiribin" – Harry James
First "Blue Prelude", then "Blue Flame" – Woody Herman
"Sunrise Serenade" – Frankie Carle
"Oh, You Beautiful Doll" – Chuck Foster
"Snowfall" – Claude Thornhill

British bands followed the same pattern, several of them using American songs for a theme. One of those was Billy Cotton with "Somebody Stole My Gal"; Fred Elizalde borrowed "Quaker City Jazz" from Jan Savitt and also used "From Out of Space," apparently referring to music being listened to on the radio. Ambrose went the American way with an appropriate "When Day is Done," at the end of an evening. Geraldo used a couple that also fit the performance, "Hello Again," and "The Clock on the Wall." That band had a jumping treatment of Duke Ellington's "Cotton Tail" that I always felt would have gotten people to perk up in anticipation of a broadcast. One I mentioned earlier in passing was the use by the Joe Loss Band of Miller's "In the Mood."

Some of what I felt were the best and most fitting themes were by such as Russ Morgan ("Does Your Heart Beat For Me," and "So Long"), Lionel Hampton, ("Flying Home"), Sammy Kaye, ("Kaye's Melody"), Kay Kyser, ("Thinking of You"), Dick Jurgens (Daydreams Come True at Night") and limitless more. I have literally hundreds and hundreds of others but even expanding the list would never come close to telling about themes for the many thousands (yes, *thousands*) of bands operating across the nation. So, I'll wrap up this segment with my all-time favorite closer that I liked well enough to use it on one of my own late night radio programs. It was by the Alvino Rey Orchestra and the richly romantic finale featured singer Yvonne King giving a breathy, almost whispered, "Nighty Night," no better way to signal the end of another show and another day.

Music made its way to our eager ears from the Aragon and Trianon ballrooms in Chicago; the Blue Room of the Roosevelt Hotel in New Orleans; the Cocoanut Grove in L.A. and Hollywood's

Palomar; the Chase and Park Plaza hotels in St. Louis and innumerable other venues from one end of the land to the other. It didn't matter much where the originating point might be, the announcer would generally always lead in with something about the "beautiful such-and-such place."

Sometimes the beauty part was accurate as in a lead-in provided me by long-time friend and co-worker, Bob Shriver. He was Denver's first TV announcer on Channel 2 in 1952, but he also did a lot of "remotes" on radio from the famed Elitch Gardens. He told me this was how he'd open.

"From the beautiful flower-trimmed Trocadero Ballroom, at world famous Elitch Gardens, in the mile high city of Denver, Colorado, at the foot of the towering snow-capped Rockies, it's the music of…"

Another note about the Trocadero concerns the Benny Goodman orchestra. The band had opened in May of 1935 in the Grill Room of New York's Roosevelt Hotel, a spot where Guy Lombardo usually held forth. Maybe the Lombardo style was part of the problem but for whatever reason, the manager thought the "new-fangled swing" was awful and two weeks' notice was given on opening night. Matters improved and a few months later, a cross-country tour was arranged.

One of the stops was Denver and the Trocadero. Disaster struck again! Customers were asking for their money back on opening night and the manager wasn't satisfied until the band played some waltzes. Reportedly, Goodman vowed he would never play in the city again and, as far as we know, he never did. But, it was on to the west coast and finally, success! – first in Oakland and then the Palomar. Youngsters on the coast had heard the Goodman band swinging on radio "remotes" and wanted more! B.G. and Company were thus on the way to his being proclaimed, "The King of Swing!"

Overall, Frankie Carle had one of the longest careers of anyone associated with big band music. It all started, as Frankie told me, "A lon-n-ng time ago," and he wasn't kidding. Born in 1903, Frankie played in his uncle's orchestra for $1.00 a week when he was only 13-years old, then tried his own short-lived outfit four years later. Then, a big boost came in the 1930s with the Mal Hallett band when Frankie got to play piano with some big names like drummer Gene Krupa and trombonists Jack Jenney and Jack Teagarden.

During our talk, Frankie enjoyed telling how his daughter got be the singer for his band in the good old days. He had been listening to a lot of demo records and to live performances but wasn't satisfied with what he was hearing. "I heard so many records that were no good and my wife slipped in a disc that I thought sounded pretty good and she suggested we go dancing that night. She took me to the place where my daughter happened to be singing with a local band. I had my back to the band and hadn't bothered to look at anybody. Finally, I heard this girl singing and said she sounded pretty good. My wife told me to turn around and see who it was and it was my daughter. I didn't know she'd been taking singing lessons while I was on the road. To tell you the truth, I didn't want her in the band; didn't want any relations, but she talked me into it. She made her first appearance in Dayton, Ohio and I didn't tell anybody she was my daughter, just announced her as my vocalist under the name Marjorie Hughes. It wasn't until three months later that my good friend, Walter Winchell, broke it in his column that Marjorie Hughes was Frankie Carle's daughter.

The first number she did was *Oh, What It Seemed to Be* and she stopped the show and we wound up with a record that made it to number one on the charts, the same thing that happened soon after with *Rumors Are Flying*."

Another of Frankie's compositions, his theme song, *Sunrise Serenade*, contributed to success of the theme for another band. Back in 1935, before starting his own band, Glenn Miller had written a number he called *Now I Lay Me Down to Weep* as an exercise for a course in arranging. It was filed away and eventually critic George Simon renamed it and wrote a set of lyrics titled *Gone With the Dawn*. It failed again.

Finally, after Miller had his band up and going, a recording session was set that included a cover recording for Frankie Carle's *Sunrise Serenade*. It was planned to have the twice-failed Miller composition, then called *Miller's Tune* on the band charts, on the backside. The story has it that someone suggested, "Hey, you've got *Sunrise Serenade* on one side, how about calling this one *Moonlight*

*Serenade?*" That's how history is made as that became the Miller theme, one of the most famous and recognizable signature tunes in the history of big band music.

## She Was Radio's First Singing Superstar

Jessica Dragonette first appeared on NBC when the network was just a month old and then became nationally renowned as a result of her appearances on *The Cities Service Concerts*. She was on the show for seven years on NBC and left because they wouldn't let her do enough operettas, acting as well as singing. She quickly wound up on the *Palmolive Beauty Box Theater* on CBS, where she got her wish and increased her popularity even more. She was a frequent guest on *The Maxwell House Showboat*, was featured on *Saturday Night Serenade* for Pet Milk and was known as "Vivian, the Coca-Cola Girl" on *The Musical Comedy Hour*. She also was frequently called "The Little Angel of Radio." Prior to her departure from NBC, an article was written about her that gave some of her philosophy about her job. It sounded like a "puff" piece from a publicity department but then, her life itself had some unusual twists. Jessica was born in India, orphaned at an early age, and was nurtured and educated by devoted nuns in the shelter of a convent. Here's the article:

"When Jessica Dragonette looks about the new NBC studios and thrills at their magnificence, she says to herself and means it, 'I must try to be as marvelous as this equipment; I must really try.'

That may be, she thinks, the secret of her success. She loves radio, she believes in it, she never gets over the miraculous wonder of it, she is proud – deeply proud – to be associated with it.

To little Miss Dragonette, whose pretty face and wide blue eyes light up when she as much as thinks about radio – radio is not a stepping stone to a stage career nor a springboard to Hollywood. No, it is an end in itself. When, eight years ago (1925 she went into radio, it was by deliberate choice. She had been the Angel voice in *The Miracle*, she had played in a road company of *The Student Prince*, she had capered in *The Grand Street Follies*, but gave all that up for radio.

No one knew much about radio in those days. It was an uncharted sea. If she remained in the theater, she knew she would only be following a tradition – but in radio she would be blazing a trail. In radio she could build her own technique. As a matter of fact, she'd have to. There was no definitive radio technique yet.

Now she looks back on those early days of radio, remembers the pitiful inadequacy of the carbon mikes she used to sing into, and is ever so grateful for the experience. Just because the equipment then was so inadequate, she was compelled to experiment, to perfect in spite of the handicaps, a radio technique, What she learned then stands by her today – although nobody must think that she's stopped learning.

That's what's so wonderful about radio to Miss Dragonette. Everybody in it is still pioneering. They haven't begun to use the facilities available, she believes. 'We're playing with a miracle,' she says. 'The whole trend of music will change. It will be better music. Even now, nobody turns on the radio and lets it play all day. Today, people select a program.'

If, as has been rumored, most sopranos are poison on the air, Miss Dragonette counters with the thought that most sopranos are poison anywhere. There are so few good ones.

Good ones realize first of all that they must not make their audience nervous. They should sing with so little apparent effort, they should be so easy that their listeners say to themselves, 'Why, I could do that. There's nothing to it.' The good ones know that radio technique requires more intensity of thought and feeling to put themselves across, that they must ignore their visible studio audience and think only of the millions outside waiting to catch their notes. There is something that Miss Dragonette, tapping her forehead, calls "radio psychology," which is the basis of all of it. You acquire radio psychology, she feels, if you're really sincere about radio.

Miss Dragonette just knows she is sincere. She is always thinking of her fans, wondering what will please them, trying so hard to do what they would like her to. Though she admits visible studio audiences disturb and distract her, she wouldn't think of refusing them admittance. They wait so long for tickets, they come from so far to see her. They are, after all, her public, always foremost in her consideration.

Because of them, she turns down personal appearance offers. If she accepted a stage job, she might destroy the illusion, she fears. Pictures, though, that's different. She might do a picture, if it were a charming one. But for Miss Dragonette, radio is an end in itself. She wants above everything else to be worthy of radio."

It would appear the NBC promotion department worked overtime on that piece. However, there were raves elsewhere also. The *Philadelphia Inquirer* once wrote:

America Has a New Love – She's the Radio Girl

"Like some lovely phantom with her exquisite voice, her mystery and charm, the maid of the air is ascending that throne from which idolized favorites of the public have held sway. As proof, consider the story of little Jessica Dragonette, a girl in her teens – they call her the "Jenny Lind of the Air,' a girl with a dimple in her voice. They hang her picture over the radio so they can pretend she is actually there when she sings."

The diminutive soprano brought semi-classical music to the U.S. in radio's early days and set what was then a broadcasting longevity record – 22 consecutive years. Listeners voted her radio's most popular performer in 1935. She was the first entertainer ever to be given a test for television, It was in 1928 and many of New York City's dignitaries showed up to see her face reproduced on a small, fuzzy screen as she sang from an adjacent studio. She died of a heart attack while being treated for asthma in 1980 at about age 70. She said in later years that her birth certificate had been burned in a fire and thus she was never sure of her exact age.

## The Show Must Go On!

The brilliant, but neurotic Oscar Levant was one of the intellectual mainstays of radio's top-rated *Information Please*. He was noted for his acerbic comments over the years, such as, "Strip away the phony tinsel of Hollywood and you'll find the real tinsel underneath," or, "I remember Doris Day before she was a virgin," and, "Every time I look at you I get a fierce desire to be lonesome." He was also a highly accomplished pianist and a good friend of composer George Gershwin.

Once, Levant was in the midst of a particularly brilliant passage of Gershwin's *Piano Concerto in F* during a performance in a college auditorium. A phone started to ring in a nearby office but Levant paid no attention to the persistent ringing. The audience, though, began to squirm. Finally, with no interruption in his playing, Oscar looked out at the audience and calmly said, "If that's for me, tell them I'm busy."

## Critic at Play

The creative half of radio's Easy Aces team was Goodman Ace. He also served some time as a theater critic. He came up with a capsule critique of the play *I Am a Camera*.

"No Leica."

Mrs. Malaprop was a character in the 1775 comedy, *The Rivals*, by R.B. Sheridan. She was noted for the generally humorous misapplication of words, enough so that using a word sort of like one that should have been used became a part of our language known as a "malapropism." Old Time Radio had no better practitioner than Goodman Ace, who wrote the ludicrous words into the mouth of his wife, Jane, on *Easy Aces*, a program that got its start on a Kansas City station (KMBC), but hit the network (CBS) in October of 1931, Over the years, he had Jane saying things like, "…up at the crank of dawn,'" "…the food in that restaurant is abdominal,' or, "Be it ever so hovel, there's no place like home."

Ace's grand-nephew, Mark Singer, wrote an article about him in *The New Yorker* that used the genre to demonstrate the hilarious style.

"The careful conversationalist might try to mix it up with him in a baffle of wits. In quest of this pinochle of success, I have often wrecked my brain for a clowning achievement but Ace's chicken always come home to roast. From time to time, Ace will, in a jerksome way, monotonize the conversation with witticisms to humorous to mention. It's high noon someone beat him at his own game, but I have never done it: cross my eyes and hope I die, he always wins thumbs down."

Among many other things, Goodman Ace became the top-paid writer on TV through efforts on *The Perry Como Show* and others. He lectured on a regular basis and wrote a column for *Saturday Review*. One of the books he wrote was titled *The Better of Goodman Ace*. He said the title raised some eyebrows and doubts at the publishers' office.

"They suggested a stronger title, but I wasn't going to leave myself open to the sneer of some browser in a bookshop, opening a book at random, reading one of the chapters, and saying, 'Is that his best?' Nobody ever says, 'Is that his better?' Protection, see?"

Ace once wrote a treatise on the mini-skirt, saying that if he never saw another thigh it'd be all right with him.

He indicated, "It isn't so bad when they're standing or walking. But, when they sit, it's the fringe benefits that get me."

He added, "The question is – if they insist on exhibiting fibulae and patellae and popliteal fossae and femura, can acetabula be far behind?"

In his *Saturday Review* column, no Sacred Cows were left unmilked – no areas of life had a safe haven from his sardonic explorations.

## You Ain't Heard Nothin' Yet!

Al Jolson was just about ready to go on the air on the *Shell Chateau* when he got a long distance phone call from a pal in a distant city.

The friend bubbled, "Hey, the broadcast was great – you were terrific, Al!"

Jolie came back, "Whaddya mean? I haven't even started yet!"

There was a moment of silence before the friend's comeback. "Well, you forget the three hour time difference. You're all through here!"

## Good Old Golden Rule Days & What's In a Name?

*Our Miss Brooks* had Eve Arden cast as America's favorite schoolmarm. Once, while playing in summer stock, her co-star decided to pull a practical joke during the play. There was a scene in which the two were exchanging dialogue and the actor arranged for a stagehand to have a phone ring on Eve's side of the stage while she was speaking. She had the presence of mind to answer the phone, then got even with the prankster by turning to him and saying, "It's for you."

Eve Arden was one of many who had a name change for show biz purposes. She was born Eunice Quedens (Qwa-DENZ) and switched for obvious reasons. Here's a brief listing of others who did the same.

Jack Benny, of course, started life as Benjamin Kubelsky, not in his oft-mentioned home town of Waukegan, Illinois, but at Mercy Hospital in Chicago. At one stage of his vaudeville career he was Ben Benny (and briefly Ben K. Benny) but when musician/comedian Ben Bernie thought that was taking advantage of his own popularity, Jack became Jack and stayed that way.

As for John Florence Sullivan, along the way he was Paul Huckle (for one night), Fred St. James, Freddy James, even Benjamin Franklin before becoming Fred Allen for good.

Name changes for Nathan Birnbaum were just as common during vaudeville days. George Burns, at one time or another, was known on stage as Eddie Delight, Billy Pierce, Captain Betts, Jed Jackson, Jimmy Malone, etc. Born as Birnbaum, George said he had to change his name often because the booker wouldn't give him another job if he knew who he was.

In her book, *Miss Peggy Lee*, the legendary star told how she became Peggy instead of Norma Deloris Egstrom. It happened after auditioning at station WDAY in Fargo, North Dakota. Station boss, Ken Kennedy, said, "You have to change your name. Norma Egstrom – it doesn't sound right. Ladies and gentlemen, Miss

Norma Egstrom? No, won't do at all. Let me see. You look like a Peggy. Peggy Lynn. No – Peggy Lee. That's it! Ladies and gentlemen, Miss Peggy Lee." It was as simple as that.

Alice Faye was born as Ann Leppert. Alice, of course, had great movie success along with her career on *The Phil Harris and Alice Faye Show* (originally *The Fitch Bandwagon*). Prior to being Mrs. Phil Harris, Alice was once married to Tony Martin. His birth name, by the way, was Alvin Morris and he was later married to dancer/actress Cyd Charisse.

I'll never forget one time doing a stand-up bit in a night club where Tony was the feature attraction. After all his success and public exposure he was still quite nervous while waiting to come on. As soon as he was in front of the audience, though, his backstage qualms went away.

## A *Real* Rolling Stone

Bob Burns was a radio and film comedian in the 1930s and '40s playing a country bumpkin who told tall tales about his hillbilly relatives. He also played a handmade instrument made up of pipe, hose and a whisky funnel. He called it a "bazooka" and the name was borrowed by World War II GIs for their handheld anti-tank rocket launchers.

Bob became a regular on Bing Crosby's *Kraft Music Hall*. There he told such stories as the one about his scientific Uncle Fud. He said that uncle went up a mountain out back of van Buren, Arkansas and found a big rock precariously poised on a cliff. He worked and worked and was finally able to dislodge the huge boulder and it went careening down the mountainside headed right straight for the town. Bob's uncle came running along after it as fast as he could go. The monster rock whammed through the livery stable, zoomed down the main drag, went crashing through the bank and finally came to rest in the back of that building. Naturally, the townspeople, who had first scattered out of the way, gathered from all sides. Bob's uncle arrived on the run, shoved everybody out of the way and proceeded to examine the boulder from every angle. Then, he straightened up and proclaimed, "Nope. No moss!"

## Give Him Good "Marx" For Humor & Her Hearing Was Okay But She Had a Bad Spell Anyway

A G-I appearing on Groucho Marx' radio quiz show, *You Bet Your Life*, told the outrageous quiz-master he was looking for a girl who didn't smoke, drink, swear or have any other bad habits. The irrepressible Groucho retorted, "What for?"

A little 8-year old girl was listening to one of her favorite radio programs on a Minneapolis station when she heard them say to write in for a "mystery gift." She very carefully wrote out her request and slowly, but confidently addressed the envelope to the station at "Many Apples, Many Soda." We understand it was delivered.

## "Hello, Anybody, Here's Morgan."

Even that stylized opening resulted from a Morganesque view of things. Henry told about in his book, *Here's Morgan! The Original Bad Boy of Broadcasting*. He said he was called in by the manager of WOR in New York and informed he was kidding around so much on the air that they wanted him to have a quarter-hour slot on Saturday mornings so he could "get it out of his system." He admitted the show was on the weird side and started with the theme song, *For He's a Jolly Good Fellow*, that led into his open of, "Hello, anybody..." That was because, as he said, "The big noise of the day was one Kate Smith, a fat girl who started her show with a condescending, 'hello, everybody...' "I, on the other hand, was happy if anybody listened in."

Henry noticed the cleansing process offered by the show worked pretty well because eventually he was on six nights weekly and making a thousand dollars a week by the time he enlisted in what was then called the Army Air Corps. Henry's autobiography came out in June after he died in May. He wouldn't have wanted to make a promotional tour anyway – would likely have lobbied for a clause to that effect.

Among the Henry-isms was the well-known baiting of the pharmaceutical industry. He talked about the town of More, Utah... said it had a couple of doctors and that started the famous ad that began, "More doctors recommend..." He lost a lot of clients through an oversupply of impudence such as his comment that an Oh! Henry candy bar was a meal in itself, "but you eat three meals of Oh! Henry's and your teeth will fall out." He even picked on cities. While working in Canada four years to avoid "alimony jail,' he said everything about Toronto was "blah." He did say the city was physically attractive, that the Royal Ontario Museum was just fine and that there were other municipal attractions you could count on your elbows. He said he was *often* reminded that the streets were clean and that one could safely walk them at night. He endeared himself to no one there when he responded, "Yes, you can walk them at night. But where would you go?"

He ended the book with a typical Morgan outlook.

"Grow old along with me, the best is yet to be."
   -Robert Browning

"Bullshit!"
   -Henry Morgan

## Some Miscellaneous Notes

A magazine called *Screen Guide* once asked Fred Allen to write a review of a Jack Benny movie. In order to keep their pseudo "feud" going, Allen wrote, "Mr. Benny first appears in a swing band, although he couldn't get a job wetting the finger of the man who turns the music for the washboard player with the Hoosier Hot Shots."

That group, by the way, became extremely popular building their following with their zany performances on *The National Barn Dance* on WLS, Chicago, a program that pre-dated the *Grand Ol Opry*. Their nutty routine would open with the ringing question, "Are you ready, Hezzie?," and he (Paul Trietsch) would reply with a swooping sound on one of his slide whistles. Hezzie also played a weird washboard arrangement, a corrugated metal washboard, with attached bells, assorted bike horns and you name it. In the period 1937 to 1950 this popular group appeared in more than 20 movies. So, Fred Allen (as usual) knew exactly what he was doing when he spoke of them in his review of Jack Benny.

Back in the 1930s, the competing radio ratings services were Crossley and Hooper. Then, as now, nothing provoked more debate and resentment than the various means of determining size of audience. Back then, it was done by making random telephone calls. C.W. Hooper himself appeared on *We The People* in 1947 to demonstrate how the sample was put together for his Broadcast Audience Measurement.

Calling a person at random, he asked, "What program are you listening to?"

The studio audience burst into raucous laughter when the voice replied, "*Amos 'n' Andy*." Hooper himself got a Hooper rating of 13 while *Amos 'n' Andy* got a 30.

Baseball great Dizzy Dean was once on a benefit broadcast with Betty Grable and the announcer urged him to say something cute to the pin-up queen. Dean said shyly (?), "Miss Grable, I'll show you my curves, if you'll show me yours!"

Later on, when Diz was broadcasting major league baseball, many schoolteachers registered protests about his atrocious use of the English language. He was equal to the occasion by telling them, "A lot of people that ain't sayin' ain't, ain't eatin'."

After leaving Washington, D.C. and before he became a big-time network star, Arthur Godfrey did a morning show on WABC, New York. The six A.M. start was not particularly to his liking and he didn't always show up on time. So, there was standard procedure for whatever staff announcer was on duty. He'd say, "This is *The Arthur Godfrey Show*. Arthur's not here." Then, they'd play records until the ol' redhead arrived on the scene.

## Take Two Kirkwoods and Call Me in the Morning

He may have been the only comedian to ever be given as a prescription. When Jack Kirkwood did a show called *Mirth and Madness* every weekday morning on NBC, the network got a letter in late August of 1944 from a group of doctors in California. It read, "Our first prescription for any patient is to listen to Jack Kirkwood and *Mirth and Madness*." Who knows, they may have been onto something even before Norman Cousins promulgated the theory of laughing yourself to good health.

The Depression that followed the 1929 stock market crash had cut into audiences for road shows Jack wrote and produced from 1925-'29 – more than four hundred original shows that played on the West Coast and through the Middle West. So, he decided to give movies a try. Nothing developed. Pretty down and out by 1932, he went past a burlesque theater in L.A. He'd never seen burlesque but bought a ticket, went in, and had a seventy-five dollar a week job three days later.

Actually, the Kirkwood radio saga had begun while he was still in burlesque. CBS affiliate KRFC in San Francisco approached him about doing a variety show. They wanted him to write and present it so he came up with *The Frivolity Show*, which went on the air in mid-January of 1938. Kirkwood continued with it through part of March, 1943 when NBC lured him away. Over the years he had a recurring role on *The Bob Hope Show*, plus many appearances on such programs as *Fibber McGee and Molly, Edgar Bergen, Jack Benny, Ozzie and Harriet*, as well as the star-loaded *Railroad Hour*.

One of the comedy bits he dreamed up was the "slow death." This was used in several westerns and had a man being shot and falling to the ground. He'd be asked for any last words and would then proceed to talk and talk and talk, minutes on end until he finally succumbed.

## Ever Hear of *The Flotsam Family*? & Speaking of Quiz Shows....

Probably not, but that was the name of a program that was once suggested as a possibility for Groucho Marx. That show never reached fruition, but a change in title and content resulted in what became *The Life of Riley*. All this happened because Gummo Marx (Groucho's brother) made contact with screenwriter Irving Brecher to see if he could come up with a program idea for Groucho. Brecher said, "I was happy doing pictures – didn't have anything in mind." Gummo was persistent, though, and kept after him. Finally, Brecher gave in enough to tell him about the *Flotsam* notion. They auditioned the program but "no sale" was the answer. Somewhere Brecher met William Bendix and suggested that Gummo get him involved in the deal. As it happened, Bendix liked the idea...some of the lines were changed and the title became *The Life of Riley*. An audition disc was cut but still nothing happened until somebody found it at the bottom of a batch of old records. At first, no one even knew who owned the idea, but eventually that got straightened out and it wasn't a "revoltin' development" after all, except for Groucho. He didn't get much of anything until a fellow named John Guedel wanted him to do some kind of quiz show. Ah, but that's another story for another time!

*Take It or Leave It* was a quiz program that lasted for a decade and had five different emcees during its run. Bob Hawk started it in 1940, but had a money squabble with sponsor Eversharp at the end of 1941. That's when Phil Baker took over and he kept the job longest, until mid-September, 1947. The final three quizmasters were Garry Moore, Jack Paar and Eddie Cantor, pretty good lineup I'd say.

Baker was another of the many radio personalities who got a start in vaudeville, even worked for a time with a fiddle player named Ben Bernie. The act did okay until Baker went into the Navy in World War I. When he got out, Baker was broke and needed some material so he could get his vaudeville career going again.

He more or less pounced on lyricist and gag-writer Lew Brown, whose work habits were not the greatest. Finally, Baker got Brown to a Times Square hotel where Brown holed up in the bathroom and occasionally called out ideas that Baker wrote down. They were making headway but next day, bedlam broke loose outside. Baker rushed out to see what it was all about. It was the Armistice and people were going wild. Baker rushed back inside and found Brown throwing confetti out the window – confetti made from the precious notes Baker had written. There went the act! Phil eventually got material elsewhere and went on from there. So, of course, did *Take It or Leave It*. It eventually had a title change to *The 64-Dollar Question*!

## A Long-Ago Bit of Subterfuge

The year was 1924. Innovations in aviation technology enabled adventurous pilots to set many records, such as the one when Army airplanes circled the globe in the flight time of 363 hours. This bit of derring-do was one of the first special events to be covered by pioneer announcer, Norman Brokenshire.

The first part was arrival of the planes at Mitchel Field, Long Island, and it was important because not only was it headline news, but it also marked the first chain broadcast. RCA set it up and publicized it by using all its outlets – WJZ, New York, WJY, Schenectady, WRC, Washington, KDKA, Pittsburgh and KFKX, Hastings, Nebraska.

Brokenshire aired the arrival that featured a greeting party of the Prince of Wales, the New York City mayor, the commanding officer of the field and a group of dignitaries from Washington. The second part was a scheduled reception that evening to be held in the officers' mess. It was to be the evening radio feature at eight o'clock and it was ballyhooed on radio and in news columns. Brokenshire took the intervening time to relax and put together all his information.

Following instructions, he went to the officers' mess about an hour ahead of time and was expecting decorations and advance hustle and bustle for the big event. There was to be an official military reception, with music and dancing, and with lovely women all decked out in their finery. To his utter dismay, there was nothing whatsoever – the lights were off and the building was empty. He raced around in a near panic and finally located a couple of enlisted men sacked out on the second floor. They knew nothing about anything and went back to sleep. Brokenshire now had less than an hour before he was supposed to be on the air with a gala description.

He found a phone and called the quarters of the commanding officer. An orderly casually informed him that the C.O. had remembered a previous engagement in New York and had decided to hold the "reception" in his own home right after the arrival ceremony. That's when Brokenshire realized that this new radio business wasn't all that big and important to the Army. But, "the show must go on," right? He raced to an enlisted man's day room, grabbed a Victrola and some assorted records, then began wondering where the celebrated fliers might be.

Two of them were located in officer's country resting up after all the previous excitement and he persuaded them to come over and let him introduce them over a background of martial music. The other aviators were in the field hospital so Brokenshire scribbled some notes that he could use as the latter two men's speeches in absentia.

Finally, all was in place – sort of. An enlisted man started up *Stars and Stripes Forever* and the operator's voice said, "You're on the air."

This relatively new announcer with the first "hook-up" of stations did it all, as Brokenshire later told. The coverage included all the ingredients…this important date in aviation history…intrepid fliers…magnificence of the scene…illustrious guests…wonderful decorations…beautifully gowned women…handsome uniforms… a receiving line (two enlisted men shuffling their feet).

Brokenshire told of the two men in the hospital, how they looked and felt, then read the little speeches he had prepared with their comments on the great adventure. Finally, for the climax, he introduced the commander of the flight, who fortunately recognized what "Broke" was facing and went along on the make-believe. He even repeated some of the things he had said at the actual afternoon reception at the C.O.'s house. It finally ended and Brokenshire nearly passed out in utter relief that it was over.

He made his way back to the New York studio and was greeted by compliments right down the line. What to do? Should he tell what happened? In the end, rather than making a clean breast of it to the powers-that-be he decided to let it ride. Insofar as we know, he never confessed until he wrote a book about his career thirty years later.

Imagination? Oh, yes! Could the later medium of television have done what Brokenshire concocted in that long-ago era? No way, and, of course, although there was an air of illegitimacy, it marked a period when radio began to grow into the giant it became. In times ahead, no C.O. would be able to do what that one did, nor would any future "Brokenshires" have to improvise in such a sensational manner.

## Aboard the Camel Caravan

The sponsor loved the show, for the title alone if nothing else. After all, the makers of Camel Cigarettes got constant sponsor recognition as they presented a number of shows under that title over the years. One of the first of this series of comedy-variety programs featured host Walter O'Keefe and it ran from 1934 through 1936 on CBS every Tuesday and Thursday evenings.

Rehearsals for the show were held in the CBS Little Theater on West 44th Street. Let's see if we can put it together the way it would have happened back in the fall of 1936.

The first to arrive would be control room men and they would begin turning things on in a glass-enclosed booth directly below the stage.

One by one, the cast straggled in – Glen Gray and his Casa Loma group, weighted down by instruments…blonde Alice Frost, perhaps bundled up in a raccoon coat…starry eyed Deane Janis, looking as though she just stepped off the pages of a fashion magazine…serious-looking Tony Cabooch, looking more like a philosopher than a comedian…fat and funny Louie Sorin…announcer Paul Douglas,,,a bespectacled and brittle-looking Ted Husing and finally O'Keefe himself, fresh from the barber's chair.

The musicians wasted no time setting up their instruments and soon the almost churchly calm of the theater was dispelled by the torrid beat of a jazz tune. Gray quietly controlled the flow and occasionally stopped to discuss a point of harmony.

In the far corner, O'Keefe and his band of thespians went over their sketches. The director chewed on a nearly extinct cigar and hovered about with stopwatch in hand, making hasty notes. O'Keefe said at one point, "No, no, it won't do! That skit is terrible. It's as flat as stale beer. We'll have to rewrite it."

The musicians continued playing away and Deane Janis joined them waiting on her cues for vocal solos. Glen Gray kept dashing into the control room to see how it was sounding on-mike.

All this went on for hours and finally the disjointed parts started coming together for dress rehearsal set to begin about five o'clock.

All noise and banter ceased. The director and an agency rep were in the control booth.

Announcer Paul Douglas made the opening announcement as the band softly played its famed signature song, *Smoke Rings*. Walter O'Keefe then broke in with his expected salutation of, "Gangway, neighbors," and the band began an infectious rhythm as Deane Janis took a vocal solo. Ted Husing delivered a few moments of crackling comment on sports – with O'Keefe, Sorin, Cabooch and Alice Frost then doing a hilarious burlesque-type bit. Eyes were glued to stopwatches in the control booth as the rehearsal wound down. It had run long. Forty seconds were sliced from the skit, a paragraph was deleted from Husing's sports talk. With other slight variations, the package was woven together into its final form.

Finally, it was just a few moments before 9:00 p.m., Eastern Standard Time. Spectators were packed into the Little Theater and performers were gathered around three on-stage microphones and they were now all decked out in formal attire.

Paul Douglas held up a warning hand and cautioned, "Twenty seconds." The band went into action and then O'Keefe stepped to the mike and said, "Gangway, neighbors. This is Walter O'Keefe – this is my one hundredth broadcast for my bosses down there underneath the Carolina Moon – this is the hundredth time I've introduced Glen Gray to you – here he comes with *Way Down Yonder in New Orleans*."

Later came some fun when everyone decided to swap jobs in honor of the one-hundredth broadcast. Walter said he'd always wanted to lead an orchestra, Louie Sorin agreed to accept Walter's host role and the audience roared when Ted Husing said, "I'd like to be Deane Janis." The whole thing was sheer nonsense but the audience loved it and loudspeakers all across the country were picking it up for listeners at home.

Then, Paul Douglas did his closing bit – about the goodness of cigarettes and the quality of tobacco – not very entertaining, but he smoothly kept it from being a bore. He finished and the host, crouching by one of the other mikes, came suddenly to life. No pause, as he said, "This is Walter O'Keefe, saying good 'nate' and thank you!" So, the show ended. And good "nate" and thank you, too, Mr. O'Keefe, for a hearty half hour of fun.

They weren't really through, though. They did it again two and a half hours later for the west coast. To paraphrase a much later TV closing by newsman Walter Cronkite, "And that's the way it was!"

## Okay, So They Gave the Election Returns, Then What?

A man credited by many as having inaugurated the radio business as we came to know it was said to have disclosed that what started his thinking was a newspaper ad in a Pittsburgh newspaper in early 1920. It supposedly called attention to a stock of radio receivers that could be used to hear radio programs being sent out from the experimental radio telephone station 8XK by Frank Conrad. This spurred some ideas in the mind of H.P. Davis, who happened to be the vice-president of the Westinghouse Electric and Manufacturing Company. Davis figured that maybe the notion of radio telephony being used for confidential communications was not full use – that maybe this was really the only means of instantaneous collective communication that had ever been devised.

So, Davis decided in early 1920 to install a broadcasting station in East Pittsburgh, but the equipment wasn't ready to operate until the fall. Various members of the Westinghouse firm sat in on conferences about the proposal and they decided that cooperation of the press would be necessary to build public interest. Fortunately, they got pledges of such cooperation from the *Pittsburgh Post* and the *Pittsburgh Sun*. So, that when the time came to get it going KDKA (the call letters they had chosen) decided to open with a big splash. It was a presidential election year why not open with election returns?

As is a well-known historical fact, they did just that on November 2, 1920. The returns were gathered at the *Post*, telephoned to East Pittsburgh and KDKA put them on the air for the audience – what there was of it, that is. Nowadays we'd call it "papering the house."

Westinghouse manufactured some primitive receiving sets and distributed them to company officers and friends. A few amateurs also picked it up but, by and large, the "audience" was miniscule and naturally everyone had to listen on earphones because there weren't any loudspeakers.

## What Next?

After that opening broadcast, the station was only on for an hour each evening from 8:30 to 9:30 and phonograph records provided most of the broadcast material for the first few months. It quickly became evident, though, that more variety was going to be necessary in order to attract any attention or make any progress. There was a band among some Westinghouse employees and it was put on the air and after a while, the KDKA Little Symphony Orchestra was formed. Before the musical groups were used the transmitting had been done from a very small room. Afterwards, an auditorium was tried but the room resonance goofed up sound fidelity. So, they tried outdoors and it was an improvement but something that wasn't going to work in the winter. With warmer spring weather in 1921, the powers-that-be decided to go ahead through summer with the outdoor setup on the roof of one of the plant buildings. They put up a tent to provide some protection and it worked very satisfactorily with good acoustics. However, as early fall came on, a windy night came upon the scene. The tent was whipped away by a big gust and radio's first "real" broadcast studio blew away into the night. Indoors it was going to have to be.

Meantime, the whole concept was starting to grow. WBZ opened September 27, 1921 in Springfield, Massachusetts and WJZ began a few days later in Newark on October 1. The group was joined by KYW, Chicago on Armistice Day, 1921.

The original WJZ studio was a converted cloakroom outside the main office at the Westinghouse meter factory. They merely crowded up the coats and got a space about 10-feet wide and around 18-feet long. There was a shack on the roof for the transmitting equipment. During the summer days of 1922, the cloakroom studio got unbearably hot and with no air conditioning available a window facing a fire escape was left open with occasional street noises drifting in. Once, with a soprano doing her thing, a wild episode of howling, screeching and spitting took place. Two tomcats were fighting outside the window and they managed to steal the show when they dashed inside the studio and completed their duet on the "live" microphone. There was brief pandemonium but finally a calm "ACN" merely announced the next number without any explanation.

During this period of time, announcers were anonymous and known only by initials. One of the first was Thomas Cowan, who was identified as "ACN." The "A" stood for announcer, the "C" for Cowan and "N" for Newark.

## "Duffy Ain't Here"

And neither was the saloon on Manhattan's Third Avenue

Just like the rest of us, Duffy's Tavern manager, Archie (or more properly, Ed Gardner), didn't want to pay any more taxes than absolutely necessary, He had been coughing up quite a bit in the way of federal levies. So, when the government decided to try and attract more tourists to Puerto Rico by declaring a twelve-year tax holiday, off went Mr. G. That's not exactly what the powers-that-be had in mind but the practical (and acquisitive) minded Gardner took advantage, using tourists as audiences for transcribing sessions of his program. An Illinois congressman labeled Gardner and some other opportunists as "tax dodgers who are continuing their raids on the treasury" and wanted the tax loophole closed. It eventually was, but Gardner had his days in the sun, so to speak.

In another note of semi-conflict, a show of December 7, 1943 opened this way:

"Bristol-Myers, the makers of Sal Hepatica, famous laxative, and Minit-Rub, modern chest rub, brings you…Duffy's."

Then, after the phone rings, Archie does his open, "Hello…Duffy's, where the elite meet to eat…" There were some protests from anti-alcohol forces who felt that "Tavern" in the name was a bad connotation, so it was briefly taken out. Wiser heads decided that was "nit-picking" and restored the title in its original form.

Another Gardner story came from Ozzie Nelson. He and Harriet signed on in the fall of 1933 to do their first weekly series on radio, a show called *The Bakers' Broadcast*. The star was comedian Joe "Wanna buy a duck?" Penner, but he wound up being replaced by Robert "Believe It Or Not" Ripley. The producer-director for three seasons was Ed Gardner, labeled by Nelson as "a tremendously talented madman." It was Ozzie's job to be the Doubting Thomas on "Believe It Or Not," with lines like, "I find that hard to believe, you'll have to prove it to me." He said that wasn't always easy because Gardner dug up most of the items that were dramatized on the air and their authenticity was often suspect.

One example concerned a story that never made the air. Ozzie was going over some music cues with the arranger when Gardner came bursting into the office and said excitedly he had positive proof of the most fantastic "Believe It Or Not" that anyone had ever even imagined.

"However, there's only one problem. I've gotta figure out a way to get it past the censors. Do you think they'll let us say "bosoms" on the air?"

Nelson replied, "Come on, Ed, just because a girl has big bosoms, that's not a "Believe It Or Not," no matter how big they are."

Gardner came right back, "Who said anything about size? It's a question of numbers…she's got <u>three</u> of 'em!"

## She Got Into Radio as the Result of a Bad Cold

Trying to list all of the credits for some of radio's busiest actors and actresses is almost impossible because many of them were all over the dial. Betty Winkler was an outstanding example of that. Here is at least a partial list of her many appearances, some as the lead: *Abie's Irish Rose, Chicago Theater of the Air, Grand Hotel, Lights Out, Joyce Jordan, Lone Journey, The O'Neills, Rosemary, This Life Is Mine, Girl Alone, Betty and Bob, The Man I Married, Curtain Time* and *Welcome Valley*. The names alone show how much she was involved for quite a period because most of those shows didn't exist later on. At one time, she had roles in seven different radio serials or soaps every week. She had several different parts on *Fibber McGee and Molly*, including Daisy, Dimples LaRue, Miss Fiditch, and Flossie. Betty was a three-time winner of the reader's poll award in *Radio Mirror* magazine as "Best Actress on the Air." It was a fine career that began with the help of a bad cold. Betty was called for an audition at WTAM, Cleveland for a part on a show called *Vivian Ware*. She went to the studio despite the cold and fever and got the job because her voice was changed in pitch as a result of her illness. She stuck after that because of natural talent. No other member of her family was ever in entertainment. Betty was born in Berwick, PA on April 19, 1914. She spent her childhood there and in Akron, Ft. Wayne and Chicago. Betty went to Western Reserve at Cleveland for a dramatic course and hooked on with the Cleveland Players repertory company at WTAM, then it was on to summer stock as leading lady at the age of 18. She went to NBC in mid-1933 and rapidly won parts on many leading programs.

Superstitions? She liked to rehearse before a mirror and couldn't broadcast with a hat on. She wore gloves to keep her fingers from sticking to the script.

## Parody of Commercials and Real Life for That Matter

Did you ever hear of the Monogahela Metal Foundry? They were busily engaged in "casting steel ingots with the housewife in mind." How about Cool Canadian Air? It was "Packed fresh every day in the Hudson Bay and shipped to your door." It so happens those were commercial spoofs concocted by the fertile comedy minds of Bob Elliott and Ray Goulding, known far and wide for their hilarious program, *Bob and Ray*. No subject was immune to their satirical approach to humor. They went about their business just as though their program was serious and was populated by a "staff," all of whom were played by the pair of comic geniuses.

To give you an idea of the diversity, Bob Elliott presented on-going characters like Wally Ballou, who was a little bit of everything – news reporter (quite inept), man-on-the-street interviewer and to certify his credentials, "winner of 16 diction awards." He would always jump the gun and start talking before his mike was on so that his opening was, "-ly Ballou here." The pair of zanies took advantage of this habit once when Ray, as an engineer, found out Ballou had started prematurely on purpose and promptly chewed out the report for making him look as though he was the one who made the mistake.

Another character was Tex Blaisdell, who was not only a drawling singer of cowboy songs but also did rope tricks on the radio. Bob was also Biff Burns, who did sports stories and always wound up his bit with, "This is Biff Burns saying this is Biff Burns saying goodnight."

There was Peter Gorey, whose character was somewhat like Gore, a Boris Karloff sound-alike, but instead spoke with a voice like Peter Lorre. He would tell gruesome headlines like, "Three men were run over by a steamroller today...." During which Bob and Ray would sometimes play a recording of *Music, Music, Music* that supposedly was being sung by Gorey.

Bob did several other take-offs, including Arthur Sturdley, based on Arthur Godfrey, and "do-it-yourself" handyman Fred Falvy. No part of everyday life was immune to their often ludicrous depictions.

Ray was such characters as Charles the Poet, a mockery of Chicago's late-night announcer, Franklyn MacCormack and sort of like Percy Dovetonsils portrayed by comedian Ernie Kovacs. The sappy verse was never finished because Ray, as the poet, would break down in laughter. Goulding did all of the female roles and generally used the same flat voice for all of them. They included the likes of Mary Margaret McGoon, who satirized home-economics expert Mary Margaret McBride. McGoon would have recipes for such bizarre dishes as "mock turtle," and "ginger ale salad." At one time, Ray (as Mary) recorded a song called, "I'd like to be a cow in Switzerland."

Soap operas were fair game for the pair and they did imitations like, *One Fella's Family*, *Mary Backstayge, Noble Wife* and *Aunt Penny's Sunlit Kitchen*, all obvious rib-tickling versions of actual programs. *Mr. Trace, Keener Than Most Persons* didn't escape their attention.

As a matter of fact, nothing much got by them. One-time major league pitcher turned broadcaster, Joe Nuxhall, had a signature sign-off, "this is the old lefthander rounding third and heading for home," which became Bob and Ray's bit from sportscaster Steve Bosco, "This is Steve Bosco rounding third, and being thrown out at home."

There were times when such characters might be sponsored by such as the United States Mint, "One of the nation's leading producers of genuine U.S. currency," or, The Croftweiler Industrial Cartel, "Makers of all sorts of stuff, made out of everything."

All of this had gotten started at WHDH in Boston. Goulding was a news reader and Elliott a disc jockey, each with separate programs. They would sometimes visit on the air and the station liked their work so much they'd call on them to do a fill-in show when Boston Red Sox baseball games would get rained out. They would joke around with studio musicians and come up with improvised comic material for however long it was needed. This caught on and they got their own weekday program in 1946, first for only 15-minutes but soon expanded into a half hour. It was called *Matinee with Bob and Ray* and Goulding explained Elliott's top billing was because "Matinee with Bob and Ray" sounded better than "Matinob with Ray and Bob."

It was virtually impossible to keep from laughing at their spoofs of broadcasting's real life world and it was generally with regret when they signed off, with their trademark, "This is Ray Goulding reminding you to write if you get work," and "Bob Elliot reminding you to hang by your thumbs."

## A Well-Deserved Honor

One of the honorees at the 1993 Radio Hall of Fame was Norman Corwin and Willard Waterman (the second *Great Gildersleeve*) listed the reasons for the high respect being given. "The Pioneer Award is presented to a broadcaster who has given at least twenty years of dedicated service to the radio industry, has been a leader in developing and improving quality radio programming. That description characterizes this year's recipient, Norman Corwin. Norman Corwin was a writer/director/producer for CBS Radio. Among his most memorable productions was the historic 1941 documentary hailing the Bill of Rights, *We Hold These Truths*, and the 1945 V-E Day patriotic special, *On a Note of Triumph*. Norman Corwin is truly a living legend."

Corwin was unable to attend, but after Willard's remarks, his letter of acceptance was read by Studs Terkel, Pulitzer Prize-winning author and broadcaster.

"Those of us who lived and worked inside the Golden Age of radio were unaware it was golden; we never suspected that the great networks and their specialties would vanish, for radio was unique in many ways. It was the first theater built for unseen and unseeing audiences, the first to command vast distances, the first to affect masses about mass effects.

I live in a region where for sport, a single hand with a lit match can destroy a whole countryside, kill people, reduce to rubble thousands of homes and shatter lives. It's another symbol of the reckless cruelty that not only damns the consequences but enjoys them. The fashions of outrageousness are many; murders, polarizations at home and abroad, children gunned down on streets, political zealots who blow up planeloads of innocents. All those in a seemingly endless pageant of malice toward all and charity for none.

What does this have to do with radio? Much. Because radio can still be, as in the past, a moral force. It has the capacity to inform, to arouse and inspire, to exalt, to celebrate, to contribute to the depleted accounts of amity and peace.

There do exist scattered islands of quality in radio, but they must be joined to the mainland. I say to all of you as friends of the Radio Hall of Fame, let's not forget that the very ether that transports our speech and music is not an invention, but a gift of the cosmos, a shard of creation itself. With these credentials, plus then needs of a sick world, there's more reason than ever to use the medium conscionably."

Corwin once stated, "The more satisfying character of what is loosely called fame is in the appreciation expressed by people who've heard you or say you've influenced them, they think for the better. That, in itself, is its own monument and reward."

## Scherzo in a Straitjacket

In November of 1941, the publication, *Radio Hit Songs*, ran an article about a very different kind of radio program.

"One of the zaniest, rollicking and yet educational programs on the air today is the National Broadcasting Company Blue Network's *Chamber Music Society of Lower Basin Street*, a sensationally popular series that bounded to national acclaim after program officials had wracked their brains to find a light show to brighten a talk-filled schedule.

Modestly introduced each Wednesday at 9:00 P.M., EST, on the NBC Blue Network, as being "no doubt world famous," the Basin Street sessions have risen steadily in favor to become the brassiest and most diverting show on the air today. A tongue-in-cheek burlesque of the classics, the series is dedicated — consecrated no less — to the perpetuation of the hallowed three B's." Theirs, however, are not the familiar Brahms, Beethoven and Bach variety. They call it, "barrelhouse, boogie woogie and the blues."

Basically, the program is a glorified jam session featuring some of radio's foremost musicians. It pokes fun not at the old masters but at the pompous stuffed shirts "who attend concerts and operas not for the music but to wallow in jewel-encrusted radiance." All involved in the "Society's" efforts are fervent lovers of the classics.

Two orchestras composed largely of the NBC Symphony Orchestra are featured on the series. One, conducted by Dr. Henry Levine, is called the Dixieland Octet or "barefooted philharmonic." The other, comprising ten pieces under the capable leadership of Maestro Paul Lavalle is billed as the Double Woodwind Quintet or "Windy Ten."

Acting as the suave "chairman" of the *Chamber Music Society of Lower Basin Street* is Dr. Giacomo (Jack) McCarthy, an otherwise respected individual, popular around eastern racing resorts.

In the most pontifical manner he informs "Basin Street" fans in a subdued voice that the lights are going down and Dr. Henry Levine "is being lured to the podium with a salami sandwich, and will now give a stirring reading of the new art form – the *Jazz Me Blues*. Continuing from the program notes written by the NBC script division's Welbourn Kelley, McCarthy adds that the work builds up to a "terrific diminuendo."

The "Society" made its inauspicious debut over the NBC Blue Network on February 11, 1940. It has built up a not only tremendous but vociferous following. This was formally demonstrated when a recent remark unleashed a storm of indignant mail that passed the 5,000 mark in little more than a week.

Said the chairman, "These sturdy little men on the sixth floor (his affectionate term for NBC vice presidents)," it was guilefully intimated, "were getting budget-minded again." But, by a wonderful coincidence, he continued, a` prospective sponsor had been found lurking in the rhythm section by a production man who had "been balancing a rubber ball on his nose."

"The sponsor," the chairman blandly added, "has asked if anyone else listens. If you must write two letters be sure to sign the second with a different name."

The letters poured in and the frantic writers offered to "eat dog biscuits," "drink eye wash," "munch sudsie soap flakes," or "anything," just as long as the program continued. If a sponsor was necessary, all they asked in return was that he extend the show to an hour.

The "Society" also caused the RCA Victor Recording Company to trim its "long hair" to the extent of having the "Basin Streeters" make two special albums for them which bear the "Society's name. Featuring Dinah Shore as soloist, the albums were made in response to numerous demands from record fans. Sales are zooming.

"Basin Street's" new "diva" is brown-eyed, ear-resistable Diane Courtney. She, too, has a classical background (and there's nothing the matter with the foreground, either), being a graduate of the New England Conservatory of Music. Just so you'll know, Diane's mother appeared for many seasons with the *Opera Comique* in Paris."

One of the more popular "chairmen" during the run of the program was <u>Dr.</u> Gino Hamilton, who was also intermission commentator with the tongue-in-cheek manner. Another singer who got some national attention on the program was Lena Horne. Dinah Shore was on the first recording by the "Society" with sax and trumpet player, Benny Carter and composer trumpeter W.C. Handy, who wrote *St. Louis Blues* and *Memphis Blues*. Handy wept when Dinah sang the latter and said, "It was never really sung before." In program lead-ins it was said that Dinah "starts fires by rubbing two notes together."

## "Bill Stern, the Colgate Shave-Cream Man Is On the Air... Bill Stern, the Colgate Shave-Cream Man with Stories Rare"

That singing opening for a sports program was just part of the unusual aspect of Bill Stern's presentation. *The Colgate Sports Newsreel Starring Bill Stern* ran weekly from the fall of 1939 until mid-year of 1951 and even though its ratings were consistently good, Stern never let the facts get in the way of what he considered to be entertainment. In their book, *The Big Broadcast*, Frank Buxton and Bill Owen referred to "flagrant fictionalization" and that may have been a very kind description.

Even Stern's own show-opening lines let you know you probably shouldn't be taking anything too seriously. He'd say, in his highly-charged, overly-dramatic style, "…featuring strange and fantastic stories – some legendary, some hearsay – but all so interesting, we'd like to pass them along to you."

Stern was always busy, broadcasting virtually every sport imaginable, so it wasn't possible for him to put together all the material for his far-fetched tales. Much of that duty fell on the shoulders of a writer named Mac Davis and more often than not he was the one who would come up with stories such as the baseball player who had a fatal heart attack between third and home and was dead when he fell across the plate with the winning run. Or, one of my favorites, that in his youth, Pope Pius XII had played baseball! How's that for a tenuous tie to sports?

In his book, *The Taste of Ashes*, Stern told how the style evolved. There weren't enough of the dramatic type stories he needed on the basis of two a week.

"Then the thought occurred to me that in movies of people whose stories lack dramatic elements the scenarios are "dressed up" to provide a punch. This is done constantly and with unrestrained imagination. In the theater it is known as dramatic license. Some magazines, particularly those catering to the motion picture trade, use the same technique without any repercussions whatsoever. Their forte is entertainment. So, too, in my mind, was this show of mine. Diversion was my stock in trade and I thrived, rightfully or not, on the same fanciful principles used by other communications media which lift audiences out of a humdrum, monotonous existence of mundane fact and insipid incident."

It all reminds me of a quotation by Sir James Matthew Barrie. It was aimed elsewhere but seemed fitting to also describe Stern.

"Facts were never pleasing to him. He acquired them with reluctance and got rid of them with relief. He was never on terms with them until he had stood them on their heads."

I recall once while working a Big 10 football game at the University of Illinois when Stern was there for network coverage. The broadcast booths were quite plain and one of Stern's first activities was to summon a maintenance man to do some remodeling of his site. He wanted a shelf built just so for some of his notes and was quite adamant about it until he got it the way he wanted.

Stern did some play-by play as early as 1925. He broadcast the first televised sporting event, the second game of a doubleheader between Princeton and Columbia in May, 1939 and in September of that year, also handled the first telecast of football action.

A story is told that once, while broadcasting a football game, Stern several times misidentified a back going for a long run for a touchdown. He realized his error just before the guy crossed the goal line and blithely announced the runner lateraled to the one who did score.

Sometime after that, horse racing's most prominent announcer, Clem McCarthy, called the wrong winner in the 1947 Preakness and had to correct it and apologize coast-to-coast for his mistake. Stern apparently badgered him about the error and McCarthy responded, "You can't lateral a horse, Bill."

## Daddy Went on a Trip and Things Changed!

The Boswell Sisters got a start on their musical careers practically right out of the cradle. Both parents were musicians and Martha, the oldest, Connie next and then Helvetia (Vet), got early exposure. However, it certainly wasn't the same music they did later. They started out playing stately minuets and some rather sedate classical selections on violin, cello and piano.

They had other notions, though, and when Daddy Boswell headed out from their southern home in 1926 for an extended business trip into Florida, the girls started playing some of the popular rhythms of the day on sax, banjo and piano. This brought on a desire to sing the tunes they were playing and all this led to their special brand of vocal harmonies in the time to come. A great many musicologists sate without equivocation that their stylings established a path for various groups to follow, the Andrews Sisters and many others, among them. The girls were separated in age by only a year between them and always did everything together, This created a symbiotic feeling that undoubtedly aided their vocal efforts.

They were three-quarters French and were brought up in a home that was rich in the cultural tradition of old New Orleans. All three played in the New Orleans Philharmonic Orchestra but close-harmony singing became ever more attractive to them. They got encouragement from cornetist Emmett Hardy.

Connie (later spelled "Connee") got polio during infancy and appeared in a wheel chair throughout her professional career. The sisters worked together until 1935, including tours of Europe in 1933 and 1935. After that, Connee worked solo and her popularity continued on radio, records and theater tours. She finally retired from touring in the 1950s but appeared as a guest star on many TV shows in the 1960s. Her radio credits included the *Kraft Music Hall* with Bing Crosby, and *Music That Satisfies* with "Street Singer" Arthur Tracy, Ruth Etting, her sisters and announcer Norman Brokenshire. The latter was sponsored by Chesterfield cigarettes on the NBC Red network in 1932.

All this was a far cry from their first professional appearances in vaudeville houses in and around New Orleans. But, those stage contacts let them make acquaintance with the microphone and that got them started on a road they traveled far, a road that might not have opened up for them if their father hadn't taken that extended business trip enabling them to begin establishing their own way through life.

## "The gaudiest, the most violent, the lonesomest mile in the world"

That's how Detective Danny Clover, played by Larry Thor, described his territory after first saying, "Broadway's My Beat." The radio crime drama ran from late February of 1949 until the first of August, 1954. The role of Clover was initially taken by Anthony Ross and the show originated in New York. However, just a few months later it switched to Hollywood and Thor played the lead.

The low-key open had its own panache with Clover intoning such thoughts as:

"In autumn sunlight the September day trots out its promises for Broadway's consideration, displays them in doorways, in push carts, in gutters, decorates them with price tags, invites you to browse – 'don't touch,' buy – 'don't squeeze,' and at cut rates of second-hand delights, the prices slashed down to any man's purse, the bold end of dreams. The vendors simper, the hawkers wink. Buy, kid. That's a winter's sun on your shoulder and the day is short, so buy. And that's whatcha do, kid, because on Broadway there's no other choice."

The opening theme was *I'll Take Manhattan* and those opening words made you want no part of it.

Clover would continue, "And at police headquarters, the September's day has arranged its wares of violence on your desk, stacked as to category, degree, grade. Because the day is still fresh, you put off the reaching for them, the touching of them, but it screams close to your ear…"

The phone would ring harshly and Clover would be introduced to the case of the day, one that often required a trip to the morgue.

When the show moved to Hollywood it was directed by the ever-excellent Elliott Lewis. He made every effort to recreate the sounds of the city, with raucous honking horns, the loudness of hurrying pedestrians, even the sound of raindrops on a drizzly day. Three sound effects specialists were required to keep pace with it all. It was a time of hard-boiled detective programs and *Broadway is*

*My Beat* was one of the best, right up to some of the closing lines by the flinty Detective Clover who had seen the seamy side of the city.

"When the night slips out of Broadway's fingers and the false dawn blurs the shadows, Broadway stands bewildered. A Carnival is run down. Only the stragglers walk it, with their step without pattern, like their dreams. And the color of their loneliness is the darkened neon, the last glow of a cigarette butt, and pavement grey. And they walk it. They never know Broadway's closed for the night."

It was quite a show, one that would likely have survived longer had it not come along as television was beginning to make its big inroads.

## In the Right Place at the Right Time

Sometime around 1933, Morton Downey had just arrived at a CBS studio to rehearse for one of his programs when the producer rushed up to him with the news that something had happened to the musical conductor. Downey, instead of insisting that another maestro be found in a hurry, looked over the first row violin section. He beckoned to one violinist sitting there and asked, "Do you think you can lead this band?" The answer came back, "Sure, I can."

That night the violinist conducted the orchestra for Downey. He was good and Mort insisted that he be made a conductor, not only for his show but for other CBS productions. The young violinist more than lived up to every expectation of Downey's. His name was Mark Warnow.

Perhaps best known for conducting the orchestra on *Your Hit Parade* during most of the 1940s, he also worked with the likes of Helen Hayes, Ed Wynn, John Charles Thomas, Stoopnagel and Budd and even did music for *Yours Truly, Johnny Dollar* in the early '50s.

When Warnow died suddenly in the fall of 1949 *Your Hit Parade* was left without a band leader. The assignment was offered to Raymond Scott and he stayed with it throughout the rest of the run on radio and on into television.

Scott's real name was Harry Warnow, and he was the younger brother of Mark. We found no specific reference as to why he changed his name but many felt it may have been because his brother achieved such acclaim first and he didn't want to be known as "Mark Warnow's kid brother."

## Name Changes Were Common

Here's one for you. His on-air name at the time was Walter Wilcox and he was the one and only member of the news staff, sports staff and was the news and sports announcer on KCMO in Kansas City. At the time, the station had only 100 watts of power and was on a split-time schedule. They were on the air from 6:00 to 9:00 in the morning, from noon to 3:00 and again from 6:00 to 9:00 p.m. The grandparents of young Wilcox lived less than a mile from the station transmitter and even if they could remember the broadcast hours they couldn't always pick up the signal. However, the station was owned by a friend of "machine politician" Tom Pendergast and "Boss Tom's" influence through a certain Senator (initials HST) was enough to eventually get the station granted 50,000 watts. By then, though, Walter Wilcox was long gone. Before he left, he twice voted illegally, on the same day! First of all, he hadn't been in Kansas City long enough to vote. Second, he had lied about his age to get the job and wasn't old enough to vote. But that didn't matter. Two Kansas City policemen took him to the polls, handed him a piece of paper with a name written on it and told him that's who he was. Wilcox went inside, was asked his name, glanced at the piece of paper and replied, "Anthony Lombardo." They looked up the name on the register and gave him a ballot. He was driven back to the radio station by the police but they returned later in the day and said his vote was needed again. Wilcox said later they at least didn't tell him how to vote – they just figured that his civic duty favoring Pendergast interests was assured because he worked at KCMO.

The station manager had given him the Wilcox name. Many radio stations in those days were afraid some of their talent might skip off to some other station. If so, the stations were determined they wouldn't take any fame with them because their name was "owned" by the originating station. The same thing, you may recall happened with "Sam 'n' Henry" at WGN in Chicago. They became "Amos 'n' Andy." The same sort of thing happened with young Wilcox. But, you know what, he moved on to considerable acclaim under his real name of Walter Cronkite, even if he did vote illegally *twice!* "…and that's the way it is."

## He Was There When it Happened!

His first action broadcast came in 1923. That's when Graham McNamee broadcast the middleweight boxing championship bout when Harry Greb took the title from Johnny Wilson. In the ensuing years McNamee broadcast under dangerous conditions – more than once he was injured. He had to make mad dashes by car and plane to get to the scene of vital happenings in time to get them on the air.

One of his mad airplane sprints had broadcasting officials behind the scenes considerably more excited and worried than his listeners had been for a long time. It was on the occasion of the famous long-count ring battle between Jack Dempsey and Gene Tunney in Chicago in 1927. There is another story concerning that disputed championship that is told in connection with Graham McNamee, but first we check on what took place at the St. Louis Radio Fair that year.

McNamee had been called to the Missouri city as one of the radio stars to appear at the show. The next day – the one on which the fight was to take place in Chicago – he was still detained at the show.

In the Illinois city, radio personnel were preparing the ringside press table for the NBC microphone through which McNamee would be providing his usual fast-moving, kaleidoscopic picture of an eagerly awaited championship bout.

The minute hand swept toward time for the main event and still no sign of the announcer. Officials grabbed telephones and frantically called St. Louis. Graham was nowhere to be found.

Finally, it was learned he had taken a plane to Chicago.

Plane riding was much less sure and safe in those days. Time was short. Other announcers and engineers fidgeted at ringside, ready to fill in if necessary.

Five minutes to go - four - three - two – one – and a broad-shouldered man elbowed his way down the aisle and slipped into his seat with seconds to spare before air time.

"Good evening, ladies and gentlemen of the radio audience…" and McNamee was on the air.

That was the famous decision championship in which there was much wrangling and accusation that if the referee hadn't taken extra time (because Dempsey didn't properly go to his corner after a knockdown) in counting out Tunney, then the Manassa Mauler would have kept his title. Some listeners even blamed McNamee for the long count. He had grown used to that sort of thing because he had been broadcasting World Series baseball from 1923 – all alone, incidentally – until 1928 and many were the deciding plays blamed on him by supporters of losing teams merely because he described them – a time-honored case of the blame-the-messenger syndrome.

Quite as dramatic in the field of heavyweight boxing was the finale of the Max Schmeling and Jack Sharkey fight. The German boxer had been dropped to the floor twisting in pain from what appeared to be a low blow. The bell rang ending the fourth round. Had the blow counted? Had Sharkey won? Here are actual excerpts from a transcription of what McNamee excitedly whipped into the microphone in those tumultuous seconds:

"Jack Sharkey is over in his corner…now for the first time Schmeling is able to take a little water, but his face is writhing in pain… it may be that Schmeling wins on a foul…I don't know yet…Yes! Schmeling wins the fight on a foul! Just a moment, I'll try to get Schmeling over here…"

McNamee leaped into the ring, microphone in hand, into the midst of a struggling mass of reporters, photographers, officials and trainers. But this was one time he didn't get a champion to speak, because the agonized German was half-carried from the ring, unable to say a word.

In August of 1935, the Soap Box Derby was held in Akron, Ohio and McNamee was there to cover it. What occurred sounds ridiculous, but it wasn't. It was serious business.

Youngsters from some fifty cities had brought their racers built from soap boxes, baby carriage wheels, etc. to compete in the race. McNamee and Tom Manning were at the mike at the bottom of the hill as the little cars, gaining amazing speed, swept down the course. Suddenly, one of the small vehicles, careening wildly, headed directly for the announcers. Before they jump aside, the car crashed into them, knocking them and the microphone to the ground.

McNamee didn't get up. He had been knocked unconscious, and stayed that way for five minutes. Small wonder, because the car, weighing 199 pounds, and bearing an 85-pound youngster, was traveling at 40 miles an hour when it struck.

Graham was taken to the Akron hospital where he was confined for three days. However, it wasn't until six weeks later, after a rest in his summer home, that the effects of a concussion completely left him.

Even before that Soap Box Derby injury, the announcer had been hurt because he stuck to the microphone.

The most thrilling of such experiences came upon the arrival of Charles Lindbergh in Washington after his daring non-stop solo flight across the Atlantic.

McNamee stood in the Washington Navy Yard behind Marines detailed to keep the crowds from breaking through to catch a glimpse of the hero. But, this was one time they didn't hold their ground.

The mob broke through the line of guards and rushed toward Lindbergh. Inevitably, down went McNamee holding fast to the microphone. By some good fortune, the mike cord wasn't broken or disconnected by the surging crowd. Heavy flying feet trod on McNamee, bruising him and tearing his clothes. Fighting his way upward, he eventually managed to regain an upright position, but not without his share of contusions.

He had not gone off the air for even a moment! While on his stomach, with feet trampling him, McNamee had continued to describe the scene.

In his own book, *You're On the Air*, published in 1926, McNamee expressed some personal feeling about broadcasting.

"We Americans are a practical people; we still want our romance, will always want it, but prefer it based on fact. And romance growing out of truth is more satisfying and casts a more magic spell. Perhaps that is why everywhere we see men of all sorts rushing into print – actors, authors, statesmen, pugilists, explorers, queens, courtesan, cooks and steeplejacks – consulting their little notebooks or ransacking their memories to tell the things they've done and seen and heard, of the great people they've met, backstairs gossip, or noble deeds performed in the fierce light that beats about a throne.

At first thought it would seem that there was little left for a broadcaster to tell. Still, we have two things on most of the other professions – a uniqueness and a certain mystery that can never die. Besides, no other calling is such a blending of romance, mechanics, and fact. And no other offers such opportunities for mingling in great happenings, for being behind the scenes at the great true dramas of the world. Constantly we see history being made.

It is unique, too, because of its numbers and youth. There are only twelve hundred broadcasters scattered among the five hundred and forty radio stations of the land; and only broadcasting was started by the first pioneers only a scant number of years ago. It seems perhaps much longer, now that so many millions are accustomed to tuning in each night; but, if you think back, you will remember that it was only in 1922 that you got your first radio set, something you put together yourself, if you were handy, or purchased somewhere under a manufacturer's label that is now forgotten. Not long after that the first radio magazine came out. In those few years fortunes have been made and lost, huge factories have sprung up all over the land, tens of thousands of radio stores have been opened, and the air is full of myriad voices spreading news and messages, music and song, to a listening world.

As for the mystery, there is little need to speak of that. Certainly it is a mystery still to me, standing by a tiny instrument of wires and springs, talking in ordinary tones and realizing I am heard by millions of people from three feet to three thousand miles away. I know you are sitting in little farmhouses or in city apartments with headphones over your ears, standing by loudspeakers in the city streets, or massed in great concert halls, all listening to what we say in quiet syllables, just as if we were talking to our wives. Yet we never see that vast audience, your massed faces, and you never see ours. We are voices out of the night, almost out of the unknown."

Columnist Ben Gross once sat beside Graham McNamee during a slow-moving, slovenly boxing exhibition that the announcer described as fast-paced, furious action. He wasn't faking, but was filled with great enthusiasm. Gross asked how he could make it sound so exciting when he knew very well it wasn't. McNamee replied, "I only tell it the way it looks to me."

## A Veteran Actress Who May Have Been the Best of All

Just imagine, a 70-year career acting in radio, stage, movies and television. That was the outstanding story of Jeanette Nolan, who died in 1998 at the age of 86. Not only marvelously talented, but she had one of the nicest personal attitudes of anyone you could ever hope to meet. She was the widow of actor John McIntire (among other things, the second wagon master on *Wagon Train*). This writer will never forget a few years back when their home was destroyed by fire in Malibu and she retained only a pistol from John's memorabilia. It happened shortly before an Old Time Radio convention and she could have easily canceled her appearance. She showed up, though, saying only that she had promised.

Her list of radio credits was astounding and included appearances on such programs as *Lux Radio Theater, Escape, Gunsmoke, Cavalcade of America, The Whistler, One Man's Family, Frontier Gentleman, Rogers of the Gazette, The Adventures of Sam Spade, Tarzan, The Sears Radio Theater, Pursuit* and the *March of Time*.

On the latter, one of her roles was to portray Eleanor Roosevelt and I believe she first met John on that program.

Jeanette's very first movie, now mind you (talk about an auspicious beginning), was in 1948 when she played Lady Macbeth opposite Orson Welles. Her later appearance on the big screen was a brief one as the mother of Robert Redford in *The Horse Whisperer*.

I shall never forget the extreme pleasure of having dinner with Jeanette and hearing some of her gentle remembrances. Like so many of the stars of yesteryear, she loved attending the various old time radio conventions and participating in the re-creations of old scripts. A goodly number of years back, she and Burgess Meredith performed a two-person script written by Himan Brown, creator of *Inner Sanctum*. Age-wise Meredith was a touch unsteady and had to be helped up onto the stage. But, when performance time came, the two were absolute magic. I still get goose-bumps when thinking about their superb performances. In my own mind, I class Jeanette Nolan with Agnes Moorehead and Mercedes McCambridge as perhaps the very greatest of all our radio actresses.

## WONDER WHAT THEY'D THINK NOW?

A magazine about the world of broadcasting, with emphasis on the technical aspects, established as far back as 1917. It was titled simply *Radio*, and your writer came across a copy from April of 1925 in which an editorial blasted away at commercialism. Of course, the first network wasn't until NBC's arrival in 1926 and things overall were often helter-skelter before that (even after that, for that matter). There was no way for the magazine to foresee all the forthcoming costs of having to pay actors, actresses, writers, directors, singers, musicians, comedians, etc. Be that as it may, a scathing viewpoint was expressed and they labeled it *Radiotorial Comment*.

"The greatest menace to the popularity of radio is its improper use of advertising. Once hailed as the broadcasters' salvation, because it promised to provide funds to meet the rising costs of studio maintenance, radiotising now threatens to destroy this wonderful new medium of public entertainment and instruction. "Whom the gods would destroy they first make mad." Surely, some of the station owners are going mad.

So insidious has been this progress of undermining general interest in radiocast programs that few yet seem to realize the danger which may come about from its abuse. The toll broadcaster is becoming increasingly bold in the direct sale of commodities, notwithstanding the implied governmental request that advertising by radio be indirect in its appeal.

From the standpoint of the good of radio we are not concerned with the ethics of the case. We are not interested in its competition with other advertising mediums. But we are disturbed by its disastrous effect in lessening the desire to listen to radio programs. People first endure, then resent, and finally shut off the offending station.

Toll broadcasting usually consists of a ten minute advertising talk interspersed between musical numbers which are announced as being under the auspices of the advertiser. For this publicity the advertiser pays from $100 to $1,500, depending upon the location of the station, the time of day and the power of the transmitting equipment.

A censor is supposed to pass upon the talk so as to tone down the intensity of its selling argument, but too often he seems to be blinded by commercialism. Consequently we are too familiar with the merits of Dr. Bluffum's magic cure for sciatica, how to use it, how quickly it gives relief, and where it might be bought. Everything is told except the price, which, as in trade association discussions, still seems to be taboo.

This evil is not yet here in sufficient force to do immediate harm. There is yet time to prevent its spread before it kills interest in radio. So far, comparatively few stations have employed to any great extent and some of the best stations refuse remuneration for putting on a program. Our stricture is intended merely as a warning to such stations as are overstepping the bounds.

Rightly conducted, radiotising may prove an effective means for financing a station. Wrongly conducted, it will kill the station's popularity. When good-will is changed to resentment a station loses its audience and consequently its value to the advertiser.

One reason for the decrease in the number of spontaneous applause cards is that many people already sense the fact that their interest in radio is being capitalized by some of the radiocast stations. While everyone realizes that some means must be found for supporting stations it is obvious that flagrant advertising will fail to accomplish this purpose.

From present indications all the stations, like Gaul, may soon be divided into three classifications according to whether they are conducted by radio manufacturers, by religious or educational institutions, or by toll broadcasters. The order of listing is probably representative of relative public favor. Unless extreme care is exercised the toll broadcaster will degenerate into the same class as the advertising movie in which advertisements are sandwiched between parts of a picture shown in public waiting rooms.

Radio is too fine a thing, it has too great possibilities in the advancement of human welfare, to be prostituted to such base ends. If this practice continues to increase, if the warnings are not heeded, the public will realize it is being imposed upon and turn to other forms of entertainment."

Somehow, the anonymous writer of that column had missed out on any classes in economics. Without a means of producing income, most of those early stations would have eventually had to fold their tent and depart the scene. As they say, hindsight is 20/20, but foresight? Well, after all, it <u>was</u> 1925 when that article was printed.

## The several gentlemen known as Deems Taylor

If you could have known Deems Taylor, you would have known a great many men in one. You would have known an eminent composer, a music critic, a journalist, a popular radio commentator and master of ceremonies, an able translator of French, Italian and German songs, a good cook, a casual carpenter, a war correspondent, a humorist. The man, Deems Taylor, was indeed a man of parts. You could go on almost indefinitely enumerating them.

There was, for example, Deems Taylor, the prophet.

"Radio," asserted the astute Mr. Taylor, "is finished. In two years it will be all washed up."

It was back in 1925, or thereabouts, that he made that astounding prophecy in an article for the old *New York World*. He proved it, too. "People," said Mr. Taylor, "will get sick of clamping on headpieces to hear ghastly squawks over the reluctant ether." Turned out to be true enough. "Besides," went on our prophet, "stars aren't going to go on the air for nothing." Right again – they certainly didn't! "And furthermore," Mr. Taylor elucidated, "the business of buying parts and assembling your own radio is a passing fad." And so it was.

Radio, however, defied his logical conclusions. For which Deems Taylor offered honest thanks.

Because, two years later, in 1927, he became the first commentator for the Columbia Broadcasting System on its initial network broadcast. So great was his enthusiasm, matched by that of his friend, orchestra conductor Howard Barlow, that they ran their program forty-five minutes beyond their allotted time. That, too, couldn't happen today!

In ten years after that eventful date, Deems Taylor became an increasingly important figure in the radio world. He supplied radio scripts, dramatizations, wrote dialogue and librettos, acted as commentator and master of ceremonies, was consultant/adviser and co-ordinator of music for numerous radio programs.

In February of 1938 he was appearing with the Andre Kostelanetz Orchestra on *The Chesterfield Hour* and also with the Philharmonic

Symphony Orchestra. He had just finished writing a book on music and was composing a new opera for the Metropolitan.

The one career he definitely abandoned was that of architecture, his original goal. What happened? Well, in his senior year at New York University he was sort of conscripted to write the music for a class play. He did it – the show was a hit and he wrote several shows. A scout heard one of them and procured a Broadway engagement. He wasn't able to sell another show but he was turned away from building with wood and stone to building with tone and harmony.

After graduating and being a devotee of three meals a day, Taylor took on whatever jobs he could get.

First, he was a commercial artist, then he worked on a couple of encyclopedias, got a job on *Western Electric News* and won a $300 prize for writing a symphonic poem. Along about 1916, Deems and Robert Benchley were editing the Sunday magazine of the old *New York Tribune* when Taylor got the notion that he should go to France as a war correspondent, even though he was an ardent pacifist. He came home in 1917 and became assistant editor of *Collier's Weekly*. It appeared he was always being thrust into jobs for which he had no proper preparation. But the Army was not to be one of them. His draft number was drawn on Armistice Day in 1918 and he didn't have to go.

To shorten the story somewhat, his first commercial radio assignment was on the *Kraft Hour* with Paul Whiteman in 1933. In '34 he did scripts and dramatizations for a ten week series of opera in English for the *Chase and Sanborn Guild*. He had a similar assignment in '35 on Sigmund Romberg's *Swift Hour*. In 1937 he did the *World Peaceways* scripts for the *Squibb* program.

He wrote a book based on some of his on-air music commentaries and discovered a lot of rewrite was necessary to make his radio comments suitable for book purposes.

He said, "We actually have two languages – we write one and speak the other. That is the essence of the trouble with most radio commercials. They're written by advertising writers who are accustomed to write for the eye and not for the ear. You'd never read a printed advertisement aloud. It would sound absurd – phony. And that's the way the commercials sound – all the fake enthusiasm.

We simply don't talk as we write – we use broken phrases, unfinished sentences, repetition."

Added Taylor, "When I'm writing my radio scripts, I always talk them aloud. I guess the people in my hotel think I'm mad! I pace up and down talking to myself. If I just wrote the thing, it wouldn't sound right when I read it over the microphone. I've always written my own scripts," he explained. "I can't sound convincing reading someone else's words. Only an actor can do that. I may be an entertainer, but I'm certainly no actor. The radio is the greatest lie detector there is. That's why political speeches on the air always sound so phony." (NOTE: Wouldn't it be something if he could hear some of today's political postulations?)

However poor a prophet Deems Taylor might have been, you could appreciate the soundness of his judgment by hearing him on the air. He was quietly sincere, human, delightful and with a rare, unquenchable humor. However slight your own knowledge of music was, there was no difficulty in enjoying Deems Taylor. And it was really a remarkable feat, making music a delight to people who knew little about it.

Radio, itself, did this, said Taylor. "It brings music to everyone. People who would hesitate to go to opera who fear they might be bored, will listen to it in their homes. That is because there's no compulsion about it. If they don't like it, they can turn the dial and shut it off. They don't have to take it if they don't want it. So, they're willing to listen to it – and they find they enjoy it."

Giving further evidence of the aforementioned sense of humor, later in his career Taylor was the occasional foil on such shows as *Duffy's Tavern*, appeared as one of the "arm chair" crime solvers on *Ellery Queen* and contributed his erudition on *Information Please*.

Not bad for an embryonic architect who became transformed into an eminent musician. What made his career all the more amazing is that he didn't come from a particularly musical family and he had had only vocal lessons at age eighteen. And although he wrote music for those mentioned class plays he didn't study harmony until two years after he graduated. With all his accomplishments it would have been easy to report, "The public "deems" Taylor first-rate!"

## Chester and Norris Became Two of Radio's Best-Loved Characters

"Chet" Lauck was "Lum Edwards" and Norris Goff was "Abner Peabody" on the delightful down-home program, *Lum and Abner*, characters and show ideas they hadn't originally intended.

In mid-April of 1931, they headed into Hot Springs, Arkansas to be on a KTHS flood relief program and they had planned to appear as a blackface act. However, there were so many of those (most likely due to the success of *Amos 'n' Andy*) that they decided to do their bit as rural characters instead. Shortly before airtime they were asked what they wanted to be called. They responded with no previous forethought when Lauck said, "I'll be Lum Edwards," and Goff chimed in, "I'll be Abner Peabody." So, they were introduced by station manager, Cam Arnoux, as "Lum and Abner." But, they had to wait a bit to get much notice because technical difficulties knocked the station off the air after ten minutes.

They began gaining more and more attention, though. This resulted in a network audition (NBC) and finally a 13-week deal with Quaker Oats for a summer replacement show. After they went through with that contract, they decided on their famed "Jot 'Em Down Store" in the non-existent town of Pine Ridge. In April of 1936, Waters, Arkansas officially changed its name to Pine Ridge.

That same year, the bucolic duo wound up number four on the national list of favorite comedians in a poll by *Radio Guide*. They beat out such folks as Fibber McGee and Molly, Easy Aces, Amos 'n' Andy and Fred Allen. They were behind only Jack Benny, Eddie Cantor and Burns and Allen.

Part of the promotion of their program involved putting out the "Jot 'em Down Store Catalogue, Calendar & Game and Party Book," described as "being a compilation of things about Pine Ridge, Arkansas and also the best darn catalogue ever put out by a store." In it, they explained why they put it out.

"For the past two-three years we been putting out a little book, full of eddication and information useful and endurin. Folks have ritten in sayin they'd like another until they must be a whole barrel of letters back in the feed room. Well, this year, when it came inventory time (which means countin what you haven't sold and wonderin when you're ever goin to) we decided to put out a catalogue fer the folks. Only have a calendar and games and parties and everthing we could think of in it, too, makin it the best catalogue anybody ever put out, I grannies.

To make everthing legal and right we have looked over other big catalogues and find out that they allus start out with some testimonies about character and when started and honesty. We have dug up some very good testimonies fer us and we will put them in right here.

Jot 'em Down Store, located Pine Ridge, Ark., got name from fact everthing on strickly credit basis so Abner couldn't make mistakes in change. Props. Lum Edwards; Abner Peabody. (That's us). First testimony from Luther Phillips. Traded with us seven years. He sez, "Wouldn't take a million dollars for my pair of leather work gloves bought yr store. They are fine."

Next from Cedric Weehunt. Traded with us since old enough to earn money. Sez, "My favorite place is the candy counter. Oh, them lickrish sticks."

Squire Skimp, who came to Pine Ridge five years ago, sez, "Nothin beats Lum Edwards and Abner Peabody's strawberry plants. I will recommend them to one and all as well as all my friends and constituents."

Luke Spears has this to say about us, "The Jot 'em Down Store is the greatest store I've ever seen and I been all over the state of Arkansas." Luke is a well traveled man so his words count.

One of our finest testimonies comes from Grandpappy Spears. He sez, "I never bin in a more comfortable place fer fightin the Civil War than the Jot 'em Down Store. I've fit ever battle from Bull Run to Appomattox settin right alongside your stove. Only complaint I kin make is you don't keep the cracker barrel handy enough to the stove."

P.S. We'll put the fi-nance report of the store later on in the book. It ain't added up yet."

The two gentle, amusing visitors eventually were bringing their kindly characters to millions of Americans every week. In about 1967, some 13-years after the program had gone off the air, Chet Lauck had returned to Arkansas and was with a PR firm in Hot Springs. He talked about those wonderful years.

C.L. We had been doing some amateur theatrics in the area when we got our chance on that Hot Springs station and right then switched over to the rural idea. After we got our show for Quaker Oats the network wanted a copy of the script but we'd been adlibbing up till then and had to come up with a script for them. We got some great exposure on the Red and Blue Networks and then a prestige thing in 1932, when we signed with Ford Motor Company for two or three years. We went from that to Horlick's Malted Milk to General Foods to Alka-Seltzer and to General Motors, one of our last sponsors.

TDOY: Was there any great difficulty in doing the shows live?

C.L. I didn't mind the actual broadcast. No sponsor would let you record – we argued with them – but they insisted on live and that's what they got. In Hollywood, we had to do two shows because of the time difference – 3:15 and 6:15 we did them.

TDOY: What single event do you remember most about your broadcast career?

C.L. Well, of course, now it's old hat, but in 1938 I believe it was, we were the first to do our broadcast from London and Chicago at the same time. I was in London, Tuffy (Norris' nickname) was in Chicago and we did the program on NBC and British radio.

TDOY: Were there any unique technical problems getting a show such as yours on the air in the early days?

C.L. No, but, of course, the old mikes – old carbon mikes – weren't as sensitive as today's microphones and I imagine a great many in our audience were still listening on an old crystal set. We used to have to create our own sound effects. We spent more time trying to improvise something for a certain sound effect than we actually did on or program.

TDOY: When you first went on the air were you surprised at the amount of hero worship radio stars were given?

C.L. I really was and I never ceased to be. I remember back – I guess back in 1933 – we started making some personal appearances. We broadcast five nights a week and then we'd go on Saturdays and Sundays and play theaters all through Ohio, Kentucky, Indiana, Illinois, that area. I never ceased to be amazed by the number of people who came out to see what we looked like. We had never released any publicity pictures showing that we were young fellows and when we did a skit in character in costume and makeup and then took it off and came back out straight there was an amazed audience. They just couldn't believe we were young. When we started making movies it use to, take about 2 ½ hours to make me up for the part of Lum. My hairline was too youthful and my hair was perfectly black and I had no wrinkles. They'd spend a lot of time putting wrinkles in my face and putting on a gray wig and a more elderly hairline. Now, I'm pretty sure I could just walk through the makeup room and right on to the set without any problem. (chuckle)

TDOY: Where did you get the many ideas for your episodes?

C.L. It was just off the top of our heads, just using an acute imagination I think we both had – <u>must</u> of had to keep it going 24 years. Of course, we'd reach an impasse on occasion and just didn't know where to go with it. We developed a method when we'd hit a center" like that and we'd just sit down and start writing and pretty soon something would evolve out of it.

TDOY: The early programs were all fifteen minutes?

C.L. Yes, then starting in 1948 we <u>did</u> do a 30-minute show for Frigidaire one a week when we had a full cast. We had Zasu Pitts and Andy Devine and Cliff Arquette and a fellow named Opie Cates – he was from Arkansas, too – had the orchestra. That was our regular cast and occasionally we'd have guests.

TDOY: Do people still primarily associate you with the role you once played?

C.L. Yes, they do and often people will subconsciously call me "Lum" and apologize for it. I tell them not to apologize – that old fellow was pretty good to me – you can call me "Lum" any time you want to.

TDOY: Is there anything you regret about your years as Lum?

C.L. Well, I think we maybe took it maybe too much for granted. It rocked on for so long that maybe we didn't give it as much effort as we should have. We had the advantage of already being established when competition came along. Maybe we didn't work as hard at it as we should of, but maybe that was good. Sometimes when you try <u>too</u> hard on a radio program, or whatever, it reflects it in the production.

TDOY: Any parting words?

C.L. I'd like to see radio come back as it once was, knowing full well it can't happen. Like I've said, and lots of others have said, radio could really stir up your imagination. It was so vivid that folks everywhere could enjoy it even if they weren't "seeing" the same thing in their mind's eye. I never understood why management in radio turned tail and ran when television came along. I still think they had the greatest medium. I think we had more loyal fans than there are in television. Not many TV shows are a "must," but for certain shows on radio the fans wouldn't have missed it under any circumstances.

## "How 'bout that?"

Melvin Israel (Mel Allen) died at the age of 82. His was one of the most distinctive voices in the history of baseball broadcasting.

He was the "voice of the Yankees" for many years and his signature line, "How *'bout* that?" delivered in his Alabama drawl, became as well-known as some of the players he talked about. He started traveling with the Yankees doing road games live in 1946. Before that, they'd been done as re-creations from the studio.

He'd always wanted to do sports and he broadcast University of Alabama football games on a Birmingham station while he was going to school getting a law degree.

After he graduated in 1936 he went to New York and got a job at CBS for $45 a week. The net requested his name change because they thought the Jewish name might become a hindrance top his career. So, he chose his father's middle name. In 1939, he became assistant sportscaster to Arch McDonald doing home games for the Yankees and Giants. A year later McDonald went back to Washington and Mel became the principal broadcaster.

Prior to his death in mid-1996, Mel was the voice on the weekly syndicated TV program *This Week in Baseball*, and was planning work on another baseball project in the week that followed his death.

One time, on a program following Pabst Blue Ribbon fights on CBS, Mel was interviewing an All-America football player. He had a habit of offering his guests one of his sponsor's cigars. This time it backfired! The football star pushed the box of cigars away and said, "No, sir, I never touch those things – they make me sick." So, even the best could be caught with egg on his face, but it didn't take away from the professionalism.

Another sportscasting legend, the late Red Barber, told in his book, *The Broadcasters*, about the sad end of Allen's days with the Yankees in 1964. Then-Yankee owner Dan Topping told Red, "I had Mel in here this morning and told him he is through – that I was tired of his popping off – that if we win the pennant I have already nominated Rizzuto to the Commissioner to announce the World Series as our representative."

Barber wrote that he was sorry to hear it – that he knew what the Yankee job meant to Mel Allen and knew what the broadcast of the Series meant to him. "His job was his life – the wife and children he never had. It was that much to the man."

Barber added, "Mel developed a habit of walking into the play-by-play booth at the last minute – I mean the very last minute. At the Stadium, his brother, Larry, would have his scorecard in order, waiting for him. On the road, Mel often penciled in the batting orders while announcing the first inning. I never asked him why he cut it so close, but I sensed it gave him an "entrance." Mel would suddenly appear out of nowhere. His chair would be empty – then he was in it – 'Hello, everybody…this is Mel Allen.'

In another portion of the book, Red wrote, "In 1954, Mel Allen was at the top of his career, an excellent announcer. The only criticism anyone ever heard of Mel in those days was his deep devotion to the Yankees and their well-being, but I always thought he had that under control. After all, the woods were full of Yankee haters, and their wrath fell mainly on Allen. There was no fault to be found with Mel's mike ability, or his voice, or his reliability."

How *'bout* that?

## A couple of close friends with compassion

Comedians Eddie Cantor and Jimmy Durante were close friends and over the years they made a lot of appearances together at benefits, on radio, etc. and they always revived some of their old routines and had a great time doing it. Once, for example, on New Year's Day, 1943, they bumped into one another in Florida. Durante said a local hotel had been taken over by the government and turned into a hospital for wounded servicemen and that it would be a good idea to go over and entertain them. So, they did, with some clowning and kidding and even reminisced about the time Cantor said he convinced Durante they should run for President and Vice-President. "We should be together in Washington, Jimmy. Think of it –with my eyes and your nose, what I couldn't see, you could smell!" They started their funfest at 10:30 in the morning and didn't wrap it up until dinner time for the patients at 5:30 in late afternoon. Cantor said they were both so hoarse they could hardly talk, especially Jimmy, who started off hoarse in his regular voice. As they walked down the street, he could barely croak but managed to say, "Eddie, tell me, don't a t'ing like dis make ya feel _good_?"

Just as they both made millions feel good for so many years!

## The Unbelievable "Reach" of Radio

Here's another quick note about Cantor. There are probably as many ways to talk about the fantastic power of Old Time radio as there are people to talk about it, but ol' "Banjo Eyes" once hit it right on the nose.

Eddie Cantor said, "To any ham who takes life from an audience, just think what this type of mass communications means. Say you played a Ziegfeld show at the New Amsterdam Theater which seats 1,600. In a week, including matinees, you play to a total of 13,000, including the standees. Play that Ziegfeld show for fifty weeks, you would play to 650,000. If you played for ten years, you'd play to six and a half million. In twenty years it would be thirteen million, and if you played for <u>forty years</u>, to packed houses, standing room only, you'd play to less people in that four decades than you played to in one night on *The Chase and Sanborn Hour*!!

That kind of statistics gives a small idea of what it was really like in the Golden Age of radio!

## A Different View on Old Time Radio and Its Many Uses
In wartime it was more than just an entertainment device

A man named Harry Bannister began a career in radio in 1930, starting in Detroit at WMBC and WJR. Brief apprenticeship there led him to WWJ as a salesman, and over a 22-year period he went on to become general sales manager and eventually general manager. In 1952 her went to New York as NBC vice-president in charge of Station Relations. In a 1965 book, *The Education of a Broadcaster*, he told an interesting story about how World War II made changes in radio operations. Here's how he described it.

"I was busy playing croquet one Sunday when I was called to the telephone. It was the announcer on duty at WWJ. He said, "Harry, just got a flash from NBC. The Japanese bombed Pearl Harbor a while ago."

The import of this news failed to register and I well remember my reaction: 'The damn fools! What did they do that for?' So, the war came to WWJ and to me.

Next day I began putting the station on a war basis. I stopped all entry to the station by unauthorized persons, which was a blow to the sightseers who came daily in droves. I canceled or changed every program that had a "free" microphone offering access to outsiders. Ty Tyson's *Man on the Street* went off. So did a number of audience participation shows which were broadcast from our auditorium. An armed guard was installed at the transmitter, 24 hours a day, and electronic controls were placed on the transmitter building doors so that admittance was possible only after recognition by the engineers on duty. Extended emergency power was provided at both transmitter and studio so that both operations could continue indefinitely if there was any interruption in the power supply.

We immediately put on the air our first programs to sustain the war effort. The number of these was to increase steadily in the next four years. We went after recruitment of doctors, dentists, nurses and other specialists. We promoted employment at the war plants, collection of scrap materials, letters to servicemen and many other causes.

Perhaps the most important and fruitful field in which WWJ could function effectively was in the sale of war bonds. The Michigan bond drive was directed by Frank Isbey, who told me repeatedly that WWJ was the most potent single instrument at his disposal, more so than any other radio station or newspaper.

Wartime operations posed many problems, but perhaps the most vexing one was personnel as many individuals were called for military duties. Quality went down as a result.

Newscast and news commentaries were added all over the schedule, there being an apparently insatiable appetite for this type of programming both by the audience and by prospective sponsors."

Operations of a similar nature took place in broadcast facilities around the nation. There were many who didn't know where Pearl Harbor was but realized the major import and possible danger.

## It Was Probably the Most Popular Radio Show of All Time

I may be one of the few (if any) people still alive who had the opportunity to meet and talk with Charles Correll, who was "Andy" of the famed *Amos 'n' Andy* program that had begun in Chicago in the 1920's. He and Freeman Gosden had begun their long-lasting series as *Sam 'n' Henry* on WGN. When they got an opportunity to branch out and syndicate the program, WGN gave them their release but said the *Sam 'n' Henry* title belonged to the station. They apparently thought they might do a similar show under that name. After much pondering over possible new names, Correll and Gosden established themselves as *Amos 'n' Andy* and no one ever heard of either Sam or Henry again.

It was a long time ago and there have been many changes in national thought patterns that caused the eventual demise of their program. They did it in blackface and in dialect and such a program is definitely politically incorrect now. However, Charles Correll told me his partner was quite bitter over the fact their show was considered racist in some quarters. It actually was a situation comedy before that term had even been invented. It would have been funny in whatever form it was presented because the situations were funny.

To give an idea of the nationwide popularity, it is said the largest audience Johnny Carson ever had during his tenure on *The Tonight Show* was the night Tiny Tim married Miss Vicki on the program and rating figures indicated 40-million people were tuned in. By contrast, when there were far fewer people in the nation, *Amos 'n' Andy* averaged 40-million listeners every night.

Correll's home town was Peoria and his first youthful job there was delivering newspapers. His father and uncles were in the construction business and when he got old enough he did work of that kind. He really wanted to be an actor, though, and to partially satisfy the longing he played the piano at night for silent movies at a local theater. He danced in contests and won often, with prizes consisting of maybe a sack of corn meal, canned goods, or whatever. He acted in local plays, sang in quartets, or did just about anything else to satisfy his longing for show business. Finally, a break came when a professionally produced show passed through and Correll got a part. He did well enough that he was offered a chance to take a road company of the production, rehearse it and stage it. He immediately accepted and it was a couple of years after that when he was in Durham, North Carolina doing rehearsals for the stage presentation. Call it fate if you wish, but that's where he met another young guy by the name of Freeman Gosden and a relationship began that resulted in a program that became a national phenomenon. During their heyday, movie theaters across the land would stop the film at air time of the radio show and put it on the speakers. Otherwise, they'd lose business with movie-goers who would have stayed home glued to their radio sets. Many department stores also piped in the broadcast.

None of their performances matched a warmly appealing episode that became so popular it was repeated each year at Christmas time. Freeman Gosden, enacting the role of "Amos," lovingly explained the Lord's Prayer to his daughter, Arbadella. It happened on Christmas Eve and Arbadella had requested the radio be turned on and was asking questions before going to bed.

It began with the sound of the radio being tuned in and the announcer saying, "The Christmas Choir continues with the Lord's Prayer." The script then continued.

Arbadella: Daddy, could you get some Christmas music on the radio?

Amos: Why, darling, this is the very best Christmas music you could get. They're going to sing the Lord's Prayer.

Arbadella: Oh, I can say the Lord's Prayer with Mommy, she's been teaching it to me.

Amos: Yes, I know.

Arbadella: What does the Lord's Prayer mean, daddy?

Amos: Well, it means an awful lot and with the world like it is today, it seems to have a bigger meaning than ever before.

Arbadella: But, what does the Lord's Prayer *really* mean, Daddy?

Amos: The Lord's Prayer…well, darling, I'll explain it to you.

Arbadella: Oh, will you, daddy?

Amos: Yeah. Now, you lay down and you listen. Now, the first line of the Lord's Prayer is this...*Our father which art in Heaven*...now, that means father of all that is good where no wrong can ever dwell. And then it says...*Hallowed be thy name*. Now, that means, darling, that we should love and respect all that is good. And then it says after that...*Thy Kingdom come, thy will be done in earth as it is in Heaven*...and that means, darling, as we clean our hearts with the love, the good, the true and the beautiful, then earth where we are now will be just like Heaven.

Arbadella: That would be wonderful, Daddy.

Amos: Then it says...*Give us this day our daily bread*. Now, that means to feed our hearts and minds with kindness, with love and with courage, which will make us strong for our daily tasks. And then, after that, the next line of the Lord's Prayer is...*And forgive us our debts as we forgive our debtors*. Do you remember the Golden Rule?

Arbadella: Yes, Daddy.

Amos: Well, that means that we must keep the Golden Rule and do unto others as we would want them to do unto us. And then it says...*And lead us not into temptation, but deliver us from evil*. Now, that means, my darling, to ask God to help us do and to see and to think right so that we will neither be led nor tempted by anything that is bad. *For thine is the kingdom, the power and the glory forever. Amen.* That means, darling, that all the world and everything in it belongs to God's kingdom...everything...your mommy, your daddy, your little brother, your sister, your grandma, you and everybody. And, as we know that and act as if we know it, that, my darling daughter, is the real spirit of Christmas.

Arbadella: That's good, daddy.

And, so it was.

The choir voices on the radio rose in conclusion to a very memorable and touching feature that could well be better for modern broadcasting than many of the programs now prevalent. It's easy to understand why Gosden was so disturbed about criticisms of their program based on accusations of racism. As a side note, noted British author/playwright, George Bernard Shaw, said after a visit to the U.S., that there were three things he would never forget about America, "Niagara Falls, the Rocky Mountains and *Amos 'n' Andy*."

The show had an unusual twist on November 22, 1935 as Gosden and Correll missed their first program in eight years. They had gone on a successful hunting trip to Maryland, bagging four turkeys and the limit of pheasants. They were so engrossed that time passed more quickly than they realized. It was almost dusk when Gosden ("Amos") said, "We'll never make it." Correll ("Andy"), who had let the hunting expedition crowd out thoughts of the program, responded, "Make what?" Then, the situation dawned on him and they decided the only thing to do was to call Washington where they were due to originate that evening's performance. Announcer Bill Hay would normally introduce them with, "Heah they ah," but he couldn't that night. Frantic network personnel dug out file biographies and Hay apologized as he spent the air time telling about the stars. So it was that the principals were absent for the 2,202$^{nd}$ episode of *Amos 'n Andy*.

In those days, the competing radio ratings services were Crossley and Hooper. Then, as now, nothing provoked more debate and resentment than the various means of determining audience size. Back then, it was done by making random phone calls. C.W. Hooper himself once appeared on *We The People* to demonstrate how the sample was put together for his Broadcast Audience Measurement.

Calling a person at random, he asked, "What program are you listening to?"

The studio audience burst into raucous laughter when the voice replied, *"Amos 'n' Andy."* Hooper himself got a Hooper rating of 13 while *Amos 'n' Andy* got a 30.

## "A Day Which Will Live in Infamy."

The day after the bombing, December 8, 1941, the nation listened quietly as President Franklin D. Roosevelt spoke to a joint session of Congress and declared a state of war. It will take you less time to read it than it did for him to deliver it in solemn, measured tones. The speech was intentionally kept to only about six and a half minutes as the President felt the abbreviated address would have greater impact that way. Here's what the world heard:

"Mr. Vice President, Mr. Speaker, members of the Senate and the House of Representatives: Yesterday, December 7th, 1941 – a date which will live in infamy – the United States of America was suddenly and deliberately attacked by naval and air forces of the Empire of Japan.

The United States was at peace with that nation, and, at the solicitation of Japan, was still in conversation with its Government and its Emperor looking toward the maintenance of peace in the Pacific. Indeed, one hour after Japanese air squadrons had commenced bombing in the American island of Oahu, the Japanese Ambassador to the United States and his colleague delivered to our Secretary of State a formal reply to a recent American message. And while this reply stated that it seemed useless to continue the existing diplomatic negotiations, it contained no threat or hint of war or of armed attack.

It will be recorded that the distance of Hawaii from Japan makes it obvious that the attack was deliberately planned many days or even weeks ago. During the intervening time the Japanese Government has deliberately sought to deceive the United States by false statements and expressions of hope for continued peace.

The attack yesterday on the Hawaiian Islands has caused severe damage to American naval and military forces. I regret to tell you that very many America lives have been lost. In addition, American ships have been reported torpedoed on the high seas between San Francisco and Honolulu.'

Yesterday, the Japanese Government also launched an attack against Malaya.

Last night Japanese forces attacked Hong Kong.

Last night Japanese forces attacked Guam.

Last night Japanese forces attacked the Philippine Islands.

Last night the Japanese attacked Wake Island.

And this morning the Japanese attacked Midway Island.

Japan has, therefore, undertaken a surprise offensive extending throughout the Pacific area. The facts of yesterday and today speak for themselves. The people of the United States have already formed their opinions and well understand the implications to the very life and safety of our nation.

As Commander-in-Chief of the Army and Navy, I have directed that all measures be taken for our defense.

But always will our whole nation remember the character of the onslaught against us. No matter how long it may take to overcome this premeditated invasion, the American people in their righteous might will win through to absolute victory.

I believe that I interpret the will of the Congress and of the people when I assert that we will not only defend ourselves to the uttermost but will make it very certain that this form of treachery shall never again endanger us.

Hostilities exist. There is no blinking of the fact that our people, our territory and our interests are in grave danger.

With confidence in our armed forces – with the unbounding determination of our people – we will gain the inevitable triumph – so help us God.

I ask that the Congress declare that since the unprovoked and dastardly attack by Japan on Sunday, December 7th, 1941, a state of war has existed between the United States and the Japanese Empire."

# Index

## A

Abbott, Bud 18
Ace, Goodman 185
Acuff, Roy 78
Adams, Cedric 56, 57, 58
*Aldrich Family* 74, 76
Allen, Fred 59, 60, 107, 164, 168, 194, 239
Allen, Gracie 69
Allen, Mel 244, 245
*Ambassador East* 7
Ameche, Don 10, 161
Ameche, Jim *10, 161, 174*
*Amos 'n' Andy* 16, 52, 65, 194, 225, 239, 250
Anderson, Arthur 30
Andre, Pierre 172
Andrews Sisters 28, 29, 220
Andrews, Archie 74, 128, 130
Andrews, Robert Hardy 11

*Aragon Ballroom* 7, 177
Arden, Eve 133, 188
*Armstrong, Jack* 9, 10, 11, 12, 67, 174
Arnold, Eddie 78

## B

*Baby Snooks* 16, 19, 134
Baer, Parley 51, 151
Bailey, Bob 149
Bailey, Jack 6
Baker, Phil 197
Ballinger, Art 4
Bannister, Harry 248
Barber, Red 244
Barnet, Charlie 175

Barrymore, John 137, 167
Bartell, Harry 147
Baruch, Andre 17, 169
Baruck, Allan 172
Basie, Count 176
Beals, Dick 128
Beck, Jackson 133
Beemer, Brace 97, 99, 100
Benny, Jack 68, 75, 146, 188, 194, 239
Bergen, Candice 49
Bergen, Edgar 49, 196
*Big Town* 133
Billsbury, Rye 10
Blanc, Mel 109, 137
*Bob and Ray* 210, 211, 212
Borge, Victor 17
Boswell Sisters 28, 220
Boswell, Connee 220
Bowes, Major 171
Brice, Fanny 19
*Broadway's My Beat* 127, 222
Brokenshire, Norman
Brown, Himan 1, 161, 231
Brown, Les 176
*Burns and Allen* 69, 109, 133, 239
Burns, Bob 190
Burns, George 188
Burroughs, Edgar Rice 136
Busse, Henry 7

## C

*Camel Caravan* 201
Canova, Judy 109, 133

Cantor, Eddie 107, 148, 197, 246, 247
Caray, Harry 153, 155
Carle, Frankie 177, 178, 179
Carter, Boake 16
Cavett, Dick 99
*Challenge of the Yukon* 100
*Chamber Music Society Of Lower Basin Street* 215
*Chez Paree* 7
*Cocoanut Grove* 177
Collins, Dorothy 6, 16
Collins, Ted 64
Colman, Ronald 16, 84
Conrad, William 53, 55, 149
Conreid, Hans 109
Conway, Tim 16
Correll, Charles 5
Corsia, Ted de 164
Corwin, Norman 213
Costello, Lou 18
Cotsworth, Staats 111
Cronkite, Walter 103
Crosby, Bing 53, 169, 190, 220
Crosby, Bob 176
Cugat, Xavier 17
Cullen, Bill 158

## D

*Dailey's Frank Meadowbrook* 175
Daly, John Charles 17
DeMille, Cecil B. 13
Diamond, Richard 149
Donald, Peter 16
Dorsey, Jimmy 7

Dorsey, Tommy 7, 43, 142, 176
Douglas, Paul 10, 201, 202
Downey, Morton 224
Downs, Hugh 157
Dragonette, Jessica 17, 181, 183
*Duffy's Tavern* 207
Durante, Jimmy 166, 167, 246

**E**
Eddy, Nelson 91, 99
Ellington, Duke 7, 177
Elliott, Bob 210
Elman, Dave 115, 116
*Escape* 51, 127, 128, 147, 151, 231

**F**
Fennelly, Parker 59
Fenneman, George 17
*First Nighter* 51, 52, 174
Flynn, Charles 10
Ford, "Senator" Ed 20
Foy, Fred 97, 100
*Front Page Ferrell* 111, 114

**G**
Garber, Jan 7
Gardner, Ed 207
*Gildersleeve, The Great* 126, 134
*Glen Island Casino* 170, 175
*God Bless America* 65
Godfrey, Arthur 45, 56, 58, 131, 195, 211
Goff, Norris 123, 239
Goodman, Benny 7, 44, 175
Gordon, Flash 133, 161

Gordon, Gale 133, 134, 138
Gosden, Freeman
Goulding, Ray 210, 212
*Grand Central Station* 161
*Grand Ole Opry* 78, 79
Graser, Earle 102
Grauer, Ben 6
Greenstreet, Sydney 148
*Gunsmoke* 51, 53, 55

**H**
*Halls of Ivy* 16, 84
*Happiness Boys* 108
Hartzell, Clarence 4
Hastings, Bob 74, 130
Havrilla, Alois 17,
Hay, Bill 16
Haymes, Dick 17
Heatter, Gabriel 88
Henderson, Skitch 16
Herlihy, Ed 6
Hershfield, Harry 20, 21, 106
Hersholt, Jean 17
*Hindenburg* 24, 25, 26, 27, 72
*Hobby Lobby* 115, 116
*Holmes, Sherlock* 17, 49, 148
Hope, Bob 16, 149, 196,
Horlick, Harry 16
*Hotel Sherman* 7
Hulick, Bud 117
Hummert, Anne 11, 19
Hummert, Frank 11, 19
Husing, Ted 80, 201, 202

**I**
*Inner Sanctum* 1, 89, 161, 162, 231
*I Love Lucy* 109, 133, 154

**J**
James, Harry 7, 44, 177
*Jell-o* 66, 69
Johnson, Raymond Edward 89, 161
Johnstone, Jack 104
Johnstone, William 16
Jolson, Al 16, 187
Jordan, Jim 83, 84
Jordan, Marian 83

**K**
Kaltenborn, H.V. 37
Kaye, Sammy 177
*Keen, Mr., Tracer of Lost Persons* 214
Kenton, Stan 176
King, Wayne 176
Kirby, Durward 3, 125
Kirkwood, Jack 196
Knight, Frank 16
Kostelanetz, Andre 99, 236
*Kraft Music Hall* 190
Kyser, Kay 160, 177

**L**
Lauck, Chet 123, 239
Laurie Jr., Joe 20, 22
Leonard, Sheldon 138
*Let's Pretend* 16, 30, 31, 33
Levant, Oscar 184
*Lights Out* 92
Lillie, Beatrice 16
Linkletter, Art 16, 58
*Little Orphan Annie* 172, 174
Lombardo, Guy 16
Lopez, Vincent 132
Lord, Phillips H. 86
Lowe, Ruth 142
Luddy, Barbara 89, 135
*Lum and Abner* 5, 123, 239

*Lux Radio Theater* 13, 14, 51, 147, 231
Lyman, Abe 7
*Lone Ranger, The* 98, 99, 101, 102, 103

**M**
MacCormack, Franklyn 211
Macdonnell, Norman 150
Mack, Nila 30, 31
Macon, Uncle Dave 78
*Madero, Johnny (Pier 13)* 133
*March of Time, The* 94, 163, 164, 231
Marshall, Herbert 16
Martin, Freddy 176
Marx, Groucho 191, 197
*Maxwell House Coffee* 69
McBride, Mary Margaret 37
McCarthy, Charlie 49
McCoy, Clyde 176
*McGee, Fibber* 83, 84, 133, 196, 239
*McGee, Molly* 84, 133, 196, 239
McNamee, Graham 5, 226, 230
McNaughton, Harry 16
McNear, Howard 54
McNeill, Don 6, 91
*Mercury Theater* 33, 40, 94, 95
Miller, Glenn 28, 29, 44, 175, 179
Miller, Marvin 89
*Mix, Tom* 124, 144, 145, 146
Monroe, Bill 78
*Moonlight Serenade* 175

Moore, Garry 9, 58, 126, 140, 166, 197
Morgan, Henry 192, 193
Morrison, Bret 26, 135
Morrison, Herb 24, 25, 27
Mott, Bob 126, 139, 140
*Mr. District Attorney* 16, 88, 102
Murrow, Edward R. 38, 39, 72
*My Friend Irma* 109, 147

**N**
Nash, Ogden 70
*National Barn Dance* 194
Nelson, Ozzie 207
Noble, Ray 16
Nolan, Jeanette 231, 232

**O**
O'Keefe, Walter 191, 202, 203
Oboler, Arch 92, 147
Oppenheimer, Jess 109
*Our Miss Brooks* 137, 188

**P**
Paar, Jack 109, 157, 197
*Paree, Chez* 7
Parker, Frank 81
Parker, Seth 86, 87, 89, 102
Peabody, Eddie 8
Pearl, Minnie 78
Penner, Joe 17
Pious, Minerva 16
Pons, Lily 17, 99, 171
Powell, Dick 149
*Preston, Sergeant* 99, 100

**Q**
Quinn, Carmel 45, 131
Quinn, Don 84
*Quiz Kids* 90,

**R**
Rathbone, Basil 17
*Rawhide* 154
Rey, Alvino 177
Robinson, Edward G. 16, 133
*Rogers, Buck* 104, 105, 106
Ronson, Adele 106
Rooney, Andy 7
Roosevelt, F. D. 160, 164, 250
Ross, David 6
Roventini, Johnny 34, 35
Royan, Roy 154
*Ryman Auditorium* 78

**S**
Salter, Harry 16
Scott, Raymond 6
Seymour, Dan 6
*Shadow, The* 11, 16, 26, 111, 134
Shaw, Artie 44, 176
Sherman, Ransom 5
Shore, Dinah 216, 217
Sinatra, Frank 142, 171, 175
Skelton, Red 41, 44, 126, 130
Smith, Kate 62, 65, 75, 169, 192
Stafford, Hanley 19, 134, 135
Stafford, Jo 47
Stern, Bill 91, 218
Stone, Ezra 74
Stoopnagel, Colonel 6, 117

Striker, Fran 99, 101, 102
*Sunrise Serenade* 117, 180

**T**

*Tarzan* 133, 136, 231
Taylor, Deems 236, 238
Taylor, Frederick Chase 117
Thor, Larry 222
Thornhill, Claude 7, 177
Todd, John 100, 101, 102
Tormé, Mel 172, 174
Tracy, Arthur 16, 220
Tremayne, Les 16
*Trianon Ballroom* 7
Trout, Bob 160
Tubb, Ernest 78

**V**

Vallee, Rudy 43, 74, 88, 176
Van Voorhis, Westbrook 164

**W**

Wain, Bea 169
*War of the Worlds* 40, 94
Warnow, Mark 16, 224
Waterman, Willard 51, 213
Webb, Jack 133
Weems, Ted 7
Weist, Dwight 164
Welk, Lawrence 176
Welles, Orson 33, 40, 94, 161, 231
*Wheaties* 9, 10, 11, 67
White, Paul 38
Whiteman, Paul 237
Widmark, Richard 11

Wilcox, Walter 225
*William Tell Overture* 101
Williams, Florence 111
Winchell, Walter 120, 166, 179
Winkler, Betty 209
Wistful Vista 83
*Witch's Tale, The* 168

**Y**

*Your Hit Parade* 6, 16, 17, 29, 224
*Yours Truly, Johnny Dollar* 224

## About the Author

John Rayburn is a veteran of 62 years in broadcasting. He served as a news/sports anchor and show host, and his TV newscast achieved the largest Share of Audience figures of any major-market TV newscast in the nation. John is a member of the Broadcast Pioneers Hall of Fame.

His network credits include reports/appearances on *The Today Show, Huntley-Brinkley News, Walter Cronkite News, NBC Monitor, NBC News on the Hour*, etc. He recorded dozens of books for the National Library Service and narrated innumerable Radio/TV recordings.

He interviewed celebrities from the fields of government, sports, entertainment, education, etc. The list includes then-SAG president Ronald Reagan, then-Senator John F. Kennedy, Jimmy Carter, Bob Hope, Milton Berle, Debbie Reynolds, Mickey Rooney, Jane Russell, Helen Forrest, Jane Powell, Art Linkletter, Hugh Downs, Charlton Heston, Arnold Palmer, Jack Nicklaus, Jack Dempsey, Muhammad Ali, Stan Musial, Mickey Mantle, Bob Feller, Tris Speaker, Tommy Dorsey, Stan Kenton, Nat King Cole, John Elway, Terry Bradshaw, Johnny Unitas, Red Grange, Rosie Greer, Leslie Nielson, Alex Trebek, Minnie Pearl, Gene Autry, Wilt Chamberlain, Oscar Robertson and hundreds of others.

www.ingramcontent.com/pod-product-compliance
Lightning Source LLC
Chambersburg PA
CBHW071704160426
43195CB00012B/1569